grace

grace

A MEMOIR

Mary Cartledgehayes

CROWN PUBLISHERS NEW YORK

Unless otherwise noted, all biblical references are from the *New Revised Standard Version (NRSV),* copyright © 1989 by the Division of Christian Education of the National Council of Churches of Christ in the U.S.A.

Grateful acknowledgment is made to the following for the use of previously published material: Excerpt from "Honey and Salt" from *Honey and Salt,* copyright © 1963 by Carl Sandburg and renewed 1991 by Margaret Sandburg, Helga Sandburg Crile, and Janet Sandburg, reprinted by permission of Harcourt, Inc. Excerpt from *Stories I Ain't Told Nobody Yet* by Jo Carson. Copyright © 1989 by Jo Carson. Reprinted by permission of Orchard Books, an imprint of Scholastic Inc. Excerpt from the song lyric "Help Me Make It Through the Night," words and music by Kris Kristofferson. Copyright © 1970 (renewed 1998) by TEMI COMBINE INC. All rights controlled by COMBINE MUSIC CORP. and administered by EMI BLACKWOOD MUSIC INC. All rights reserved. International copyright secured. Reprinted by permission of the Hal Leonard Corporation.

Published by Crown Publishers, New York, New York.
Member of the Crown Publishing Group, a division of Random House, Inc.
www.randomhouse.com

CROWN is a trademark and the Crown colophon is a registered trademark of Random House, Inc.

Printed in the United States of America

DESIGN BY BARBARA STURMAN

Library of Congress Cataloging-in-Publication Data
Cartledgehayes, Mary.
    Grace : a memoir / Mary Cartledgehayes.—1st ed.
    1. Cartledgehayes, Mary. 2. United Methodist Church
(U.S.)—Clergy—Biography. I. Title.
BX8495.C357 A3   2003
287'.6'092—dc21   2002007974

ISBN 0-609-60834-7

10 9 8 7 6 5 4 3 2

First Edition

To the memory of

FREDERICK BREVARD HAYES

grace

chapter one

THE FELT INSIDE A YAMAHA PIANO IS MADE OF WOOL
from the underside of sheep sheared on a cold day. If the piano is not
tended to properly, moths will eat holes even in this exceptionally tight
felt. As a result, the tone of the piano becomes tinny. I know these
things because Joe Turner explained them to me when he came to tune
the piano in my living room in February of 1998.

The piano doesn't belong to me. It belongs to my husband, Fred.
He bought it in 1974 from Case Brothers, a music store in the small
town in South Carolina where we live. According to the receipt he keeps
in the bottom left-hand drawer of his desk, he paid $1,575.00 for it,
plus tax. Fred had three children from his first marriage, one or two of
whom took piano lessons. After Fred's first wife died and he and I married, one of my two daughters took lessons for a few months.

Otherwise, the piano was ignored. I'd dust it from time to time,
and every year in December my friend Terry would bring over a briefcase
filled with sheet music and play for an afternoon. The remainder of the
time the piano simply sat, taking up space, upright, unplayed and
unloved, graced only by whatever lamp fit on top of it.

After nearly twenty years of living with the piano, I decided to have
it tuned. I had a hostile relationship with musical instruments, knew
nothing about their needs or possibilities, but I was tidying up my life
and wanted everything in perfect order because my soul was weary unto
death—an unfortunate position for anyone to be in, but even worse
for me, because I'm a clergywoman, an ordained minister, a priest, a
preacher, a person of the cloth.

When, six years earlier, at age forty-two, I'd entered divinity school,
my theology reflected the ennui of Qoheleth the Teacher in Ecclesiastes:
"Vanity of vanities! All is vanity." We are born, and sometime later,

having strutted and fretted our hour or year or thirty years or ninety upon the stage, we die.

After three years as the sole pastor of a church of 180 members, plus several of their kin and a number of persistent visitors—three years spent preaching, baptizing, marrying, burying, and visiting house to house—I'd concluded that life, the passing interval between birth and death, is a blank slate upon which people construct themselves. Some people use thick pieces of white chalk to construct careful equations in parallel lines. Others of us clutch in our fists all the pieces of multicolored chalk we can hold, dragging them randomly yet vigorously across the slate and then standing back to see if there is any pattern at all.

To see the holy, you must have the capacity to see the patterns surrounding you. By 1998 I was blind to patterns. I couldn't tell what, if anything, carried the power to heal and to save.

Nothing, it seemed.

Or everything.

But more likely nothing.

▲   ▲   ▲

Joe Turner rang the doorbell at exactly one o'clock in the afternoon, as scheduled. A long, lean man with thinning gray hair, he wore gray pants, a white button-down shirt, a blue tie, and a navy sports coat. Joe started grinning the moment he spotted the piano at the far end of the living room.

"A Yamaha," he said. "You couldn't ask for a better piano."

He strode to the piano, gestured for me to remove the lamp on top of it, opened the lid, and reached in to extricate a three-inch neon-orange plastic space cadet, which he handed to me.

"I've tuned a lot of pianos in my time," he said. "Some friends and I added up the exact number at a piano tuners' convention a few years ago. We figured out I've tuned more Yamahas than any other tuner in the country. Yamaha makes a fine piano." He offered me a look inside. "You've got moths. See the holes?"

I did, indeed, see the holes, half a dozen of them bored so deeply into the brown felt that the base wood showed through. Another dozen holes were smaller, mere indentations in the felt.

"I've never seen any moths around the piano," I apologized. "I didn't know they were here." Actually, I hadn't known pianos contain felt. Wood and air would have been my guess for what was inside.

"If you've got a piano, you've got moths, even with a Yamaha." That's when Joe explained about the wool coming from the underside of the sheep. "They do the shearing on a cold day because a sheep's wool is tighter in the cold. That way you end up with a tighter felt. But moths are going to get into the felt, no matter how tight it is. That's why you have to have it mothproofed every twenty years." Joe bent down to open the panel underneath the keyboard. Inside was an array of vertical strings and, at their base, more moth-eaten brown felt.

Joe fingered the piano keys in what seemed to be a random pattern. "It's out of tune, all right," he said.

"I thought it might be. I wasn't sure."

Joe nodded. "Now let me tell you your options. I can tune the piano to itself, right now, today while I'm here. Or I can tune it back to its original range. To do that I'll have to take the action assembly home with me to work on and bring it back to you. That'll cost more."

"How much would it cost for you to do that?"

"About three hundred dollars."

"What do you think?" I asked. "Is the piano worth it?"

"Ma'am," he said, "it's a Yamaha. I could sell one like this today for ten thousand dollars."

·   ·   ·

Joe left, carrying the piano's insides with him. He returned on Monday with the action assembly and his son Joe Hal Turner, a smiling, dark-haired young man who looked to be in his early thirties. While Joe Hal replaced the action assembly and dusted the piano's felt with yellow mothproofing powder, the elder Joe chatted with Fred and me.

"Learning to tune a piano takes a long time. It takes two years before you even know if your ear's good enough to learn the trade. And then it takes another three years to learn how to tune on your own. First piano I ever tuned alone, I worked on it for three weeks, and when I was done it was further out of tune than when I started." Joe laughed at the recollection of his novitiate.

I underwent a novitiate, too, but mine was different from Joe's. First congregation I ever pastored, I worked on it for almost three years, and now I was further out of tune than when I started. I felt as though I'd spent my life reading things that didn't need to be read, thinking things that didn't need to be thought, and doing things that didn't need to be done. The things I'd believed in, worked toward, and achieved seemed insignificant, the sacrifices a waste of time. I had been called into the ministry, had given my heart to the institutional church, did everything I could to conform to and respond to its demands, but it wasn't enough; no matter how much I gave, it wasn't enough; it couldn't be enough because *I* wasn't enough. Coming to terms with the truth hurt like hell, which is why by February 1998, when I still had four months to serve as pastor, I was pretty much fucked.

I'd called the piano tuner because I'd decided to normalize my life, and putting my house into order was the first step. My friend Molly and I were working together on the project at separate locations, I at my house, she a hundred miles away at her house. Our friendship arose at the intersection of our similarities and differences. We'd met at an inter-denominational conference on preaching in 1995. I'm of average height with brown hair and green eyes; Molly is five feet ten inches, has red hair she usually keeps corralled in a ponytail, and eyes the same honest blue as Fred's. I had grandchildren; she had three children under the age of six, two of them still in diapers. Even though she was younger than I, Molly knew much more about being a pastor. A seminary graduate at age twenty-four, she'd pastored three congregations since then. She'd become my guide, mentor, and salvation as I struggled with the complexities of a first pastorate. For instance, she could tell me without looking it up that *yashab* is the Hebrew word for "God sitting down in the temple in Jerusalem." She knew when you officiate at your first funeral and don't know what to do next, all you have to do is stand still and look pastoral, and the funeral director will give you a hand signal. She also knew that the day the church door closes behind you after you've preached your last sermon, your relationship with the congregation is severed as completely as though you'd never been there at all.

Between us, Molly and I had read every book in the public library on household organization. I leaned toward the analytical ones that begin with sentences like "First take all the clothes out of your closets, stack them on your bed, and go through them one at a time." Molly, meanwhile, was immersed in Julia Cameron's books, and she doesn't remember if it was *The Artist's Way* or *The Vein of Gold* from which she learned that the more you rid your life of things you don't need, the more creative you can be. The thought reminded her of something she'd heard theologian Justo L. González say more than once when she studied with him in seminary.

"Have you heard of him?" she asked.

I had. His book *The Story of Christianity* was the text for my church-history classes, and I was also familiar with his three-volume series called *A History of Christian Thought.*

"González said if you have things you don't want or need, you're keeping them from their rightful possessors. He says we need to pass them out of our lives so they can reach the person they really belong to."

I had a house full of things I neither wanted nor needed, but passing them out of my life wasn't easy. You get used to living a certain way, surrounded by certain things that give you comfort even if they're of no real use. I had to start my cleaning out with easy items. The first to go were the records, including the itemized inventory left over from a house fire we'd had in 1986. It was satisfying to rid myself of that reminder of the past, so I continued to sort through the papers hibernating in our three metal file cabinets. In one day I got rid of four feet and seven inches of outdated, unnecessary documents, papers, and journals.

Vitalized by success, I took on the family photographs stored upstairs, downstairs, and in my lady's chamber. I collected photos for weeks and even then didn't find them all. Six months later strays were still turning up at the back of dresser drawers or under couch cushions. I grouped the photos by decades, then by years, and then by months. I held intense conversations with myself about acid-free photo storage and finally bought a dozen albums at Wal-Mart, arranged the photos chronologically in them, wrote the corresponding years on the spines, and lined them up tidily on the bottom shelf of the bookcase in the living room.

When I finished, I had a pile of leftovers, the ephemera of my life: grade-school report cards, college transcripts, wedding announcements, important church bulletins, newspaper clippings. I slid the papers into individual clear vinyl sheet protectors and put them all into a notebook. I bought a second notebook and filled it with paperwork from my family, including the after-Christmas thank-you notes my twin nephews sent me the year they were in first grade and a magazine article about my brothers' restoration of a World War II airplane.

My next project was household artifacts. You'd be surprised how many things five children leave behind when they move into homes of their own. I shipped and/or delivered grade-school, high-school, and college yearbooks to their respective owners: Fred's first wife's sterling silver flatware and crystal stemware to her daughter; a scrapbook compiled, with much whining, as a school assignment by my younger daughter during the 1984 presidential election; a math book with a nineteen-stanza poem titled "It" written in the margins of chapters four through seventeen to one of Fred's sons; and a sleeveless green organza dress my older daughter wore in the spring of 1969 when she was a pudgy orange-haired baby.

"Why are you getting rid of all these things?" asked Fred. (This from a man who kept the twenty-year-old receipt for a piano in the Active file in his bottom left-hand desk drawer.)

I told him cleaning out excess is said to be a sign of good mental health. The undertaking frees you up physically and emotionally, makes room for whatever new things the universe is brewing up for you. He knew I was ready to taste the new brew.

I didn't tell Fred that I'd have thrown away the perfectly good piano, too, if I'd had that option. Did I mention the piano was only played one afternoon a year? Did I mention it was the most demanding piece of furniture I'd ever encountered? Pianos are delicate, I was told. Their backs have to be against walls, and not just any old wall will do. Pianos are like fragile elderly relatives; they favor inside walls where they're safe from drafts, which means I'd never been able to rearrange the living room lest I disturb the Yamaha's tranquillity.

I considered passing the piano on to one of Fred's children, but there were complications. One of them lived two hours away, one eight hours away, and one on the other side of the country. To get the piano to any of them, I'd have to hire a truck and muscular movers and work out pickup and delivery times. Besides, none of the children had expressed a desire for this or any other piano.

My biggest problem, though, was Fred. He liked the piano. He thought it belonged to him.

I finally decided that if I was stuck with the damned thing, at least it was going to be in tune. I called Molly for the name of a piano tuner. She'd gone to a church yard sale the year before with ten dollars in her pocket. An hour later her pocket was empty, and she was wheeling home a Hobart M. Cable upright piano that had done service in a Sunday-school classroom for seventy or eighty years. When I asked her who tuned her piano, she'd given me Joe Turner's phone number.

▴   ▴   ▴

Much later, after I announced to my congregation that I was leaving, after I'd dyed my hair purple and had learned to play Tchaikovsky, I read *The Music of the Spheres* by Jamie James. The author says the ancient Greeks believed that "music and the human soul are both aspects of the eternal." It's a stirring thought, but when I called Joe Turner to come tune the piano, I could no longer deal with the eternal. It was enough to pare life down to the moment's essentials. My hope in doing so was that I might once again be able to discern what was trivial and what, if anything, was redemptive. One of the essentials, since I couldn't get rid of the piano, was to make sure it was used for the purpose for which it was intended, and so, after the piano-tuning Turners finished their work and went on their way, I joined Fred in the sunroom where he was watching a basketball game on television.

"Do you know what we've got in the living room?" I asked.

"What?"

"A ten-thousand-dollar lamp stand."

He nodded and kept watching television. Just to be friendly, I blew lightly on the top of his head and sent flying the few hairs that covered his bald spot. "Somebody needs to take piano lessons," I said.

I expected Fred to jump on the idea. After all, he'd played "Rhapsody in Blue" in a recital forty-nine years earlier, when he was fourteen, and he'd always said that when he retired he was going to take up the piano again. Didn't that make him the ideal candidate?

Fred thought not.

That left me.

chapter   two

––––––––––

THE PIANO WAS ONCE A WEAK-BONED CREATURE. AS invented in 1711 by Bartolomeo Cristofori in Italy, it was crude, more the essence of piano than the instrument we now know. That first model had fixed keys that struck hammers that hit wire strings that reverberated into music. Early pianos required constant tuning, because their frames were too tender to hold the necessary tension. That inherent flaw was rectified in 1790 by an American, John Hawkins. Hawkins, who was trying to build an upright piano, thought to use iron for the frame. A century later, steel was used for the strings for the first time. The modern piano is thus constructed of wood, felt, steel, iron, and tension. A standard model has 230 strings, each of which carries a tension of between 150 and 300 pounds. The total string tension is thus approximately thirty tons.

Piano tuner Anita T. Sullivan, in her book *The Seventh Dragon,* says this about the tension: "If a piano were to relax, as we humans keep trying to do, it would be something else altogether. A piano is full of suppressed desires, recalcitrance, inhibition, conflict. Yet because its opposing forces are carefully balanced, they are still. And the still space, though small, is where music can spin its way through into our dimension."

Pianos don't explode from the inside out because the tons of tension are carefully balanced so that within the tension there is a place that is still.

Nice language. Religious language, even. Christians speak of the trinity, God in three persons, traditionally named as "God the Father, God the Son, and God the Holy Spirit." It's the Holy Spirit that captivates me, because the Holy Spirit is simultaneously tension and stillness, the wild winds of a hurricane and the chilling peace when the eye passes over. The Holy Spirit blows where it pleases, as it pleases. It is uncontrollable and uncontainable. Sometimes it's a violent wind. Sometimes

8

it's a sigh. In either case, the metric tons of its tension are finely balanced, and within the tension is a place that is still.

In my personal life, I had lots of tension but no fine balance, no place that was still. As I learned later, neither do pianos most of the time. The laws of physics guarantee that every piano will not only go out of tune but will, eventually, lose forever its ability to hold a tune. It's the nature of the beast, as unavoidable as the concept of original sin in classic theology. From the moment of the final tuning in the factory, each piano begins a descent, eventually fatal, into discord.

To understand why, I read some background material on the structure of the piano. In his book *The Piano Owner's Guide,* Carl D. Schmeckel describes the three units that make up a piano. The structural unit, consisting of the wooden piano back, the metal plate that contains the tension placed on the strings and absorbs the strings' vibrations, and the tuning pin block, is the frame onto which everything else is hung. The tone unit includes the soundboard assembly, the strings, and the hammerheads. The mechanical unit is made up of the keyboard assembly, the hammer-action assembly, and the damper-action assembly.

When an alteration occurs in any of the three units, the piano goes out of tune. The most common alteration is the entrance of foreign invaders, at least according to conversations I had with a group of piano tuners/technicians via their professional association's website. One day I read a posting about a Rottweiler getting stuck in a piano.

A Rottweiler stuck in a piano. Imagine that.

Actually, I couldn't imagine it, so I posted a message asking if the story was true. While I was at it, I asked what the strangest item was that anybody had found in a piano.

Apparently dropping, shoving, blowing, wedging, and hiding foreign objects in pianos is a national pastime. One piano technician, a man named Conrad Hoffsommer, sent me an alphabetized list of 183 different items he'd found. The list began with A for acorn and ended with Y for Yahtzee score pads. In between were balls (golf, super, and wood), a bow tie, doll shoes, nails (finishing, paneling, and roofing), pins (bobby, hat, safety, and straight), religious medals, the tail from a Pin the Tail on the Donkey game (oh, that's where it went), and a toothbrush.

Hoffsommer's list looked exhaustive, but it wasn't. A technician named Lisa Weller found a music stand shoved into a Steinway. Andrew Remillard found a 1940s newspaper from Czechoslovakia and an old birdcage; inside the birdcage were mid-nineteenth-century coins from Great Britain. Bob Bergantino once found an automobile headlight. John Dewey knew someone who found a teaspoon bent to form a heroin cooker.

Food turns up regularly, including ice cream–cone tips, raisins, Cheetos (poked in, the tuner said, by an enterprising three-year-old), a desiccated chicken drumstick, a Hershey's Kiss, and an entire lunch box–sized bag of Cool Ranch Doritos.

Animals turn up, too, most often dead. Tuners reported sightings of spiders, roaches, carpet beetles, a dead squirrel (once), a dead kitten (once), rats (entirely too frequently), and nests of mice, both quick and dead.

Carol Beigel once got a call from a woman whose cat had its foot stuck in the bass strings of a new grand piano. As the caller spoke into the phone, the cat howled in the background. (Note: if this ever happens to you, spread the strings apart with a wooden spoon.) Carol had a colleague who answered the phone one day to a question about the hissing of piano pedals. It turned out new construction was going on in the neighborhood, displacing the birds and the beasts, and an enterprising copperhead snake had made a new life for itself inside the piano.

Pianos serve as safety-deposit boxes for some people. Marijuana joints are not uncommon discoveries, nor are wads of cash. Bill Simon from Phoenix told me that in the fifties or sixties a man from New York found a jade figurine dating from the Ming dynasty in a piano he'd bought from Goodwill for a hundred dollars. Bill had also heard of a Stradivarius violin found in the bottom of an upright piano by the piano's new owner, but then again, said Bill, the story might be an urban legend.

Other items found were even more valuable: a Christmas card from an aunt who'd died a few years earlier; a book report tragically lost in 1964, the discovery of which so pleased the piano's owner that she immediately phoned her sister to let her know it was found.

David Ilvedson e-mailed me about the time he and a helper moved a baby grand piano. They tipped it over onto the moving board, and, said David, "Clinkity, clink, clink, out falls a diamond ring. I call in the woman who owned the piano and give her the ring, and she stares at it with these sad eyes. She said she had lost a good friend over that ring.

She had accused her friend of stealing it. All these years it had lain hidden in the action."

Almost anything, it seems, can find its way under a floorboard, under glass, or into a piano.

But not a Rottweiler.

The Rottweiler story, it seems, is a popular practical joke. A novice piano tuner gets a phone call, somebody yelling about a Rottweiler stuck in a piano. The tuner rushes out to the rescue. When he reaches the address, the home owner, who most likely has neither a dog nor a piano, stares blankly when asked about the Rottweiler. The practical jokers who made the phone call are usually hiding nearby, laughing.

▲   ▲   ▲

Foreign bodies inside a piano disturb the tension, and the disturbance of tension sends the instrument out of tune. A single bobby pin changes the tension in the mechanical unit, which causes the tension in the tone unit to shift, which adds additional stress to the structural unit. Over time the whole system breaks down.

Pianos aren't the only things to go out of tune physically. People do, too. Take Terry, for instance, my friend who played the piano in my living room every December. Terry took lessons from her mother, Helen, who was a classically trained pianist. Terry loves the instrument; it allows her to say things she has no other language for speaking.

In the 1970s, when Terry was in her twenties, she was diagnosed with rheumatoid arthritis. At first the disease didn't have much impact on her piano playing, but little by little her ability degenerated. Surgeons did what they could to salvage her hands. They repaired a snapped tendon, replaced a worn-away knuckle, trimmed bone spurs, and recommended physical therapy, which Terry practiced religiously. The day came, though, when she couldn't play anymore. The conformity of her hands had changed. Passages she'd played since childhood were beyond her reach.

Terry says someday she might select a few pieces of sheet music and memorize a new method of fingering in order to play them. Not now, though, she says. It would be too painful to do so now, when she's still grieving what she's lost.

Sometimes when people go out of tune physically nothing can be repaired, replaced, or trimmed. Beth Flynn was one of those people. In the summer of 1994, my last year in divinity school, I worked for three weeks as a student intern for the congregation I would later pastor. On Wednesday of my second week, Beth was driving home from work when her car ran off the road and into a tree. A brain scan at the hospital showed she'd had an aneurysm. Now she had no brain activity.

The next day the pastor with whom I was working had to leave town; his father was having a medical crisis. The pastor asked me to stay in touch with the Flynn family at the hospital.

I checked the church's pictorial directory to be sure I'd recognize them when I got to the intensive-care waiting room. If I'd met any of them, it was only briefly as they introduced themselves and shook my hand on the porch steps after a Sunday service. By then I knew Beth was in her early thirties and not married. Her mother, Bertha, worked at a funeral home. Her father, Alva, ran a shift at a textile mill. Beth had two brothers, Jimmy and Chris, both of whom were married.

When I got to the neurological intensive-care waiting room, one of the brothers steered me to an empty chair beside his father. Alva and I sat together for half an hour or so. Neither one of us said much. At one point he pulled a picture of Beth out of his wallet.

"She's beautiful," he told me.

"She is," I agreed.

A repeat brain scan the following day confirmed that Beth had no brain activity. The Flynns began to say the words "organ donation." Bertha held my hand while she talked to me about it.

"I know Beth wanted her organs donated. She worked at the funeral home with me part-time on the weekends, and she and I discussed these things. She told me if anything ever happened to her, she wanted her organs to go to help someone else. But Alva's not ready yet."

A little later, Alva asked me to walk back to Beth's cubicle with him and Bertha.

At the time I was a raw recruit into the ministry. Previously, I'd seen only one dying patient in intensive care, Fred's former father-in-law. I'd been surprised on that visit to learn that there's a stillness around a deathbed—a place of stillness within the tension, I'd now call it—and nothing to fear.

That time my only task was to support Fred emotionally. Now, walking down the corridor with Alva and Bertha, I had a formal job to do. I mentally rehearsed prayers and hoped I was ready for whatever was coming.

The whisper of the respirator was the only sound in Beth's cubicle. She lay unmoving, her head wrapped in white cloths, a white blanket pulled up over her shoulders. All I could see were her face and hands. She was, indeed, beautiful.

The air smelled of gentleness, heartbreak, and peace. I touched Beth's toes. Her parents and I spoke quietly. The three of us held hands as I prayed out loud some fumbling thing about grace equal to every need and leaning on the everlasting arms.

The next day a hospital representative met with the family to discuss organ donation. Bertha, Alva, Jimmy, and Chris decided together to sign the documents that would let Beth go and, at the same time, would let aspects of her life, or at least her physical body, continue.

Years later Bertha told me that she and her two daughters-in-law, Candy and Kathy, were sitting at the dining room table that evening and she had said to them, "I never go into Beth's room. It's hers, and I don't intrude on it. But I need the two of you to go in there and see if you can find something, anything, that shows her desire that I do this so I'll know and it will be easier."

"It wasn't two minutes later that one of them, I'm pretty sure it was Kathy, came back out and said, 'Ms. Flynn, look what I found.'"

Kathy offered Bertha the piece of paper in her hand. Beth had recently renewed her driver's license, and the document showed that she had agreed to be an organ donor.

Two days later Beth's respirator was removed. Her organs were harvested.

▲   ▲   ▲

I have a copy of the letter Bertha and Alva received from the South Carolina Organ Procurement Agency. The letter says Beth's kidney (she was born with only one) went to a thirty-year-old. Her liver went to a sixty-four-year-old. Her heart went to someone with eleven grandchildren, her pancreas to a diabetes research agency, her eyes . . . well, the Flynns weren't given specifics, but her eyes are out there somewhere.

Beth's heart beats on.

Her eyes see on.

Her liver continues its task of purification.

▲ ▲ ▲

The first verse of Isaiah 40 reads, "'Comfort, O comfort my people,' says your God." Beth's continued life is little comfort to those who still grieve her death, yet it is all the comfort the world can offer, and it must be enough.

▲ ▲ ▲

A piano. A human being. They are not so very different. Structural unit, mechanical unit, tone unit. Mind, body, soul. In either case, if one unit goes out of tune, the whole is unbalanced. The structure can not hold. Something has to give, or someone has to stop, or someone has to go.

chapter three

HOW ON EARTH DOES A BRIGHT, CAPABLE, RELATIVELY normal middle-aged woman end up in the ordained ministry? As with most questions having to do with spiritual matters, the answer lies as much in the past as in the present.

The idea first popped up when I was a little kid. I grew up on an island in one of the Great Lakes. One day my sister, Amy, and I were walking home on the asphalt road that began at the main dock on the southern tip of the island where we lived, ran past our house, turned right at the pear trees, passed the marsh and an assortment of summer cottages, and eventually disintegrated into the rocky shore of Lake Erie. The sky was blue, the clouds were puffy, and we weren't wearing winter coats, so it wasn't fall, winter, or early spring. In those seasons in northern Ohio the sky is gray, and heavy coats are required. It couldn't have been summer, either, because the tar in the road wasn't bubbling from the heat, tempting our toes to prick the bubbles and our mother to scold us for ruining yet another pair of shoes or—worse—for taking off our shoes and coming home with toenails clotted with tar.

May: let's say it was early May. I must have been ten going on eleven, old enough to imagine adulthood yet not so old that my brother Douglas had left home for high school on the mainland. It was 1960. Douglas was thirteen, Amy not quite twelve, and Charlie only days away from his first birthday.

By that time I was as tall as Amy. Her Easter Toni permanent would have washed out of her straight hair by then, but my naturally curly hair would still have held its corkscrews. We'd have been pale from a winter spent in boots, mittens, scarves, and hooded parkas, but pink-cheeked from all the oxygen we inhaled in our ambles through the fields, pastures, woods, lanes, and roads on the 786-acre island. Two little girls following our feet and our thoughts from one place to another.

Amy had announced her plan for what she would be when she grew up, replacing her long-held intention to be a ballerina. After laying out her future as a veterinarian, she asked, "Well, then, Mary Jo, what are you going to be?"

I replied, with no forethought whatsoever, "I'm going to be a minister."

Amy accepted my statement with her usual equanimity. "Like Reverend Lee?"

"Yes."

"Oh. Okay, then."

▲　　▲　　▲

Reverend Lee Lindenberger was all I knew of the ministry in 1960, which is to say next to nothing, even less than most children because of the isolation, both geographical and social, that came with living on the island, which was so small that I attended a one-room schoolhouse through the eighth grade. In eight years I had only one teacher, Mrs. Kuemmel, except for a few months when she was ill and a substitute filled in. The only time anyone shared my class level was the fall of fifth grade. That year a boy named Johnathon joined me, but just before Thanksgiving he and his family moved to the mainland, and things returned to normal.

If you wanted to be part of a religious community on the island, you had to be either a Roman Catholic or an Episcopalian. My father ferried the half dozen Roman Catholics to Mass on Put-in-Bay, a village on South Bass, the next island over, on his boat in the summer; in the winter, they met in a corner of someone's living room. We Episcopalians met in the one-room schoolhouse every week for Sunday school. Once a month Reverend Lee flew in from Put-in-Bay to conduct a church service. On the Sundays he was there, the blackboards and the teacher's desk at the front of the schoolroom receded from view when the altar table was dragged out of the coat closet and stationed a few paces to the left of the upright piano on the south wall.

Reverend Lee was an old man, at least twenty-five or twenty-six. He wore a stiff white round collar and a long black dress, and over the dress a sheer white pinafore with lace at the hem. His clothing contrasted with the wardrobes of every other man I'd ever seen, especially in the winter when male islanders were heavily layered: T-shirts, long underwear, insulated pants, wool plaid shirts, wool sweaters, and hooded parkas, generally brown or green, although my father's was red. The men smelled like gasoline, coal smoke, and pine trees. Reverend Lee had no scent. And boots: the islanders wore bulky, lace-up boots, thick enough for warmth and strong enough for stability in snow, ice, sleet, and slush. I believe Reverend Lee wore galoshes. I also believe, accurately or not, that he removed his galoshes prior to the service and stood before the congregation—the three Cartledge children (my baby brother was not yet born) and the half dozen adults who made up the Protestant faithful—in smartly polished black leather shoes.

Reverend Lee was foreign to me, ethereal, barely real. His actions—the solemnity of his voice when he pronounced the invocation over the bread and wine of Holy Communion, the grace with which he lifted the chalice, his attention to a ritual that seemed inconsequential in light of chickens to be watered, spelling words to be memorized, and roads to be walked—surrounded him in mystery. It must have been his otherness, and possibly the lace, that prompted me to say, "I'm going to be a minister."

I didn't know anything about the church, or about the ministry, or about life in 1960. I didn't know that the Episcopal Church didn't ordain women and that it wouldn't do so until pressured to by highly publicized "irregular" ordinations in 1974 and 1975. I didn't know that some of the first female priests would be spat at and bitten as they offered the bread of communion, nor did I know that one of the first female bishops would arrive at a church for a scheduled visit only to find the door bolted and, when she finally gained admission, the sanctuary emptied of altar cloths and the cross, with every light extinguished, in protest of her consecration.

I didn't know I'd give birth to my first baby in 1968, six weeks after my nineteenth birthday, and to my second baby in 1973, and that by the end of 1974 my second divorce would be final and I'd be finished with anything to do with God. I didn't know I'd be single for six years, that I'd meet and marry a blue-eyed southern widower named Fred, or that ten years into our marriage I'd present myself as a candidate for the ordained ministry in the United Methodist Church. I didn't know I'd be the senior and sole pastor of a church and spend half my time wondering what in the hell I was doing there, or that finally, on my next-to-the-last Sunday in the pulpit, I'd realize that whether I ever pastored another church or not, for the rest of my life I'd be a minister, a person set apart above all else for the task of seeing and proclaiming the holy.

How could I have known any of those things in 1960? I was a kid, a green-eyed girl with stubbed toes, elbows I couldn't control, and scabs on my knees. The curly blond hair I was born with had only recently darkened to brown, but I was already trying to distinguish between the trite and the sacred. It took me nearly forty years to reach a conclusion, but the answer only makes sense in the present if you understand the past: the past time, the past place, the past people. And so that's where I'll begin, in the past, with the year 1922.

My father's parents were Mornington and Mona ("Gregory, that was," as she put it) Cartledge. They lived in England in the county of Derbyshire in the village of Tideswell. Tideswell is listed in the Domesday Book of 1086 and is renowned for its parish church, which was built in the fourteenth century, is dedicated to St. John the Baptist, and is known familiarly as the "Cathedral of the Peak."

My grandfather worked as a laborer in a limestone quarry, raised sheep, and built houses and drystone walls. He was a strong man, and quiet. If I'd had sons, I intended to name one Mornington, after Grand-dad, partly because I loved him and partly because I assumed his name had been handed down across succeeding generations in the family. My daughters were grown before I learned the real story. It seems my great-grandfather liked the horses, he did, and on the day of his son's birth he happened to be at the racetrack, he was, and he happened to bet on a horse, indeed, which horse happened to win the race, praise God, and the name of the jockey who rode the horse who won the race that put the money in Great-grandfather's pocket was . . . you'll have guessed this by now . . . Mornington.

My grandmother Mona was forced by poverty to leave school at the age of twelve to go to work in a textile factory, where she cut fustion for military uniforms. She was a tiny thing, no more than five feet tall, with blue eyes that gleamed with delight or interest or malice, as the occasion demanded. In September 1922 Grandma had three fits in the course of giving birth to her only son, Douglas (no-middle-initial) Cartledge, my father. He was an only child for fourteen years until his sister, Mary Astrid, was born. Three years later, he joined the British navy.

Meanwhile, on the American side of the Atlantic, Charles and Lily (née Brown) Harkness had already welcomed their first and only child,

Joanna Belle, she of the flaming red hair, on May 26 of the same year. The Harknesses and the Browns lived just outside Pittsburgh, Pennsylvania, where they were coal miners, midwives, store owners, and town councilmen. When the mines closed in 1928, Charles, Lily, and other family members moved to Detroit, Michigan, where he went to work on Mr. Henry Ford's assembly line and she in one of the huge downtown department stores, until 1929 when everybody lost their jobs because of the stock market crash.

My mother used to tell us children, especially when we were whining about having to do chores like shoveling out the chicken house, that we came from strong stock. Such an inheritance precludes neither intelligence nor the capacity for mysticism. My grandmother Cartledge, for instance, saw things. She saw shapes in clouds—a cow, a duck, a panting terrier—the way we all do, but she saw other things in other places, too.

"Look!" she once said to me, pointing to the fading coals in my aunt's fireplace grate. "There's the bust of a woman, and a beast nearly intent on devouring her."

The sight recalled to her mind the time she was passing by the fire on the way to bed, glanced in, and said to my grandfather, "There's King George. What's he doing in the fire?"

The next morning she learned the king had died in the night.

Another time, in November of 1941, during the Second World War, Grandma was at one of her brothers' houses having a cup of tea. My father had been home on leave from the service and gone back to war. He was stationed in the Mediterranean Sea on the aircraft carrier HMS *Ark Royal,* one of the ships involved (prior to Daddy's arrival) in the sinking of the German battleship *Bismarck.*

Grandma glanced at the leaves in the bottom of her teacup.

"Look, there's Doug with a kit bag," she said. ("Although it can't have been a kit bag," she confided when she told me the story. "I think they didn't carry them in the second war.")

Her brother scoffed at her. "Don't be thinking Doug's coming home. He was just here."

When Grandma got back to her own house, the radio was playing. As she started up the steps she heard the announcer say the *Ark Royal*—my father's aircraft carrier—had been sunk by the Germans. She stood on the steps, unable to move, listening.

"How long was it before you learned Daddy was safe?" I asked.

"I don't remember."

As my father recounts, he, along with 1,539 other officers and men and a big ginger tomcat, was transferred from the sinking *Ark Royal* to a destroyer, the HMS *Legion*. The *Legion* unloaded in Gibraltar, where they boarded the HMS *Nelson* for the trip to Scapa Flow, Scotland. From there the men, still dressed in their tropical shorts and shirts, were transferred to an unheated train to take them to Portsmouth, where new, warm uniforms and railroad passes were waiting. Daddy changed clothes and caught the train for home, proving his uncle wrong and proving something, although I don't know quite what, about my grandmother's visions.

When Father's six-week leave was up, he was reassigned to a different squadron. The following April he was sent to Canada. The skies over England were off-limits for flight training—too much danger of being shot down—so he went to flight school at the Grosse Isle Naval Station near Detroit, Michigan. My parents met and married in February when he got his wings. Mother says the Methodist minister almost cried as he performed the ceremony, and I can see why when I look at their wedding pictures. They were so young, the smiling American girl in the lace wedding dress and the lanky English boy in his naval uniform.

A week after the wedding, my father was returned to England and from there dispatched to Trinidad, where for eighteen months he trained navigators. Meanwhile, Mother was in a war plant making parts for Pratt & Whitney engines.

After the war, the two of them reunited in Daddy's hometown of Tideswell. They plotted out their future. My father enrolled in Reading College to study agriculture. Everything fell apart a month or so later when my mother got word that her mother was dying of cancer back in America. After much agonizing, Mother returned home. Weeks later, her mother died.

As soon as he could scrape enough money together, my father joined her. Then came struggles to find work—not easy to do when most jobs were reserved for veterans, which meant American veterans, not British ones—which ended with their eventually settling on Middle Bass Island in a four-bedroom farmhouse with a mortgage.

By then they had babies. Douglas's birth in 1947 delighted everyone. Amy's the next year didn't; she and Mother both nearly died during the home delivery. They were hauled in the back of a truck to the island airstrip and loaded onto the Ford Tri-Motor airplane that served the islands. The local hearse was waiting at the airport to take Mother to the hospital. Either the ruts in the road or the air pockets jolted Amy out of her stubborn breech position; once at the hospital she was born easily, and healthy.

I don't care to imagine how my parents felt when Mother realized half a dozen months later that she was pregnant with me, but I assume "ecstatic" is not the appropriate word. Luckily, when I was born in 1949, I turned out to be a very nice baby, and so the next day my parents took me home.

"Home" was Middle Bass Island, one of the Lake Erie islands that lay to the north of the Ohio mainland and to the south of the Canadian mainland. Erie is the smallest of the Great Lakes, the five freshwater lakes formed at the end of the most recent ice age. Glaciers, by their movement, carved out the basins of the lakes and, by their melting, filled the basins with waters. The islands in the Lakes are geologic accidents, spots of land spared the glacial grinding. From the air, Lake Erie's islands look like pancakes poured on a griddle by a not particularly coordinated four-year-old.

Commodore Oliver Hazard Perry fought numerous sea battles near Middle Bass during the War of 1812. In 1815 the war ended with the signing of the Treaty of Ghent, which established the permanent boundary between the United States and Canada. In 1854, according to Robert Dodge's *Isolated Splendor,* Joseph de Rivera St. Jurgo bought the three Bass islands (North, Middle, and South) along with four smaller islands nearby and soon began cultivating grapes. The 1874 county atlas showed that 3,154,109 pounds of grapes were harvested from the Bass islands in 1872. Rumor has it they were stops on the Underground Railroad and later became havens for whiskey runners during Prohibition.

In the 1950s, the winter population on the island was roughly twenty-five people, fifty if you counted dogs, cats, cows, and sheep, maybe two thousand if you counted rabbits and pheasants. Two family wineries offered employment for some residents. Fishing was a year-round industry, with gill-netting in the spring, party-boat fishing excursions in the summer, and ice fishing in the winter. Tourism was a beginning industry, although the word is too grand for the reality, which is that two families with property facing the lake built a number of concrete-block cottages that they rented for a week at a time to vacationers who wanted to fish and/or swim.

Our family was settled once I was born, or so it seemed until nine years later. On Christmas morning of 1958, after Amy, Douglas, and I had opened all our gifts, my father said, "We have another present for you, but you're going to have to wait until May to see it."

I suppose they could have given us something practical, like a pony or a box of chocolate-covered cherries, but they didn't. Charlie was born on May 31. Daddy took us along when he went to retrieve Mother and the baby from the hospital in Port Clinton. I remember clearly the ride home on the *Erie Isle,* the ferry that crossed from the mainland to the island. Normal trip length, excluding high winds and waves, was an hour and fifteen minutes. We spent the time below deck, which was a trade-off: the pitching of the boat was subdued, but the clatter and fumes from the diesel engine were heightened.

Mother looked different holding a baby. Pleased with herself. Content. The baby himself, at nine pounds and a few ounces, was bigger than a puppy but smaller than a real person. I didn't know what to make of him. I touched his dimpled fist with my first finger. His skin was soft.

Charlie may not have been a practical gift, but he was an awfully nice one. As soon as Mother would let him out of the house in our keeping, Charlie went along on all our adventures: to the post office to get the mail, to the woods for a wander, to the backyard to dig for worms. For road trips we installed him in his aged, elegant, black leather pram, which was roomy enough to hold not only Charlie but also a pile of blankets, my Mary Hoyer doll, Amy's Honey doll, and a stray family of kangaroos.

Amy and I didn't always walk and push the baby carriage. Some days we'd ride our bicycles and take turns giving the carriage handle a push to keep it moving. One day we accidentally had some clothesline with us, so we knotted it around the back of my bicycle seat, looped it over the carriage handle a few times, and then knotted it on Amy's bicycle seat. It worked smoothly.

A few days later we came up with an even better idea.

"Nick! Come here, Nick!"

Our dog, Nick, a black-and-white spaniel mix, was one of those dogs that seems always to be smiling. He was friendly and fast; my father once clocked him running beside our car at forty-five miles per hour. When we beckoned, Nick sat down and waited happily as we tied the rope from the carriage handle to his red collar. We began walking, Amy, Charlie in his carriage, Nick playing lead dog, and I, and were quite happy with the arrangement until Nick noticed a rabbit in a field at the side of the road. He took off after the rabbit.

Luckily, the combined weight of the carriage and the baby slowed him down. We caught them both before Charlie toppled into a ditch.

We never tried that maneuver again.

Thirty years later I made the mistake of mentioning Charlie's carriage rides to my mother. I thought she was going to wallop me.

"But, Mom, we thought you knew."

"No, you didn't. You waited until you were on the other side of the tiger-lily bed to tie the rope, to be sure I wouldn't see."

Geez. You would have thought that the baby belonged to her instead of to Amy, Douglas, and me.

"But Charlie liked it, Mom. Really, he did. We wouldn't have done it if he hadn't been laughing."

Mother was not mollified.

▲　　▲　　▲

In truth, Charlie was a godsend, a spangle of luxury in our cloistered midst. There was nothing austere about our upbringing—we had electricity, running water, radios, television, record players, a home-movie camera, and parents filled with wit and curiosity—but we were different from people on the mainland. They could go to concerts and recitals, wrestling matches and basketball games, church socials and movie theaters. We were pretty much finished with entertainment once we took our bows at the end of the school's Christmas program.

In the winters before Charlie's arrival, evenings stretched long. My father didn't want our brains to atrophy from boredom, nor did he want us to be culturally deprived, missing out as we were on live performances of *The Nutcracker* and the film rendition of *The Shaggy D.A.* He was also concerned about our insularity. His war service had shown him the breadth of the world, and he wanted us to know that breadth.

Accordingly, one winter he built a ham-radio set and taught us three older children Morse code, using what he'd learned in a three-month radio course during the war. At dinner he'd tap out messages on his plate, and we'd translate. Finally we became fluent enough in the language that we could, under his supervision, communicate with other ham-radio operators. It was fun when those operators sent us cards post-marked from exotic locations like Indiana and West Virginia.

Many evenings I would sit on the scratchy red couch picking fuzzy threads, timing my pulls so Mother wouldn't notice and swat my hand. Amy and Douglas sat with me on the couch or in armchairs (we were not a floor-sitting kind of family). My father, who'd had classical violin lessons from the time he was six until he left for military service, would carry a straight-backed chair in from the dining room. He'd sit, rub his bow with the piece of rosin tucked inside a fragment of purple velvet, balance the violin on his thigh for a tuning, and then position the instrument between his chin and collarbone. He would play and Mother would lead the singing: "Pack Up Your Troubles in Your Old Kit Bag," "K-k-k-katie," "Mairzy Doats," "Oh, What a Beautiful Morning," "Side by Side," "It Had to Be You," and more, dozens and dozens of songs into the night, songs of war, of peace, of love.

Amy, Douglas, and I would natter over which song Daddy should play first. He'd watch us and listen, and then his eyes would twinkle and he'd start to play, his arm sliding the bow back and forth, the heel of his work boot pumping up and down as he kept time. We'd play a home version of *Name That Tune*, competing to be the first to recognize the tune and begin the singing.

After a couple of hours, we'd start to tire, slump against each other, stare into space. My father was not patient with his children's inattentiveness.

"Sing!" he'd say. "Why aren't you singing? And why aren't you smiling? You're having fun, goddamn it."

We'd rearrange our faces into what we hoped looked like pleasure and sing dutifully, hating the damned violin and longing for bedtime.

Can you grasp that in the winter there was no escape? The thermometer hunkered below zero for days at a time, and ferries couldn't run because of the thick ice on the lake. We could have caught the Ford Tri-Motor operated by Island Airlines, which made daily flights to deliver the mail, groceries, items ordered from the Sears, Roebuck or Montgomery Ward catalogue, and human beings—but flying required disposable income my family reserved for other things.

▲   ▲   ▲

Easter Sunday was the outward and visible sign that winter might some day end. Douglas, Amy, and I would get up early, discover our Easter baskets, and stuff ourselves with marshmallow eggs, the hard-boiled eggs we'd dyed the evening before, yellow marshmallow Peeps, jelly beans, and a bite or two of our chocolate bunnies' ears. Then we'd get ready for church and go out in the front yard under the maple tree to be photographed, Douglas in his new suit, new shoes, and new tie, Amy and I in new dresses, new patent-leather shoes, new white gloves, and new pink-flower-bedecked white straw hats that scrunched our Toni permanents even more tightly into our skulls.

As soon as the photo session ended we'd run into the house to don our winter coats, boots, and scarves. We'd pile onto the back of the Model A and Daddy would drive us down to the dock to wait for the *Sonny S.* to come around the point to take us to South Bass, the island a mile to the south of us, so we could go to St. Paul's Episcopal Church. The *Sonny S.* was a fishing boat; only on Easter Sunday did it operate as a church boat.

Some years we had good weather for Easter, which meant no blizzard, no high winds, and no freezing rain, but even in the mildest years the temperature was below freezing, the wind was gusting, and the lake was tossing white caps. On the boat we'd hang on to each other and clutch at the rails until we got our sea legs, and then we'd stand still, roll with the boat, and laugh the passage across the lake while the three or four ladies with us (my parents stayed home to do whatever it is adults do when they have only one morning a year in which their house is child-free) sat shivering and nervous on their benches.

The church service was spectacular. First of all, there were so many people, at least forty, and, not only that, there was a choir, and the choir members wore robes, royal-blue ones topped by white smocks. Adding to the amazement was the fact that we sat in pews rather than at school desks, and, wonder of wonders, the pews had mechanical units at their base that unfolded. The first year we went to St. Paul's we thought we'd discovered a footrest, but then a woman, a stranger who smelled good, scowled at us and told us it was for our knees, not for our feet.

I'd watch adults come in and take their place on the kneeling pads, put their elbows on the back of the pews in front of them, fold their hands, and bow their heads. It was a curious posture.

"What are they doing?" I asked Amy and Douglas.

"They're praying."

I tried to imagine what adults might say to God.

Good morning, God. How are you today?

Thanks for the Easter basket.

God, did you see those barbaric children with their feet on the kneeling pads?

The church had stained-glass windows, tall and narrow, and the priest was so far away I couldn't see his face. Everything was so unfamiliar, and fascinating, that the worship service itself never registered.

The next big event after Easter was May 31, Memorial Day. It was the first day of the year we were allowed to go swimming, and it marked the beginning of the summer holidays. Vacationers, some of whom had children for us to play with, filled the island's cottages.

One family of vacationers—the Wilsons—were our special friends. They came up from Lancaster, Ohio, four times each summer and stayed for a week at a time in their vacation home, a decommissioned school bus refitted with beds and a kitchen counter.

Mr. Wilson, Elmer, played the guitar. Mrs. Wilson, Gladys, played the spoons and sang in a confident soprano. Gladys and Elmer had five children, three of whom were still of an age for family vacations: Leslie, whom I met when he was sixteen and who I thought was a blond-haired, banjo-playing god; Penny, who played the guitar and had red hair and was between my age and Amy's; and Roger, who was the youngest and not yet musically invested.

By day we girls—Penny, Amy, and I—lived in the water: water-skiing, with Elmer in the boat as captain and coach, or lounging in the lake on a tractor inner tube large enough to hold all three of us at once. In the evenings my family would migrate the half mile north to join the Wilsons in Albert's kitchen.

Albert Gmelch owned the two-story redbrick Georgian house in which he lived, plus the lakefront property on which the Wilsons' school bus and a dozen or more other vacation-home buses, trailers, and cottages were situated. The rooms in Albert's house were high-ceilinged, high-windowed, and crammed with heavy furniture. The house, while spacious and no doubt elegant when built, did not boast bathrooms. To get to the bathroom, you had to walk across the driveway—where in the daytime, chickens scratched in the dust and ruffled their feathers—to the far side of a dilapidated garage.

Outside the outhouse door was a sack of lime, which the adults scattered prodigiously to counter odors. On the other side of the wall behind the wooden toilet bench was Albert's chicken coop. After you knocked down a spider web or two, entered the outhouse, and sat down, you'd hear a few questioning clucks from the nesting hens on the other side of the wall. As outhouses go, it was exceptionally pleasant.

Albert's kitchen was just large enough to hold all the music makers. My dad, with his fiddle, and Elmer, with his guitar, would take the wooden chairs on the far side of the kitchen table near the wood-burning cookstove. Albert would settle into his chair in the far right corner, from where he'd nod his head in time to the music and pour drinks when he thought the fiddler and the guitar player looked a little dry. Leslie, the banjo-playing god, would stand to the left of the cookstove with his five-string.

Sometimes Penny would play the guitar while Elmer played the mandolin, but most of the time she, Amy, and I squeezed together on one chair and sang along with our mothers. We sang the songs we'd practiced in the bleak midwinter, and more: "Alexander's Ragtime Band," "I'm in the Mood for Love," "Heart of My Heart," "Has Anybody Seen My Gal?," and "Beer Barrel Polka." Once in a while we'd try a contemporary song like "Moon River," but after the first few notes, the musicians would give up, disgusted with the slow pace, and help themselves to a beer or a shot of whiskey, biding their time until the women and girls finished singing.

The dining room adjoining Albert's kitchen was used, no doubt, for formal dinners when the house was new. Now Albert used it for storage, primarily of outdoor equipment. Some evenings it held a rowboat. Most of the time it held at least one outboard motor balanced on a notched board over two sawhorses. As a result, my mental repertoire of song lyrics are all overlaid with the smell of outboard motor fuel, a mixture of gasoline and oil, a smell that still sets me humming the rare times I catch a whiff.

▲   ▲   ▲

Even as a child I suspected I had no real gift for music. It's not that anybody ever told me so; I reached my conclusion on the basis of seemingly incontrovertible evidence. For instance, in Albert's kitchen, Penny was sometimes invited to sing solos, never me. One winter Mrs. Kuemmel, the island schoolteacher, decided the Cartledge girls should sing a duet. She assigned Amy and me a piece of music called "Santa Lucia." Mrs. Kuemmel listened to us sing "Santa Lucia" twice, or maybe it was three times.

"Let me have the music," she said.

We never saw it again.

Miss Carrie High, who was in her nineties and smelled like ginger cookies, was the pianist at Sunday school. She'd group Douglas, Amy, and me beside her so we could see the words in her hymnal. We'd sing "In the Garden" or "Saviour, Like a Shepherd Lead Us" or "The Beautiful Garden of Prayer," and when we finished she'd clap her delicate hands, smile, and say, "Beautiful. Beautiful." After she became too frail to attend Sunday school, though, we were no longer invited to stand beside the piano and sing. Skimpy evidence, perhaps, but enough to make me nervous.

In school, music class was limited to a mere fifteen-minute segment on Friday afternoons. Class time was devoted to the study of and testing on a narrow red book that contained brief biographies of classical composers—Bach, Beethoven, Brahms, Handel, Chopin, and perhaps a few others—and information about musical nomenclature, the only bits of which that stuck were the mnemonics for the lines of the treble clef ("Every Good Boy Does Fine") and for the spaces ("FACE"). In the red book I learned about people like Wolfgang Mozart, who was composing and performing almost before he was out of diapers. I concluded that if you hadn't demonstrated musical accomplishments on your own, with no formal training, by age six, you'd be wasting your time trying to play an instrument.

Around that same time I got confused about my place in the church. My siblings were baptized as babies, but I wasn't. I suspected it was because my parents, instead of birthing me in the normal way, discovered me in a ditch by the side of the road and took me home so Amy and Douglas would have something to play with. How else would you explain the fact that everybody in the family except me could hop on one foot, blow bubbles with their gum, and get through supper without knocking over a glass of milk?

I was somewhat appeased when Charlie and I were baptized together. It was an auspicious day. Even my father was there for the service, sitting sideways at the student desk, his legs too long to fit anywhere except in the aisle. Reverend Lee had me lean over the baptismal bowl, which Douglas had filled with well water from the tap at the back of the room. I felt the icy water drip through my curls as the pastor intoned the baptismal formula: "In the name of the Father [drip] and the Son [drip] and the Holy Ghost [drip]." Then he pulled a hunk of hair at the back of my neck to make me raise my head. After the service we had a party at home with a glamorous cake imported from a bakery on the mainland. The icing read, "Charles Joseph, 10 months—Mary Joanna, 10 years."

I felt connected to the church for the first time, but the feeling lasted only until the next spring when Reverend Lee came to our house on a number of consecutive Sunday afternoons to conduct confirmation class for Douglas and Amy. I was right there at the dining room table with the three of them, and I paid attention to every word Reverend Lee said, and I memorized the Apostles' Creed and the Lord's Prayer just like they did, but when the great day of their reception into the church occurred, the two of them walked up to the altar table and were admitted into church membership, I was stuck sitting at my desk. I was eleven, and the rules said you had to be thirteen to join the church. Somehow the rules were relaxed for Amy, who was twelve, but I didn't warrant a dispensation.

From then on Amy and Douglas got to take communion. I didn't, because you had to be confirmed to participate in the Lord's Supper. I probably imagined them looking down their noses at stupid little me (surely joining the church made them too holy?), but my feeling of inferiority was real. So was my disappointment when Reverend Lee didn't reappear in our dining room the next year, when I was twelve, to prepare me for confirmation, or the year after when I was thirteen. I suppose if I'd told somebody what I wanted, something would have been done, but I didn't have the words, and so it wasn't until 1963, after I graduated from grade school and left the island for high school, that I tasted the bread and wine of Holy Communion.

So that's how it all began, not just my interest in the Church but also the disquieting notion that the institutional Church might not really want me.

chapter four

WHAT DO YOU DO WITH NINTH-GRADERS WHEN YOU HAVE no high school for them to attend? Islanders resolved the question in one of three ways. Either they sent their children to a private boarding school, or they sent their children back and forth on school board–funded rides on the Ford Tri-Motor airplane to the high school on South Bass Island, or they found families on the mainland with whom their children could board.

Douglas and Amy began their high-school careers off-island but ended up graduating from Put-in-Bay High School. I began and completed high school in Wooster, Ohio, coming home only for holidays, summer vacation, and a few weekends in the winter when I could catch a ride with family acquaintances headed up to go ice fishing.

I had just turned fourteen when I left for school. There were well over a thousand people in the student body, with more than 350 in the ninth grade alone. I thrilled in the excitement of finally seeing what a school locker looked like and of learning how to work my combination lock, and I thrived on being part of the wave of students rushing up and down wide staircases between one class and the next.

Football season was a grand adventure, what with the pep rallies, the bonfires, and the signs (GO, WOOSTER in the school colors of blue and gold) my new friends and I had lettered on posterboard. I went to the Homecoming football game with a boy, and at the gate to the football field he bought an enormous yellow chrysanthemum with a dark blue pipe cleaner in the center twisted into the shape of a W for me to pin on the lapel of my coat.

I was agog at the difference between football and basketball. Basketball was so much noisier, with everyone packed together inside a gym where the babble of excited voices, the squeak of the players' shoes, and the throb of the dribbling ball echoed in ever-escalating waves. I was surprised to find the players so near that I could watch the Roman Catholic boys make the sign of the cross on their chests before attempting a free throw (it never seemed to help) and even see the sweat dripping off their foreheads.

My musical incompetence was confirmed at one of those basketball games. One night the crowd started singing "The Star-Spangled Banner." Halfway through the song, a boy I knew turned to look at me and said, "Would you please stop singing off-key?"

Off-key? How could I be singing off-key? I didn't even know what it meant.

In ninth grade, I still believed keeping the beat and getting the words right equaled musical ability. Now I knew otherwise. I stopped singing in public. But more proof of my incompetence lay ahead.

I was taking Ninth-Grade Choir at the time. When registration forms for the next year's classes were distributed, some friends told me I should sign up for Senior Choir, made up of tenth, eleventh, and twelfth graders. Tryouts were mentioned casually, as though they were merely a formality. A few weeks later I got a note saying what time I was to go for my audition.

I walked into the green-walled room off the school office. The Senior Choir director pointed to a piano. On the piano was a music book open to a song, a simple song, a song with no chords and not all that many notes, a song as easy to sing as "Mary Had a Little Lamb," if you knew how to read music.

"All Senior Choir members can sight-read," said the director, "so I'd like to hear you sing this piece. Feel free to pick it out on the piano if that will help."

I couldn't sight-read, and I couldn't have picked anything out on the piano without a brain transplant. Also, I was too embarrassed to speak. We sat together in silence for a while, and then I suppose he excused me.

I might not have been destined to play music, but I could appreciate it. Every few weeks we had an assembly at school. The entire student body gathered in the auditorium to hear a speaker or to witness a talent show or to watch their compatriots get inducted into the National Honor Society. The most extraordinary assembly I ever attended, though, was held in the gym, not in the auditorium. A local college, the College of Wooster, had a corps of bagpipers who played during half-time at their football games. One afternoon the corps presented a concert at the high school. Half a dozen bagpipers—or was it a dozen?—dressed in black, gold, and white tartan kilts, pumped their bagpipes and marched in step up one side of the gym and down the other, then crossed the width of the gym, pivoted, and marched across it again.

You haven't heard bagpipes until you've heard them played in concert in an enclosed gymnasium. The sound hits the bleachers first and then the back walls, and it ricochets from there up to the ceiling and down to the floor. The waves bounce, collide, and bounce some more, like a thousand crazed Ping-Pong balls let loose in your bathroom. The music assaults you from every direction, and it takes a week for your head to clear.

The friends I was sitting with at the assembly winced and covered their ears. I covered my ears, too, but I was faking delicacy. I loved the way the music seemed to fill the universe. Ever since, when I hear the sound of bagpipes I find myself grinning.

▲   ▲   ▲

The new friends I was making in high school frequently invited me to church with them on Sunday mornings and to their youth group meetings on Sunday nights. Pretty soon I settled in with the Methodists.

I hesitated the first time the communion tray was passed.

"No, go ahead, it's okay," said the friend sitting beside me.

I can't say taking communion that first time changed my life. The bread, it turned out, was just a flat, oval cracker that turned gummy in my mouth. I had to use the wine—really just grape juice—to wash it down. But it was nice to be included. I never joined the church, but I went to Sunday school and the service, sang in the youth choir (where no one commented on my voice), was an officer in the youth fellowship group, and performed in the youth drama group. We were encouraged—pushed, even—to go to other denominations' worship services, to read, to wonder, to think, and to ask questions. For three years running, the church sponsored a youth-group work camp near Cherokee, North Carolina. There the boys repaired things while the girls taught Bible stories and songs to the local children, Native Americans in a poor area of the Appalachians.

It was on a trip to Cherokee that I first saw someone give his heart to Jesus. Our carloads of teenagers and adults camped out overnight in a church in Kentucky on our way south. That evening we went to a church service in what must have been a barn. Our group sat on benches at the back of the room. A small congregation—twenty? thirty?—huddled close to the preacher at the front. At the end of his sermon the preacher made an altar call. "Just As I Am" played in the background.

Come to the altar. Give your heart to Jesus.

Nobody moved.

Jesus can take away your sins. All you have to do is come forward. Jesus is calling you now. He wants you just the way you are, sins and all.

I didn't quite know what the preacher was after, but I felt the tension rising, rising, until it was nearly unbearable, and then finally someone stood up, a young man, and he walked to the front and knelt, and then other people did the same, and the song played over and over while we kept singing, "O Lamb of God, I come, I come!"

The service finally ended, and our group escaped. When we got back to the church where we were camping out, one of the adult leaders tried to put into perspective what we'd seen.

He said, "I'm proud of all of you. It's easy to get caught up in the emotionalism of that kind of service, and none of you did." He said Methodists believe faith is not the emotion of a moment but a clear-headed decision to be a disciple, to love mercy and justice, and to work for the greater good. We Methodists are nothing if not pragmatic.

▲   ▲   ▲

We were good kids, the class of 1967, even though we had the reputation for being the rowdiest class in the history of Wooster High School—a reputation I suppose we earned. After all, when we were eleventh-graders, the boys in my advanced English class *did* compete every time the teacher turned her back to see who could land a spitball between the eyes of the portrait of George Washington high on the wall. Most days the floor, walls, and blackboard would be spotted with slimy white globs by the time the bell rang. And then there was one time after an assembly when my classmates *did* rip down the hundreds of signs posted on the corridor walls and fling them across the floors.

On the other hand, it was my senior year before I heard someone say he'd smoked marijuana, and even then it was an older man, a first-

year college student home for fall break. I'd certainly heard the word
pregnant, but I was two pregnancies away from saying it out loud. We
were at the tail end of fifties gentility and just ahead of the sixties riots.

Life got fuzzy in the summer of 1966. I was dating a boy named
Bob, and after work he and I and a group of friends would get together,
go down to the lake, and build a beach fire. The boys would drink, and
the girls wouldn't, and boyfriends and girlfriends would kiss a little and
talk a lot.

Canada was a major topic of conversation.

"Would you or wouldn't you?" the boys would ask each other (the
girls didn't venture opinions; we, after all, were girls). Would you go to
Vietnam to fight, or would you head for Canada?

The American body count was in our faces, and the police were
turning fire hoses on people in the South, and the churches were being
very, very quiet. The things I'd been taught—to ask questions, to love
America (my father, who became a naturalized citizen in 1955, was very
clear on this country's virtues), to love my neighbor as myself, and to
respect differences—seemed to have no public value in the summer of
1966.

▲   ▲   ▲

By the next summer, everything was different. I'd graduated from high
school summa cum laude and was headed to Ohio State University on
full scholarship. I started dating someone much too old for me, a college
senior who was headed for the army as soon as he graduated. After two
semesters, I dropped out of college, at his behest, to marry him. The best
I can say about myself is that I was a silly child. Unable to imagine my
own future, I embarked on his. It could have been worse—ungrounded
and confused as I was, I might have joined SNCC (the Student Nonvio-
lent Coordinating Committee) or taken up arms with the Symbionese
Liberation Army—but it could have been better: I might at least have
finished college.

By the time I got married, I'd given up on God. My husband, who
was gorgeous (dark-brown hair, fair skin, and blue eyes), was also totally
antiestablishment. He dreamed of building a house in the distant hills of
the west, a place of safety to wait out the coming revolution. His certainty that religion was a crock of shit was significantly stronger than
my suspicion there might be some truth to it. He was too much older

than I for me to realize how very young he was or to know that he, like everyone else on the edge of adulthood, was testing out feelings, ideas, and possibilities. We were children struggling with adult realities, and the greatest of these, for us and for our contemporaries, was Vietnam. Well, one reality did surpass the war: my pregnancy and the birth of my first daughter.

At age nineteen, in the middle of the night in an apartment in Alabama, I sat in a yellow-slipcovered armchair feeding my baby and watching the presidential-election results. A year later my husband and my brother were both in Vietnam. I read the morning newspaper and watched the nightly news, anxiously awaiting peace negotiations. Instead there were reports on negotiations over the shape of the table at which the peace negotiations might take place.

Should the table be round? Should it be square? Should it be oval?

Why would anybody care when there was a war on? How could the government keep fiddling when each nightly news broadcast ended with the toll of Americans killed that day? How could something so petty as the shape of a table determine the duration of the war and the deaths and lives of so many people?

I was still very young then. I know more now about power plays, about strategizing and establishing parameters. I know the rules of the game determine its outcome; that the one who makes the rules wins; that wars are won and lost long before anybody shows up in a treaty room. And while I know those things, pettiness is still my enemy.

I stood the tension as long as I could, and then I took the coward's way out: I fell in love with a tall, gray-eyed, silver-tongued, guitar-picking southerner and stopped thinking about the war. I got divorced. A month or two later I got married again, having learned nothing in the interim. Three weeks later we headed to his hometown for Thanksgiving. Late that afternoon we stood in his brother's front yard, talking. That's when I decided I could live in the South. To be outside at the end of November, with the sun shining so warmly I didn't need a coat, or even a sweater, was a new, and incredible, experience. On those superficial grounds, we made the decision to move to his hometown.

That marriage lasted five years. After the second divorce, I lived with my two daughters in affluent poverty: the kind where you reside in government-assisted housing because you can't afford the rent on any other kind of apartment; the kind where you don't drive to the far side of town because if you do, you'll run out of gas before payday and you've only got two dollars left after you paid bills and bought groceries and what if there's an emergency; the kind where you cut your own hair by holding up one curl at a time and chopping at it with your sewing shears because a trip to a beautician costs as much as a cute dress, and you love cute dresses and curly hair can take a lot of hacking and still look okay; the kind where you can afford to stop at a fast-food place once a month or so for supper but you always get the food to go because the Kool-Aid in your refrigerator is cheaper than fountain drinks.

The poverty is what made me a feminist, although at the time I'm not sure I even knew the word. I was working as supply-room manager at a textile company, reporting to the senior engineer. I wasn't making much money; the men working in similar capacities were making substantially more. I asked the senior engineer about a raise.

He was a good old country boy with an education. He laughed heartily and genially. "Sure. No problem. You'll get a raise as soon as you get back from Sweden."

"Sweden?"

"Yes, Sweden. That's where they do the sex-change operations."

In other words, I wasn't getting a raise because I was a woman. My indignation wasn't based in theoretical constructs about the role of women; it was based in having children whose feet kept outgrowing their shoes. And yet there was nothing to be done about my salary. Didn't I know this was simply the way the world worked?

▲   ▲   ▲

Luckily, affluent poverty is the fun kind, the kind where disaster is only one paycheck away and you're forced to pay attention to every detail, every penny, every decision, because the future—your children's, your own—depends on it. Once you learn how to live within that tension—and I did learn, well—every bill paid becomes a victory, every birthday present a sacrament.

My life was okay except for my despair at the failure of my marriages. It's like this: one divorce, you cope. You admit your failures and his, recognize youth and stupidity played a large part, believe you learned what you needed to know, and choose to go on.

The second divorce damn near kills you. It forces you to recognize that you're the problem.

I'm not saying my divorces were all my fault. I'm saying that no matter whose actions precipitated the divorces, I'm the one who chose to marry the men I married. I loved my first husband for his certainty, for the way he chortled when he heard something funny, for his curiosity. I loved my second husband more deeply—treasured him, was desolate when I had to leave him, left because I saw no option for stability or tranquillity with him. The pain of separation forced me to admit I was incapable of sustaining a relationship. I saw a therapist for as long as I could afford it (three sessions, maybe four), and then I stopped. I'm a sensible woman, in and among my idealistic tendencies, so I made a sensible decision: I wasn't going to get involved with any more men.

I was only twenty-five, but I was a strong-minded twenty-five. "Bullheaded" is the word my parents use for their children. It's appropriate: strong people beget strong children who beget strong children. And it's a good thing I was strong, because there I was, a twice-divorced failure, with two children, no money, no life, and no prospects.

I gave religion a shot after my second divorce when Evelyn, my former sister-in-law, invited me to go to church with her. She told me she was Church of God of Prophecy. I didn't know anything about that denomination, but how different could it be?

The service began in the ordinary fashion, with hymn singing, a prayer or two from the preacher, and some Bible readings. It was during the sermon that events took an unusual cast. All the people in the congregation were sitting in the pews minding their own business, perhaps even listening to the sermon, when a tall, slender middle-aged woman wearing a dress patterned with dark flowers against an ivory background stood up and began shouting. A moment later she was in the center aisle, striding up and down, up and down, up and down, her arms waving in the air, indistinguishable syllables streaming from her mouth.

She scared the bejesus out of me. I thought she was having some variety of medical emergency, and I couldn't understand why nobody was rushing from the sanctuary to call an ambulance.

On our way across the parking lot after the service I broached the subject with Evelyn. "What happened in there?" I asked.

"The Holy Spirit came upon her, and she was speaking in tongues" was the answer.

"Oh," I said.

Oh.

Ah.

Holy Spirit.

Speaking in tongues.

It was five years before I went to another Sunday service.

I'm not saying I never went to church at all. Offhand I remember attending at least two weddings. One was my friend Terry's, the other her sister Maureen's. The weddings took place in the United Methodist Church their family attended, which is how I ended up going there in 1980 when the curtain between me and God opened: it was the only church where I knew how to get to the sanctuary from the parking lot.

But that came later. First I had to figure out how to live as a single mother. I took a secretarial job with a law firm and a year or so later became the firm's real-estate paralegal. I worked full-time and overtime to pay the bills, and as soon as I could afford tuition, I started taking a class or two per semester toward my unfinished college degree. After a few false starts, I declared English as my major, opting for words, my first and deepest enchantment. I liked the rhythms of texts; the thrill of coming upon an unfamiliar word; the way you acquire information almost by osmosis even when you're reading for pleasure; the way people who don't exist—people the writer invented, people who weren't, aren't, and never will be real—sometimes become as real to me as my hands.

My children made a lot of sacrifices during that time. They were, after all, so young—six and two—when their dad and I separated. They needed time with me and attention from me, and I gave them all I could, which is to say not enough. It was never enough, even though I sewed their school dresses and Halloween costumes and bought their shoes and picked them up from day care and cooked supper and gave them baths and called them outside in the evenings so they could watch with me a particularly beautiful sunset fade to dark and then tucked them into their beds and gave them kisses. How could it be enough? There was only one of me.

Well, one and a half, actually. My best friend, Mary Flowers, who is my daughters' cousin and only five years younger than I, carried as much of the weight as she could. Every year in the late summer, she'd take my children shopping for school clothes, and she was their ally in makeup and ear-piercing discussions. I hid their Christmas presents at her house, and she'd deliver them at five A.M. on Christmas morning so she could see my daughters' faces when they woke up and realized Santa had come. She took Tara and Jennifer with her when she went to the beach, and we took Mary along when we went to the island on summer vacation. Every other weekend when my children were at their dad's, she and I went out partying. We'd head for one of the two bars we judged respectable enough for us and order Kahlua and cream in a tall glass. Mary could drink as many as she pleased, but I always had to stop halfway through my second drink because the right side of my face had turned numb. We'd talk with whomever looked interesting, and at closing time when our conversational companions suggested continuing the evening, we'd offer directions to our favorite all-night breakfast establishment, where we'd eat, drink coffee, smoke cigarettes until dawn, and then tell them good-bye.

Okay, we may not have said good-bye every single time. But we always waited until we were more or less sober before we made any decisions.

By the time I'd been divorced three or four years, life was good, although I expect my daughters felt the same way I did as a child: that I was a princess deposited with ruffians, for the good of the state or some other equally noble reason, and soon my real parents, statuesque, with buffed fingernails, would return to remove me from my vale of woe.

Life went on. In and amongst motherhood, work, and school, I also dated, ubiquitously yet selectively. The ubiquity was inevitable, since two months was the maximum time I'd date anyone. I liked the time of discovery in a relationship when you go places, do things, talk, listen to each other laugh, watch each other move, get to know each other. As time passes, though, because of the very nature of relationships, things have to change: the relationship either grows or withers. I preferred to pull any relationship up by the roots and toss it in the compost pile. Because I knew anybody whose company I enjoyed was a person with whom I was incapable of sustaining a relationship.

▲   ▲   ▲

So how did I end up back in church? How does it happen that someone for whom God is a nonentity chooses to orient her life differently, to enter into the great swirling waltz of religious faith?

Don't blame me.

It was an accident.

I didn't mean to do it.

It wasn't my fault.

Six years after my second divorce, I finally had a life. My children were healthy; I'd bought a brand-new car, a gold Chevette with a standard transmission and no air-conditioning, so the payments were low and the gas mileage high; the hours I needed to graduate from college were steadily accumulating; and I had right at three thousand dollars in a savings account. And then the God-thing happened, and it was the difference between the moment when you look into a tube of Pick Up sticks and the sticks are tidily arranged, their colors muted by shadow, and the moment when you dump the sticks from the tube and watch them scatter, red, yellow, blue, green, in a glorious heap for you to ease your way through, one careful movement at a time.

It started in casual conversations that spanned a six-month time period. One friend happened to mention that she went to church.

"Why?" I asked.

She told me that for a while she and her roommate were so poor, they couldn't afford to buy food, yet they'd sometimes come home to find sacks and sacks of groceries outside their door. They never found out who brought the groceries, but the food kept them alive and so did the knowledge that somebody was watching them and caring for them. Somehow for my friend, God got wrapped up in the groceries, and that's why she went to church.

Another acquaintance, a woman with two adolescent daughters, amazed me with her cheerfulness, even though her teenagers were taxing every emotional resource she possessed.

"How are you doing this?" I asked her. "How are you managing?"

"I drag them to church every time the doors open," she said.

"And does that help?"

"I don't know, but I have to do something, and it's the only thing I know."

The third conversation was with someone I was dating, which means I'd been seeing him less than two months and was indifferent to his opinion on how I should live my life. We were lying in bed one afternoon when my girls were visiting their father. He must have asked where I went to church, and I said I didn't go to church, and he said, firmly, "You and those children need to be in church." I just looked at him, and he looked back at me, and then we went on to talk about other things.

A final conversation was with Helen, the mother of Terry and Maureen, the women whose weddings I'd attended at the Methodist church.

Helen was good to me. Her kitchen table was a sanctuary where I could sit and drink coffee and feel cared for and safe while my children beat out music on Helen's piano or laboriously printed their initials beside treasures they found in the catalogues she kept in a kitchen drawer. Helen knew I didn't go to church; neither did any of her children at that time except Maureen. She was okay with that, understood distance and angst and that gaining maturity is hard work, but one day she said to me, "I hope someday you'll get to experience the happiness I've known in sitting with my children in church."

▲ ▲ ▲

Even I, heathen that I was, couldn't ignore the links between these conversations. I considered going to church, but I didn't think much of it. I knew what to expect inside the doors: a cadre of people who knew each other well, weren't interested in outsiders, and chattered about topics that had nothing to do with my reality.

I started thinking about God instead. The question I came back to, repeatedly, for months, was *What would it mean if there really were a God, if, instead of being the invention of trite minds, God really did exist?*

I might have gone on holding this conversation with myself indefinitely if it hadn't been for a day in November 1980, when I was on my way back to work after picking up my dry cleaning. My experience that day is inexplicable. Scholarly research has established that a person's religious experience is dependent upon his or her religious formation. In other words, what you see is what you become. For instance, if my staunchly Christian grandmother Mona had lived to be a hundred thousand years old, she would never have spoken in tongues. In fact, if she'd been with me the day I saw it happen, Grandma would most likely have strode forth from her pew, grabbed the hollering woman by the elbows, slapped her into silence, and pronounced, "Woman, get hold of yourself. You're in church."

By the same token, I have no answer to the faith question tossed out from time to time, especially in the Deep South where I live, "Have you given your heart to Jesus?" Where I come from, that's not how commitment works. Where I come from, you study and think and then make a decision about faithfulness rather than being swept off your feet like some love-sickened calf of an adolescent.

Given all that, my experience in November 1980 is, as I said, inexplicable. All morning I'd been deliberating my God-question—*What if God were real? What then?*—and I'd just retrieved my dry cleaning, pulled out onto a four-lane road, and shifted into third when (and I know this next part is far-fetched, but I can't help it; it was real) the roof of my car became transparent and a shaft of golden light bathed me in luminescence, and I could see each individual ray of gold even while the rays were surrounding and containing me. I started laughing, laughing out loud, because, you see, I now knew the answer: God was real. And then I started weeping, but then I stopped and started laughing again instead because all of it—the warmth, the light, the peace, the rays—all of it was the most magnificent cosmic joke in the history of the world, and the joke was on me. The moment went on for hours, although it was long over by the time I got to my office, which was only five minutes away from the dry cleaners.

I learned later that the proper terminology for such an event is "conversion experience," a phrase I'd never heard in northern Ohio, an area far too pragmatic for such elevated notions. If anyone said she'd been touched by the Holy Spirit, she'd have been known forever after as "that nice woman who's a little touched in the head." Nonetheless, it happened to me.

The moment ended, but the dazzle remained. I had an answer to my questions. Yes. God existed.

I had no framework for my experience; it was as outlandish as the possibility that human beings are transported up into Martian spacecraft. I didn't talk to anybody about it. Instead, I thought. And what I thought was that if God is real—a point on which I now held absolute certainty—then I needed to be in church.

The next Sunday I took myself there.

chapter five

———

CHURCHES IN AMERICA PRETTY MUCH ALL SMELL THE
same. The hymnals are part of the aroma, with their hundreds of printed
paper pages compressed between fabric covers. Wood is another part, I
suppose: the pews, the pulpit, the altar. There are the residual cleaning
smells: Murphy's Oil Soap or Pledge spray, ammonia for the windows,
brass polish for the altar cross and the collection plates. The stained-glass
windows contribute in that they generally aren't meant to be opened, so
the smells of paper, wood, cleaning supplies, and transient worshippers
remain, largely undisturbed, Sunday after Sunday, year after year.

I like the smell of a sanctuary. I feel safe within it, and happy. I
don't know if everybody does or if I have these feelings because my
schoolroom and my sanctuary were the same room when I was a child
and I loved the room because one of the happiest days of my life was the
day in 1955 I finally, finally started first grade there.

I felt awkward my first Sunday back in church in 1980. I didn't
know when to sit or stand. I faltered my way through hymns I'd never
heard before. I didn't know when or why the Holy Ghost had changed
its name to the Holy Spirit. When I recited the Apostles' Creed with
the rest of the congregation, I was disturbed because they left out a line.
The version I knew states that Jesus "was crucified, dead, and buried; he
descended into hell; on the third day he rose again and ascended into
heaven." The Jesus in these people's creed hadn't been to hell and back.
All he did was die, get buried, and rise again.

I thought I was in the wrong place until the organist started playing the closing hymn, "The Old Rugged Cross," and I could shut my
hymnal because I knew all the words. The hymn is filled with words
and phrases like "suffering and shame," "despised," "stained with blood,"
"trophies," "crown"—words I don't have much use for. But it does have

one word I love—"cherish"—and it does have a steady, lilting-in-the-midst-of-sorrow tune.

I went back to church the next week to sing some more. That week I took my daughters with me, and from then on we were in church Sunday after Sunday. December passed, and January, and in February the pastor of the church came to call. His visit surprised me; I didn't know pastors visited people. He told me quite a few things about the church, asked me a few questions, and then told me the names, ages, and occupations of every single adult male in the congregation. I was perplexed; the last thing I needed was to meet one more asshole in a suit. I knew enough of them already.

In March I went to the first-ever meeting of a group called Single/Single Again that a kindly layperson had organized. Fifteen or twenty of us huddled near the refreshment table in the fellowship hall, a room that could hold two hundred people. After half an hour of eating cookies, we all decided to go out for pizza. I was interested to hear the man sitting next to me, a blond guy, mid-forties, in a suit, order a beer. I didn't know people who went to church were allowed to drink. (In retrospect, that was really stupid of me—as though I expected church people to be differently human than us ordinary folks.)

I had a good time watching and listening to Fred, the blond guy, put the moves on a woman seated near him. I chatted enough with him to learn he'd been a widower almost a year. He mentioned that he'd paid a deposit on a cruise he was going to take in August.

"Have you ever been on a cruise before?" I asked.

"No, but this one looked interesting. It's all single people."

I grinned. Sunshine, salt air, single people, food, alcohol: a recipe for a good time, indeed.

Fred grinned back.

Ten days later he and I went out for dinner. I learned he was born in 1935, was the oldest of four children, and had lived his entire life in North Carolina and South Carolina except for a two-year stint in El Paso, Texas. He managed the southeastern region for a national chemical-distribution company and spent two or three nights a week out of town, checking in on one branch office or another.

Over dessert, Fred asked what had brought me to worship services. I hadn't told anybody about my Chevette and its roof and the light—it was too intimate and still too new—and was surprised when I started describing it to him.

He said, "Nothing like that has ever happened to me. I've heard about it happening to other people, though."

"You have?" Oh. So I wasn't the only one.

"I've always wondered if something was wrong with me because it didn't work that way for me."

"You have? I thought it happened to me because I'm so thick-headed that it was the only way God could get my attention."

We left the restaurant and went to a club for a drink. He ordered a bourbon and ginger with a wedge of lime; I, my standard Kahlua and cream. Our drinks were half gone when he asked why I'd gotten divorced.

I studied him, wondering how a grown man could be so stupid. What kind of question was that for anybody to ask on a first date? I decided it was my solemn duty to prepare the poor fool for dates with other divorced women. I gave him the short list.

Fred blinked and mumbled something meaningless. A few minutes later we somehow drifted to the topic of heaven.

I said, "I don't much care one way or another whether it exists," and he said, "Oh, it exists," and then he told me why he believes it does.

He knew from the day his wife was diagnosed with a brain tumor that she would die, but after she had surgery, there was a time of hope, and then there was no more hope, only illness, and she was sick for a very long time, three years all together. When she was in the hospital for the last time, he knew she was dying, but he'd been without sleep and without sleep and without sleep and finally he went home. The ringing of the phone woke him. He knew she was dead before he picked up the receiver.

When he got off the elevator at the hospital and started down the hall to her room, his pastor approached him and said, "She's with Jesus now."

Fred brushed past, enraged by the statement, and went to his dead wife's bedside.

"She never smiled much, but when I looked into her face she was smiling. That's when I knew there's a heaven. The smile on her face proved it to me. Heaven's real, and so is death. When life's over, it's over. When I buried her, she was wearing nothing but a dress and a pair of panties. And the one thing I've learned since then is that death is permanent."

Fred spoke quietly, reflectively. I sat silent, with tears standing in my eyes, and felt the first pale glimmer of love, without even knowing it.

After that night we talked on the phone every few days, depending on his travel schedule, and dated regularly. It isn't accurate to say I liked him or loved him (I barely knew the man), but I felt an assurance about him, and about myself. I knew something important, no matter how improbable, connected us.

We'd been dating a month or so when I introduced Fred to my children. The next day I regretted it.

I called him from work and said, "I don't think we should be spending this much time together."

"Why's that?"

"Because I don't want my children to get to know you. My emotions are one thing; my children's emotions are something else entirely. I can take what comes, but I don't want my children to get hurt."

The next morning he called me back. "My daughter needs a dress for the prom. I was wondering if you and your children would like to go out for pizza with me and my children, and then we could all go to the mall together to look for a prom dress."

He couldn't see me shaking my head no, but he must have heard the edge in my voice when I asked, "Did you even hear what I said yesterday?"

"Yes. I heard everything you said."

Silence while I thought things through. He was a decent man. He'd taken my statement seriously, and now he was clearly upping the ante.

What to do? What to do? Stand still, retreat, or move forward?

"Okay, Fred. Yes, I'd like that."

The four children laughed and carried on at the pizza place, and then we all went to the mall. His daughter tried on several dresses before she came out of a dressing room wearing a very pretty light blue dress, floor length, with a fitted bodice, narrow shoulder straps, and a flowing skirt.

"It looks beautiful on you," Fred said to her, "but it's too big."

I stepped over to her to check the side seams and the back zipper.

"It's not too big," I reported. "It's too long." I knelt down on the floor to inspect the hem. "See? It just needs turned up an inch or two." I folded the fabric up far enough that her feet were visible and turned my face up to see Fred. "Nothing to it. I could hem it in an hour."

He was staring down at me, his cheeks flushed. He later told me that the moment I knelt down on the floor to help with his daughter's dress was when the glimmer of love he felt for me became a flicker.

▲   ▲   ▲

The love burst into flame the first time we made love.

We'd been dating for two months. My children were at their dad's for the weekend. Fred and I had accidentally gone to see a dreary movie and afterward ended up giggling our way down the hallway to my bedroom. That semester I was taking two classes, and I had to shove all my textbooks and notebooks off the bed to make room for Fred.

The sex was fun, and easy. Afterward he sat up cross-legged on the bed and stroked my body for the longest time.

I was lying on my stomach, luxuriating. "Do you know what the worst part of this is?" I asked him.

"The worst part? No, what?"

"It's going to get better."

His hands stopped moving. "It is?"

"Of course. Sex always gets better after the first time."

"I have trouble imagining that."

"Me too."

▲   ▲   ▲

When I got up the next morning, the first thing I did was dial Mary Flowers' number. I was sobbing when she answered the telephone.

"Mary, can you come over here?"

"Where are you? What is it?"

"I think I'm in trouble."

"Where are the children?"

"They're at their dad's."

"I'm on my way."

She reports that I was sobbing when she arrived.

"Tell me why you're crying, Mary Jo."

"I don't know."

"Did something happen?"

"Fred and I had sex last night."

"Oh, good. It's about time. But why are you crying?"

"I don't know."

"Is it something he did? Did he hurt you?"

"No, it was wonderful. He's wonderful." Sob, sob, sob.

"Then why are you crying? I've never seen you like this. He's just a guy. We know how this works. It was just sex."

Now I was babbling as well as sobbing, saying things like "he said" and "I said" and "then he" and "then I" and "this one's different," and finally Mary Flowers made sense of what I was saying, and she said, "Oh, shit."

Oh, shit, indeed.

▲   ▲   ▲

A week later Fred told me he loved me. We were inside my apartment near the front door. I was leaning back against the wall. We'd been kissing, my hands on his waist, his hands cupping my shoulders. He was looking a little pale, and I was about to ask him if he was feeling all right, when he said, "I love you, Mary Jo."

I stared into his blue eyes. He looked expectant, as though waiting for me to say something. I stared. He waited. I stared. He waited some more.

"You have to go home now," I said.

He blinked. "What?"

"You have to go home now."

"Why?"

"Because I think I'm going to throw up."

I wanted him to leave so I could heave, and then I wanted to fall asleep and when I woke up I wanted this conversation never to have taken place.

Fred shook his head. "You're not going to throw up."

"Yes, really, I think I am." I shifted my body several feet away from him, readying myself for a break for the bathroom. He could see himself out.

Fred said again, gently, "You're not going to throw up. You're going to be okay. Here: let's sit down on the couch and talk for a minute."

We sat. He held my hand. His lips were moving, but I couldn't hear him for the sound of the wind howling around my ears. I felt as though I'd plummet into an abyss if I took a step either direction, into the truth or into a lie. I loved him, yes, but to say the words was to speak a promise, a commitment to endurance across time. I was afraid to do that . . . but I couldn't lie into those eyes, either.

Ten minutes. Half an hour. An hour. Fred was no longer pale. He looked healthy, and happy, and not at all troubled by my verbal paralysis.

I started to imagine saying the words to him, and I felt a jolt of terror each time. In the end, though, I had to make a decision. Fred is a patient man. He intended to stay until I responded one way or another.

Finally, I just said the words: "I love you, too."

As soon as I spoke, the wind stopped howling, and then I started laughing, and I leaned to kiss him, and I said the words half a dozen times in a row for the sheer pleasure of it, and Fred's eyes began to water, and we sat together on and on into the night, saying the words, laughing, kissing, and finally I sent him home.

▲   ▲   ▲

When a man like Fred speaks of love, he also means fidelity, which may explain why he had a crisis two days later. He was still scheduled to take that cruise in August, which he expected to be filled with food, alcohol, and many bronzed unmarried people in bathing suits. He'd planned to get laid while on board, although he phrased it more delicately, saying, "I assumed with a ship full of single people having a good time, I might meet a woman to enjoy the evenings with."

For weeks he vacillated over whether or not to cancel the cruise. The man had been married more than twenty years. He'd been single only one year. He wanted to party. And who could blame him? Besides, as he told me more than once, he'd already paid the deposit, which he'd lose if he didn't go.

I knew if Fred's and my relationship continued, it would deepen, and if it deepened we were heading toward a permanent commitment. At that point, there'd be no cruising. I decided to make things easy for him, so one night I told him, "If what you need to do is go out and fuck half the county, then go and do it. I'll still be here when you get finished."

I meant it. I was thirty-one with two fine children, three thousand dollars in the bank, a new car, a stable job, and an English degree to complete. My life was full, and I was in no hurry.

Fred canceled the cruise. Two weeks later, on the Saturday of Memorial Day weekend, he asked me to marry him. I said yes.

▲   ▲   ▲

Fools that we were, Fred and I got married in the miserable heat of August in South Carolina. Mary Flowers was my maid of honor, and the five children our attendants. The rehearsal took place the morning of the wedding. I, being somewhat over-the-top with the whole bride business, sobbed through much of it.

Finally the pastor told me to stop it, so I did.

After the rehearsal I remembered a phrase from the Korean Creed, which I read in the back of the hymnal every Sunday when I got bored. "Grace equal to every need," it says. I repeated the words to myself throughout the day.

We have a photograph taken in the church vestibule moments before we proceeded down the aisle. Jennifer is first in line; her hair is shining golden and she's giggling. Tara, just behind her, isn't trying very hard to hide her disgust at having to wear baby's breath in her hair. Mary Flowers, darkly tanned and tense, has a tear glistening in the corner of her right eye.

Terry wasn't there. She was nine months pregnant with her first baby, and it was just too hot. Her mother and her father were there, though.

Afterward Helen hugged me and asked, "When was the last time you wore baby's breath in your hair?"

We both knew the answer: it was October 14, 1976, the day Terry got married, when I was a bridesmaid and Tara and Jennifer were her flower girls.

▲   ▲   ▲

My girls and I moved into Fred's house, which wasn't exactly a shrine to his first wife but came close. He didn't empty her closet until the week after he asked me to marry him, and it was July before he'd taken down the ornately framed eighteen-by-twenty-four portrait of her in her wedding gown. I wanted to rearrange the bedroom furniture, but Fred explained that every configuration had been tried, and this was the only one that worked. Inanimate objects began to take on complex emotional substance, and the greatest of these was the piano in the living room. I suppose I could have moved the damned thing over Fred's objections, but he and I had so many other things to argue over that I never got around to it.

Because of course we argued. The patterns of our separate lives had disintegrated, and as yet we had no new structure with which to replace them. There were all those children living with us, four of them teenagers (one of Fred's children having decided to take that semester off from college), which meant Fred and I were not only adjusting to the first year of marriage; we were also adjusting to seven personalities under one roof.

Actually, if we'd set out to enter into the most difficult marriage possible, we couldn't have planned things better. We had the age difference (fifteen years), the cultural differences (southern vs. midwestern), the political differences (Fred voted for Richard Nixon at every opportunity, whereas I draped my mirrors with black crepe when Reagan was elected), and the personality differences (he had logbooks in which he'd recorded every check he'd written since 1963; I had ten years' worth of bank statements stuffed into one manila envelope with a split seam). Add five children to that, and disaster takes up position in the limb of a tree and awaits the right moment to strike.

Fred and I were too blitheringly in love to care about the obstacles when we got married, but it wasn't long before we had to come to terms with them. I don't remember the argument—something to do with one or more of the children, I'm sure—but I do remember standing at the dresser pulling my clothes out to shove them into a suitcase and then stuffing the suitcase full of Fred's clothes, too, because I couldn't imagine going anywhere without him.

And then he was standing at my right elbow.

"Please, put the clothes down," he said. "Please, can we talk?"

Later he refolded the things and returned them to their proper place, and from then on we still made mistakes and still annoyed the hell out of each other as often as not, but we knew we were in this, together, permanently. Part of the reason was God: We were both certain God intended us to be together (although, in retrospect, God probably expected us to have better sense than to marry five months after our first date). The second was the sensuality of our relationship. I'm not speaking merely of the sex, which did, indeed, keep getting better. I'm also talking about how Fred would come home for lunch, take off his suit coat, drape it over a chair back, unbutton the sleeves of his white shirt, and fold the cuffs up past his wrists, and I'd nearly swoon at the sight of his wrist bones.

I officially embraced Methodism a few months after Fred and I got married. Before doing so, I went through an adult confirmation class, and I read two books, each of them published every four years by the United Methodist Church, immediately following its quadrennial legislative gathering. *The Book of Discipline* documents the Church's theology and polity (the latter term is church language for administrative structure). The section titled "Doctrinal Standards and Our Theological Task" interested me the most. I learned there that Methodism is "grounded in Scripture, informed by Christian tradition, enlivened in experience, and tested by reason." Reason? Reason is good. I have a brain. I like using it, even when it comes to God. I have energy, too, a trait the book suggested was consistent with Methodism, saying, "The underlying energy of the Wesleyan theological heritage stems from an emphasis upon practical divinity, the implementation of genuine Christianity in the lives of believers." I learned that John Wesley, the founder of Methodism, was interested in doctrine only insofar as it was significant for Christian discipleship and that "love of God is always linked with love of neighbor, passion for justice and renewal in the life of the world." The important words were there, words that convinced me that these people knew the same God I'd been introduced to: passion, energy, justice, renewal. And I loved the practicality of it all.

The other book I read was *The Book of Resolutions,* which sets forth Methodist understanding on social and justice issues, including labor unions (for), literacy (for), racism (against), homelessness (against), and inclusivity (for). One of the first things I turned to was the resolution on abortion. I'd been pro-choice ever since March, 1973. Jennifer was eight weeks old. My period was due. It didn't arrive. Instead, the veins in my breasts became so dark they seemed to have been tattooed on, and my body started feeling odd, in a too-familiar way.

I was pregnant. If my only option had been to die in my own blood on the dirty floor of a medical quack's office, I'd have gladly done so rather than have a third child.

It didn't come to that. Two weeks later while I was at work (I operated a polyester-texturing machine in a double knit–manufacturing plant), I had a spontaneous abortion. From then on, I was committed to safe and legal abortions.

The position of the United Methodist Church wasn't as refined as mine, but one sentence gave me room to become a member. It said, "In continuity with past Christian teaching, we recognize tragic conflicts of life with life that may justify abortion." I didn't completely agree with the statement—I don't believe a fetus is a life, nor that abortion needs to be justified—but at least the denomination acknowledged the complexity of the issue, and their resolution was respectful.

In the adult confirmation class, nobody spoke in tongues, gave their hearts to Jesus, or made ugly remarks about Democrats. It was my first exposure to the jargon of the faith, the peculiar language in which the words I knew took on new meanings. The word *create,* for instance. When the pastor said only God could create, I questioned his reasoning. Artists, after all, create.

No they don't, he responded. Only God creates.

All righty then. I let it go, accepting the fact that he and I were talking out of different definitions. A few weeks later I joined the church on profession of faith, and life went on. For ten years Fred and I sailed along, the way you do with a house full of teenagers, sometimes moving ahead at full speed in bright sunshine with a tailwind, other times lashing ourselves to the deck while the wind howled, the seas raged, and we waited to capsize. Together we went through basketball games, swim meets, driving lessons, chicken pox, high-school graduations, college applications, drug problems, sprained ankles, splinters, torn cartilages, bloody noses, broken bones, broken hearts, double- and triple-pierced ears, car wrecks, arguments over pickled beets and minced onions, and a thousand games of Scrabble.

Some days I felt as though I were a yellow helium balloon and Fred's careful hold on my string was all that kept me connected to solid ground. Other days I felt as though I were a mountain climber and Fred an anvil I was dragging behind as I grunted my way up the slope. We endured, sometimes empowered by the energy we sparked off each other, other times too drained to divide the furniture and Christmas ornaments for a divorce settlement.

I finished college in 1983 and decided to write full-time for a year. If I didn't get anything published, I'd find something else to do. I wrote a children's picture book, a science-fiction book for teenagers, and a romance novel, and in between I asked myself questions about the Bible stories I was hearing in church on Sundays. The God-thing captivated me, and so did the stories. My background as an English major, the way I'd always responded to characters on a page as live, breathing human beings carried over into what I was reading and hearing. I carried questions around with me, mulling over things like *Why would Lot's wife have looked back on the city she was fleeing? How come God gave Moses' sister leprosy when their brother Aaron, Miriam's partner in crime, got off scot-free?* And then there was the big question surrounding Jesus' gender. What was the significance of his maleness? The Roman Catholic Church used his maleness to justify an all-male priesthood. Did that make sense? Did he have to be male? Why was he in the first place?

It took me at least two years of contemplation before I found an answer, one that was remarkable for its simplicity. Jesus was male because only males had standing in the society in which he lived. I wrote a short story retelling the nativity, in which the Christ child was born female and when the kings arrived to see the savior they set the straw on fire, killing mother and infant. Writing it wasn't like writing at all; it was as though the story had been circling the universe and I simply pulled it down onto the page. When I sent it to the only journal I thought might be interested—a Christian feminist magazine named *Daughters of Sarah,* out of Chicago—I even put a note in saying I didn't know if this story was self-evident or had already been written by someone else. *Daughters* bought the story, titled "What Child IS This?", and published it as the centerpiece in their tenth-anniversary issue in December 1984.

I was spending time in those early years of marriage with a friend named Anne Herbert. Anne had been in China in the 1920s as a medical missionary. Now in her late eighties, she was still vibrant, still committed. She included me on jaunts to her family cottage at Lake Junaluska, North Carolina.

I was sitting beside Anne at Lake Junaluska the first time I saw a woman officiate at Holy Communion. Reverend Rosemary Brown, an ordained minister in the Tennessee conference of the United Methodist Church, was tall, elegant, white-haired, and gifted. She preached with a passion I'd never seen before, and at the end of the sermon she began the ritual of the Last Supper. Not until she lifted the loaf of bread to eye level and tore it in half did I realize I was weeping.

Watching her, everything I understood about communion exploded. Holy Communion looks different when a woman's hands, a woman's arms, a woman's body enact the event. When I was growing up, my mother baked, took, broke, and offered bread, and so had other women I knew, and so had I. For the first time I saw the Supper as supper, a real meal, a meal to nourish and strengthen everyone at the table.

▲   ▲   ▲

One afternoon in my last semester of college, I was standing in a campus hallway waiting to discuss a term paper with Dr. Nancy Plummer Moore, one of my English professors. While I waited, I read the flyers posted outside her office. The Population Action Council, headquartered in Washington, D.C., was sponsoring a nationwide essay contest on the subject of overpopulation.

When Nancy opened the door to let another student out of her office and me in, I asked, "Do you think I should enter this contest?"

"Why, certainly. You'd have a good chance of winning." Nancy had been telling me for several years that I was both brilliant and a gifted writer. I was attempting to take her opinion seriously.

I proceeded to read everything I could get my hands on regarding population issues, wrote five completely different versions of essays, had Nancy read two of them, wrote a final essay from scratch, sent it in, and won the contest. In the summer of 1984, I got my reward: an expense-paid trip to Mexico City for an international meeting on population issues held in conjunction with the United Nations Population Conference.

Being in Mexico City jarred me. It wasn't the policy speeches, many of which rejected any forms of family planning, including contraception, so much as something that happened one night as I was walking with some new acquaintances. We were half a block from my hotel when I caught a flash of movement in a recessed doorway. Thinking it might be rats, I looked more closely. Crouched in the doorway was a very young woman, clearly bunked into that concrete corner for the night. She was wrapping a scrap of cloth more tightly around the infant asleep beside her.

They were human beings, and I'd mistaken them for rats. In that moment of recognition, I understood how poverty dehumanizes both the poor and the wealthy.

In the way one thing leads to another, while I was in Mexico City I heard about Forum '85, a meeting scheduled to parallel the United Nations End of the Decade for Women conference in Kenya the next summer. In July of 1985 I stepped off a KLM flight into the terminal in Nairobi. I was one of more than thirteen thousand people from around the world who made it there to attend the workshops and seminars and to view the exhibits on alternative technologies, nutrition, child welfare, and more.

Forum '85 ran from July 10 to July 19. On the last day, I stood under the striped sky of the Peace Tent, a blue-and-white-striped awning that was the central gathering place and the site of many of the activities. The smell of canvas mixed with earth, sweat, Magic Markers, passion, and rattan. Doves soared on purple batik wall hangings. Posters asked nuclear questions: *If it's so safe, why not your backyard?* On my far left were a series of hand-stitched tapestries from Chile on which blue flannel women, gray wool mountains, red polyester flames, and back-stitched barbed wire depicted the violence in Chile since 1973.

That afternoon I heard a woman from Sweden tell of marching for peace in Moscow, in Paris, in Minsk, in Washington, D.C. "We felt if we had enough disarmament, we would have enough water and food and health care for all peoples," she said.

A Canadian woman spoke of her activities for a nuclear-free north and admitted, "I alternate between terrible despair and feeling that we're taking a few small steps."

I drifted across the campus and saw two women knitting together under a tree, one with pink yarn, one with blue. Under a neighboring tree, two cameramen slept. A woman in purple and a bearded man claimed the rest of the shade; the woman changed her infant's diaper and nuzzled its neck. I walked on, to the center court, where veiled Iranian women swore, "We will never submit to any kind of peace which America imposes on us."

Near the entrance to the Peace Tent, a mammoth fabric-covered globe had appeared that morning with a message scrawled across the surface: *As a woman I have no Country My Country is the whole world* (sic). Through the day more inscriptions were added: *What we all want is peace. I want peace for my children. Together—nothing is impossible. White women must sort their white men first. We dwell in possibility. Apply sanctions against South Africa. Peace! Please!* Signatures told the international story: Hilda, Flo, Mikami, Maggie, Yaza, Manzuii.

As the afternoon faded, people moved toward center court for the closing ceremonies. A few short speeches, and then the celebration. Tribal dancers drummed, stamped, and whooped. A group of children sang in an unknown tongue, raising their crutches high. Kindergarten-sized children sang, first in Swahili and then in English, "This Little Light of Mine." An all-female gospel rock group from America, Sweet Honey in the Rock, performed. They were followed by a lone woman, an Australian aborigine, who sang in her native language. Her melodies were so compelling, I wanted to join her in song, but I couldn't catch the words.

We stayed for hours, as though we were at a party that's over but nobody is ready to go home. I'd seen Kenyan troops threatening to close down the Forum after a Vietnamese woman spoke out against U.S. policy. I'd gone to a seminar on organized religion where I heard a Jewish woman from New York speak while inches away from me women from the Palestinian Liberation Organization muttered, "Murderers, murderers." I'd heard rumors of spies taking notes and names so that governments could bring reprisals against the speakers. I'd had my silhouette examined by metal detectors each time I entered a restaurant, the conference center, or a hotel. I was exhausted and overwhelmed when I finally boarded the plane for home.

When Fred picked me up at the airport in Atlanta, I was still drained. He filled me in on events while I was gone. I barely spoke. I thought maybe the next day, after I'd had a good night's sleep, I would tell him everything I'd seen, but that day faded into the next and the next and the next, and I still couldn't find a place to begin.

Mexico City had been peripatetic, all smog and horn-blaring automobiles crowding the streets. Nairobi, on the other hand, had been clear and quiet: no smog, the cars replaced by groups of men walking, seemingly aimlessly, up and down the sidewalk in front of the Kenyatta Conference Center. It was in Nairobi I first saw armed soldiers running through an airport; first met a woman who'd walked across half a continent because she believed a women's conference might provide information to alleviate the suffering in her village; first saw free speech abrogated in the name of democracy when Kenyan police officers attempted to arrest a group of speakers because they were criticizing U.S. policy.

I knew before I left home that I lived in a big world, but Nairobi became a microcosm of the whole, a location where poverty, incipient violence, hopefulness, and despair coalesced.

The despair was my own. The problems, the hatred, the suffering: I grasped that they are too deep, too wide, too broad for solution; that they cannot and will not ever be resolved. The only way to prevent the agonies human beings inflict on each other, I concluded, is to annihilate the human race.

How could I have named such a thought to Fred? It was unconscionable even to me, which is why that trip to Nairobi formed my life. Everything I've done since 1985 has been, in one way or another, an attempt to find enough grace in the world that I may believe that life—not mine alone, but everybody's—is worthwhile.

I responded to my societal desolation in the same way I responded to my personal desolation after my second divorce: I simply kept going. The Nairobi conferences received some attention in the local press. My phone started to ring, with people wanting to hear me speak about the conferences, and I agreed to a number of speaking engagements. One of those was at a college in a nearby town at a seminar called "The Witness of Women in the Nuclear Age." Dr. Helen Caldicott, the Australian physician who wrote the book *Missile Envy,* was the keynote speaker. I was on a question-and-answer panel with Johanna W. H. van Wijk-Bos, a professor of Old Testament at Louisville Presbyterian Seminary in Kentucky. Later that day Johanna said something crucial to my spiritual formation.

There must have been a dozen people swirling from room to room in the college chaplain's house, where we'd all been invited for dinner. Somehow Johanna and I ended up alone in the kitchen filling our plates with spinach salad. She told me, "Everything I know of war I learned through my aunt's arms around me when the Nazis marched through Amsterdam."

Johanna's statement, so matter-of-fact and poignant, convinced me that the only way we experience creation—life, whether at its most beautiful or its harshest—is through our own bodies and the bodies of other people.

▲   ▲   ▲

I decided I wanted to know more about church history, about poverty and justice, about God and life. I studied church history, Methodist history, and feminist theology. I served on various committees in my local church, became an officer in the women's group, and joined the board of directors for the local Bethlehem Center, a Methodist mission agency.

I also set aside my embarrassment over my singing abilities long enough to join the church choir. Watching the faces of the people in the choir as they sang reminded me of what I'd learned in my parents' living room and in Albert's kitchen: that lifting my voice in the company of other people is a rare and rich joy.

The choir absorbed me into their ranks. As long as I sat between two strong altos, I had a good chance of hitting the notes correctly. I did assume, though, that the night the choir director said to the room as a whole, "If there's a note any of you can't sing, just mouth the words," he was speaking for my benefit.

▲   ▲   ▲

I preached for the first time on Mother's Day, 1986. It was Woman in the Pulpit Sunday, an event initiated in the South Carolina conference to acclimate women to the idea of standing in pulpits and congregations to the sight of women doing so. I didn't ask why I was invited to preach that year; I suppose somebody who'd heard me speak in another setting was on the committee and suggested me. When the pastor asked me, I cheerfully agreed, and it was probably all of two hours before I started to panic. Stand in a pulpit? Me? Preach? Me?

The pastor had told me which texts from the Bible were to be read that day. One of them was the story in the last chapter of John where, after the resurrection, Jesus gave instructions to one of his disciples. He asked, "Do you love me?" and, when Simon Peter said yes, Jesus responded, "Feed my lambs."

Jesus asked a second time, got the same answer, and this time said, "Tend my sheep."

After the third time, Jesus said, "Feed my sheep."

I don't remember much, beyond my terror, about that Sunday, except that just before I went out to preach, a frail, elderly choir member who'd lost his wife a few years earlier spoke to me, I guess because he saw the stress on my face.

"Just go out there and tell it like it is, girl," he said.

And that's what I did. I told the congregation about the time Douglas, Amy, and I all went home for a visit with our spouses and children in tow. It was chaotic, as you'd expect with a small farmhouse packed with adult siblings revisiting their childhood while their children were over the edge with exhaustion from travel and excitement. Whenever a child wandered into the room with blood dripping from a hand or toe, the way they do, one of the adults bandaged the wound and sent the child placidly back outside to play. When I pointed out to Mother that none of the children seemed to care who did the fixing up, she swooped her arms into a big circle.

"It's because they're our kids," she said.

I think that's what Jesus was talking about, I told the congregation. *When he said to feed his lambs, tend his sheep, feed his sheep, he wasn't talking about doing something to somebody out there, separate from us. He was saying they're our kids, the great family of God.*

It felt right standing in the pulpit. I'd been challenged, horribly, but the congregation had responded to me. I'd been doing poetry readings for a while by that time, courtesy of Dr. Nancy Moore's invitations to address her English classes, and I knew when a poem worked right because a silence came into the room, a connection in which we were all breathing together and nothing existed except the rhythms and the meanings of the words blending together. The same thing happened in the pulpit.

What did it mean? Was there something I was supposed to do with the discovery that I was at home in the pulpit?

No, I decided. *Or maybe yes.* But if the answer was yes, there was nothing I could do about it. We had all those children, after all. I was hardly a model of Christian faith or practice. I had no patience with our teenagers, groused about them to my friends, screamed at them to their faces from time to time. And then there was the business of my vocabulary: have you ever heard of a clergyperson who says things like "goddamn it" and "fuck it"? Preaching, ministry . . . obviously those were tasks suited for people holier than I.

Not only that, I felt little in common with most people in the congregation. None of them seemed bored out of their minds during the worship service the way I was. God's power, energy, dazzle: I couldn't feel them reflected around me. If I felt out of place as a layperson, how much worse would it be if I were ordained?

Clearly, the ministry wasn't for me.

At twilight on December 27, 1986, I was in the bathroom cleaning my contacts. Fred was lying across our bed chatting with me. The children were scattered around the house, all except Fred's older son, who'd gone out with friends.

Our first indication that something was seriously wrong was the sound of footsteps pounding up the stairs from the den. Then we heard an urgent voice: "Dad. Dad. There's smoke downstairs."

I dropped my contact in the sink and ran to see. The door on the far wall of the den was closed. Behind it were the laundry room and a bedroom. Beneath it, smoke was seeping. Fred reached the door first. He turned the handle, pushed, and vanished inside a cloud of smoke. He stepped backward into view, pulling the door closed.

I moved into crisis mode.

"We have to get out now," I said briskly, and out we trooped through the back door, several of us barefoot, one of us carrying our dog Brandie. We hurried across the street, pounded on a neighbor's door, set the dog down, and went back outside to await the fire trucks. I heard a downstairs window explode and saw flames leap out of it. I saw smoke churning and billowing through the upstairs windows. I wondered if the house was going to burn to the ground, wondered if neighboring houses were going to catch on fire, wondered why I hadn't grabbed a set of car keys, wondered where in the hell the fire trucks were. It was hot, and loud, and impossible.

▲   ▲   ▲

Three hours later, the fire chief allowed us to reenter the house to gather a few belongings. Night had fallen. The power was out. Downstairs the den, laundry room, and one of the bedrooms were charred.

I lifted my purse from the kitchen counter, and the image of the purse remained, a light space within the darkness. We'd thought we'd retrieve a number of items, but what do you take? Purses, it turns out. Wallets. Car keys.

We spent the night at a friend's house. The next morning I borrowed a pair of her underpants and took a shower while Fred went to the drugstore. He returned with seven toothbrushes, seven hairbrushes, seven combs, seven tubes of toothpaste, seven cans of deodorant, and four hair dryers.

That afternoon we moved into the residential hotel suggested by our insurance company. When we went to bed that night, I lay still with images of flames and of smoke damage playing in my head. I thought Fred was asleep until he cleared his throat and said, "I want to say something, and then I don't want to discuss it."

"Okay."

Fred said, "I would not have survived emotionally, physically, or spiritually without you." A pause. "And now I'm going to sleep." He rolled away from me and pulled the blankets up to his neck.

Silence, except for the muted mumble of children's voices over the television they were watching in the living room. I lay staring at the ceiling. To think on our first date I'd thought this man was open with his feelings.

I wanted to respond to Fred, but he'd shut me off. Besides, what was there to say?

▲   ▲   ▲

Odd, isn't it, how we human beings crave a logical explanation for chaos? We waited for the fire chief or the insurance people to say, *The fire began at this outlet,* or *This lamp shorted out,* or *This candle set a curtain on fire,* but nothing of the sort occurred. Instead we were told that in 50 percent of cases, the cause of a given house fire is never discovered. We kept asking through all the days and weeks—three months' worth—during which we wrote inventory lists of our possessions, documenting the brand name and type of each item, date purchased, amount paid, replacement value. Every item in the house: the cans of corn in the kitchen cupboard, the eyebrow tweezers in the bathroom cabinet, the sweaters and boxer shorts, the books and tapes, the rocking chairs and couches, the ornaments still hanging on the Christmas tree.

Not everything we owned was destroyed by the fire. The damned piano, for instance, went off to the music store for reconditioning and came back when the house was once again inhabitable. The pool table was safe, too, because it was stored in our garage. The only other items preserved were the ones strong enough to withstand boiling water and pine cleaner. The upholstered furniture, the carpet, the brass chandeliers, our clothing and computers and tax documents, the ornaments hanging on the Christmas tree: gone, all gone.

Soon after the fire, we stopped at a department store so I could get something decent to change into at bedtime. I was sorting through the selections, only peripherally aware of the wide berth other shoppers were taking around Fred and me until he pointed it out. I watched a couple of them.

"Why are they looking at us like that?"

He shrugged. "Maybe it's because we stink."

"Oh, my God. We're vagabonds, aren't we?"

Vagabonds: us. Grimy, redolent, not fit to be near decent people.

So the fire was part of my going into the ministry, because now I understood differently the Bible passages about being unclean, about being outcasts. And then there was the resurrection piece. I'd never been much interested in the resurrection—okay, fine, Jesus died and was raised, but that was a long time ago, and the Holy Spirit is operating here and now—until the fire. Watching my house being reconstituted from the stench and darkness, I finally grasped why people long for the restoration of a broken, rotting corpse into something whole and clean.

▲   ▲   ▲

A year later Terry's father, Bill, died. Helen, his wife, had died a year earlier. A perfectly healthy fifty-five-year-old woman, she'd collapsed for no reason an autopsy could determine. Bill's health, already poor, declined further. By October he was living with Terry and her family; by November he was dying. I managed to break away from Fred and the children after lunch on Christmas Day to go to Terry's. The doctor had made a house call and said death was only hours away. I had to leave after only a few minutes to fulfill a family obligation, but I promised myself I'd return that evening.

At very close to the stroke of eight o'clock that night, Fred and I had met our obligation and were walking to our car. All day long I'd been nearly frantic to get back to Terry's. Now I waited for my adrenaline to kick in, waited to feel again the urgency that had surged all day. Somewhere between one step and the next I noticed it was gone.

I stopped walking, stood still, looked around as though the urgency might be standing in the driveway beside me, waiting to be beckoned in. I couldn't feel it. It wasn't there.

I glanced toward the sky, which on that clear night had billions of stars, and I practically sniffed the air in search of the danger that had stalked me all day, and there was none anywhere—no danger, no urgency, no hurry. All was calm. All was bright. Bill was fine. I knew it as surely as I knew the weight of my own footsteps.

When we got in the car, Fred said, "So are you going to Terry's when we get home?" and I said, "I don't know. Everything feels different now," and he said, "What do you mean?" and I said, "I don't know." I'd just set my purse down on the kitchen counter at home when the phone rang. When I heard Terry's voice, I knew. I asked what time, and when she said eight o'clock, I told her I already knew that, even though I couldn't have known, and she said, "Yes," because she believes in my capacity for connection to her, to Bill, to the force of life.

It was the first time I experienced the sense of elemental connection to—what? Shall we call it spirit? And if we do, whose spirit did I connect to? Bill's? The Spirit of God? The spirit of life? It didn't matter; it was enough to know that the holy had touched me.

The touch of the holy: for some people it never happens. For others it happens once in a lifetime. For me, it happened twice, and because it happened twice I knew it could happen again. I began to watch and wait and see, and gradually the watching formed me to the point that I could not only see the holy and call it by name, but I could point it out to other people: *Did you see that? Did you feel that? Pay attention; it's here.* Ultimately, I had to acknowledge where the moments were leading me.

chapter six

IN THE FALL OF 1988, I GOT A CALL FROM NANCY Hardesty, a woman who jump-started the feminist movement in conservative Christian circles when she, with coauthor Letha Dawson Scanzoni, published a book on biblical feminism called *All We're Meant to Be.* After we'd met at a spiritual retreat, Nancy had encouraged my work and answered my innumerable questions about publishing. She was now phoning to say she'd been to the annual meeting of the American Academy of Religion. While there, she'd spoken with a publisher who was looking for manuscripts.

"You need to send her a proposal," Nancy told me.

"I do?"

"Yes. You're ready to write a book."

I was? How did she know that? "What would I write a book about?"

We talked through options. I settled on the simplest, most structured of our ideas. When I did readings from the poetry I'd written about women in the Bible, listeners always had lots of questions when I finished, wanting to know the story behind the poem and how I made sense of it the way I did. What about if I started each chapter with a poem, and then wrote an essay expanding on the poem? And I could throw exercises in at the end of each chapter in case people wanted to use the book for spirituality groups.

"Write the proposal," said Nancy, and, when the proposal was finished, she said, "Now write the book." I did.

▲   ▲   ▲

To Love Delilah was published in 1990. In the months prior to its release, both Fred and Mary Flowers seemed intent on destroying my peace of mind.

"You know they're going to burn crosses on your yard," Mary would say to Fred when she dropped in for a visit, and he would respond, "There's nothing to worry about. I've checked three times to be sure our home owners' policy is up to date."

"That's not funny," I'd fume.

"We're not joking," they'd reply.

It was hard for me to take their concerns seriously, because I was reared with the notion that if and when you read anything, up to and including the Bible, you are supposed to *think*. What I thought was that even though Jesus said more than once that we're to love each other, Christians believed they had a "stay out of hell free" pass when it came to the women in the Bible. Eve, Lot's wife, Herod's wife: they were all fair game for hatred. Others (Mary Magdalene, for example, who is still sneered at as a prostitute, even though generations of translators insist no such word appears in the original texts) are victims of shoddy scholarship. In *Delilah,* I pointed out some of these errancies, and I offered a love's-eye view of the women. How could that be incendiary?

Mary explained it more clearly a few weeks after the book came out. A friend of hers had gone to prayer meeting the night before at a local Baptist church. Afterward, she reported to Mary that the planned topic of conversation had been replaced with an hour-long denouncement of *Delilah,* which had garnered a two-page spread in a local newspaper.

The people at that prayer meeting were furious. How dare a woman interpret scripture? How dare she, or anybody, make evil women the topic of her writing? And, most of all, how dare I suggest we try to love and learn from these women? The book was an abomination in the sight of the Lord, and so was I.

"Had any of them read it?" I asked.

"Of course not. They'd never read something like that. Mary Jo, I told you some people were going to hate you for writing this book."

"But it's not like I'm saying anything heretical."

"To them you are. They think God wrote the Bible, and they think the only possible interpretation of those passages is the one preachers have repeated to them their whole lives. For you to suggest there's another side of the story—as far as they're concerned, that's blasphemy."

Nothing came of the stomping and snorting at the prayer meeting, except I gained a new clarity regarding the rigidity of the Christianity some people inhabit. My only recourse was to study more, think more, write more.

▲   ▲   ▲

I'd hoped the publication of the book might disperse a dream that had plagued me for several years. The dream begins with me in the doorway of a sitting room with ceilings twelve feet high. The room is large enough to hold three or four flowered couches, half a dozen occasional tables, a Victrola, and more antimacassars than fifteen people working double shifts could crochet in a year.

I walk to the far left side of the room and open a door. Facing me is a flight of stairs with the treads painted air force blue, although much of the paint has worn off.

I climb the stairs to find myself in the barn behind my parents' house, staring up the hay chute. Douglas, Amy, and I used to slide down it when we were kids. A nail a third of the way scratched me on the back when I was nine or ten. In the dream I'm required, in what I suppose has some sort of reverse-birthing significance, to crawl up the hay chute.

I struggle upward, even though I'm much too big and much too worried about the nail. At the top I crawl out into an octagonal room floored and paneled in golden brown. Picture windows fill three of the walls. It's dark outside, but I can see the glimmer of moonlight on tree leaves and a sparkling river.

My immediate response is *I hate this room. It's ugly.* Then I take a step forward and catch, barely, the scent of a food I love, maybe popcorn, maybe tapioca pudding, and I think, *Oh, I love this room. Why can't I ever remember to come in here when I'm awake?* I want to live in the room, to eat at the plank table that stands between me and the windows, to work at the oak desk in the left corner. I want to invite everyone I know into the room so that they, too, can feel and smell the grace.

I'd supposed the dream meant there was a hidden aspect of myself that needed release and assumed the release of the book would solve the problem. It didn't.

Months later I had lunch with an old friend named Eileen who'd gone into the ministry a few years earlier. She asked me, as she had at each of our meetings for the last several years, "Well, Mary Jo, have you recognized yet that you're called to the ordained ministry?"

As always, I laughed and shook my head no. "That's the dumbest idea I've ever heard. Have you read my book? Did I tell you some people think it's heretical?"

"Some people can't tell the difference between heresy and creativity. The Church needs you, and you need to be ordained."

I couldn't imagine a less likely candidate. Did I mention I'd been divorced twice before Fred and I got married? Did I mention I'd not only heard most of the dirty words in the English language but could use them in a grammatically correct fashion in sentences? Did I mention I have a great laugh, I'm a clotheshorse, and I'm not pious? Did I mention five children? Granted, none of the children were still at home, and the one who'd struggled with drugs had steadied down and seemed okay, but it's not as though the children were completely emancipated, either. Fat chance I was called to the ministry.

What Eileen was waiting for, and what I was not allowing for, was an epiphany.

In the language of Christianity and of literary criticism, epiphany means a singular moment, an event powerful enough to re-form and transform a person (or a literary character) from that time on and forevermore. I don't have singular epiphanies; I have multiple epiphanies, serial epiphanies, transformative moments piling higher and higher upon each other, rolling like earthquakes across the terrain of a lifetime, destroying and creating again, again, and again.

I had another epiphany in 1991 at Annual Conference, the state-wide meeting of United Methodists held late every spring. The preacher for the ordination service was Leontine Kelly, the first African-American woman bishop in the United Methodist Church. I'd read some of the bishop's sermons, but I wasn't prepared for the power she ignited in the basketball arena where the ordination service was held. She began at a podium; before she ended she was moving back and forth across the stage, a microphone in one hand, her other arm extending either outward toward the gathered crowd or upward toward the heavens. I can still hear the timber of her voice when she caroled, "Have you not known? Have you not heard? The Lord our God is an everlasting God. He does not faint or grow weary."

Listening, I believed every word she said. I also believed *she* believed every word she said. She was so alive, so vibrant. I'd never seen anyone else preach like she did, like she meant it, like it mattered.

Afterward Fred and I went outside to smoke, and Eileen joined us.

She was annoyed with herself. She could have been ordained that year, but she'd put it off; the church she pastored had been devastated by Hurricane Hugo, and she hadn't had time to prepare the required documentation. "I wish I could have had Bishop Kelly's hands on my head for ordination."

As Fred and Eileen discussed the sermon, I mused over the questions the ordinands had been asked earlier in the day. John Wesley, the Church of England priest who accidentally founded Methodism, developed the questions, which have been asked of every candidate for ordination since the beginning of the denomination:

1. Have you faith in Christ?
2. Are you going on to perfection?
3. Do you expect to be made perfect in love in this lifetime?
4. Are you earnestly striving after it?
5. Are you resolved to devote yourself wholly to God and his work?
6. Do you know the General Rules of our Church?
7. Will you keep them?
8. Have you studied the doctrines of The United Methodist Church?
9. After full examination do you believe that our doctrines are in harmony with the Holy Scriptures?
10. Will you preach and maintain them?
11. Have you studied our form of Church discipline and polity?
12. Do you approve our Church government and polity?
13. Will you support and maintain them?
14. Will you diligently instruct the children in every place?
15. Will you visit from house to house?
16. Will you recommend fasting or abstinence, both by precept and example?
17. Are you determined to employ all your time in the work of God?
18. Are you in debt so as to embarrass you in your work?
19. Will you observe the following directions?
    a. Be diligent. Never be unemployed. Never be triflingly employed. Never trifle away time; neither spend any more time at any one place than is strictly necessary.

    b. Be punctual. Do everything exactly at the time. And do not mend our rules, but keep them; not for wrath, but for conscience' sake.

Fred and Eileen were still discussing Bishop Kelly's sermon when I interrupted them.

"Wouldn't any Christian say yes to those questions?"

"What questions?" Fred asked.

"The ones the candidates were asked. Are you going on to perfection and do you know the Rules and the doctrines and do you approve of our church government, and are you determined to devote your time to God?"

I can still see Fred's and Eileen's eyes widening, and how they turned simultaneously to look at each other and then, slowly, turned back to stare at me.

Fred said gently, "No, Mary Jo. Everybody wouldn't answer yes to those questions."

They waited, as though expecting me to say something else.

"Are you sure?" I asked.

"Yes."

"Oh."

Still they waited. What did they expect? I was forty-two. I'd only just begun writing; I didn't want to stop. We were members of the country club, for Christ's sake.

"You two need to give it up. It's not going to happen."

▲   ▲   ▲

A few weeks later Fred's company decided to downsize and offered him, along with dozens of other people of a certain age, an early retirement package. He was fifty-six, too young to retire, but middle managers were being eliminated and senior executives were out of favor because of their high salaries and benefits packages. We talked it over, and over, and over, back and forth, up and down, all around the town. Fred did a fair amount of agonizing.

"What do you want me to do?" he asked one day.

"Fred, I can't answer that. It's your decision."

"You know our financial situation will change. We won't have the money coming in that we do now."

"Okay."

"You're not taking this seriously."

"Yes, I am. So our financial situation changes. I'll fire the cleaning lady, and you can resign from the country club. Problem solved."

He shook his head at me. "It's not that simple."

"All right, fine. Think of it this way. If you take this package and six months from now decide you want to be working, get another job. But if you reject the package and six months from now wish you'd retired, you're stuck working there for another six years."

For the next three days, all I heard out of Fred was the click of the calculator keys from his office. Then he spent two days on the telephone to corporate headquarters, requesting information about continued life-insurance coverage, the vesting of his current stock options, and health coverage. Finally he put a legal pad down in front of me. The first page was divided in half with a pro list on the left and a con list on the right. The second through sixth page had a list of questions, with the answers written underneath. The seventh through infinity pages had numbers on them.

"I've run all the numbers. If I retire, we can manage financially as long as we're very careful and don't have any exorbitant expenses. It'll be tight for a few years until I can start accessing my IRA, but we can do it."

"And is that what we want to do? Do you want to take the package?"

"Yes."

His official retirement date was September 30. We managed to avoid exorbitant expenses for all of ten days.

▲   ▲   ▲

By then I'd stopped attending the thousand-member church where Fred and I met. Instead I was spending Sunday mornings at a two-hundred-member church where a new acquaintance named Christine was the pastor. We'd met at Eileen's wedding, and the next week Fred and I decided to go hear Christine preach. After that, I returned Sunday after Sunday, drawn there for no discernible reason. I decided to transfer my membership there, which made no sense at all.

"Why would you do that?" Fred asked me.

"I don't know. It's like something's pulling me there."

In August I went to a national meeting of United Methodist women held on the Ohio State University campus. At lunch one day, I told one of the other attendees that I wanted to move my church membership but how silly it seemed. I was on the board of a local mission agency, I explained, and it seemed likely I could do more financially and otherwise for the agency from within my huge church than from within the smaller church.

"Ah, but that would be whoring," she said.

Her word choice startled me. Whoring? How? It's not like anybody was paying me. I brooded for several weeks before I reasoned it out. I thought God was drawing me to the new church, but I was resisting because of a potential financial benefit. So was that whoring? Maybe, maybe not, but it was too close to the edge for my comfort.

One of the speakers in Columbus was the Reverend Dr. Chung Hyun Kyung. A Presbyterian clergywoman, university professor in Seoul, Korea, and author of a groundbreaking book on Asian women's theology called *Struggling to Be the Sun Again,* Dr. Kyung had delivered the plenary address at the 7th Assembly of the World Council of Churches in Canberra, Australia, in January of that year. Afterward, a firestorm erupted for, among other reasons, her self-description as a syncretist (somebody who believes that God is present in everything that exists) and her belief that it is an act of violence to tell nonbelievers they'll go to hell if they don't accept Jesus Christ as Lord. I'd read that she was receiving, in what is surely one of the greatest perversions of Jesus' teachings, death threats from angry Christians. Dr. Kyung looked calm and happy each time I saw her standing at a lectern or walking across campus. I wondered how a person can look that serene when her life is threatened.

I also heard the Reverend Linda Hollies preach. She told the Exodus story of the parting of the Red Sea and said, "In order to get across, the people had to put their toes in the water first. They had to trust what God was doing."

Integrity, serenity, trust embodied in three more epiphanies to tantalize me, epiphanies lying in wait to reveal their mysteries, their intention for me.

▲   ▲   ▲

In the early autumn I went to Charge Conference at the small church. Charge Conference is the local congregation's annual business meeting and is filled with committee reports. It's conducted by the district super-intendent, an ordained minister appointed to oversee the pastors and the churches in a particular area. This year the district superintendent made an announcement at the bishop's behest. He said the United Methodist Church was facing a crisis, that within ten years between 50 and 80 per-cent of ministers currently ordained would reach retirement age, and there weren't enough candidates coming into the ministry to replace the retirees. He said the candidates were out there, but the churches hadn't done enough to identify or encourage them.

"One of the tasks of Christianity is to name the gifts and graces we see, and it's time for us to get serious about it. Otherwise we're going to have a whole lot of pulpits left vacant in the coming years."

I was already aware of the shortage of ministers, not just in the United Methodist Church but in other major denominations as well. I liked the idea of our actively encouraging candidates for the job. Nobody's going to come to a party if they're not invited. People aren't going to know the ministry is where they should be if nobody tells them so.

When I got home from the meeting, I told Fred about the announce-ment and read to him from the *Book of Discipline* about the ordained ministry and about the tasks pastors perform. (Not all ordained minis-ters are pastors, nor are all pastors ordained. The term refers to those people who are appointed by their bishops to offer spiritual and tempo-ral leadership to one or more congregations.) Pastors, according to the book, preach, teach, marry, bury, and administer the sacraments and other means of grace; oversee the educational program; offer an example of ministry to people with disabilities; lead outreach programs and membership classes; visit the sick, the aged, and others; are active in ecumenical and community concerns; order the life of the congregation; help with goal-setting and program planning; encourage racial and eth-nic inclusiveness; train leadership candidates in the church; are active in denominational programs; supervise the church's programs; administer the *Book of Discipline;* and certify the accuracy of all financial and mem-bership reports.

Good God. Who could possibly do all those things? It sounded like parenting multiplied to the nth power. I'd been a parent for twenty-four years, since I was nineteen years old. The last thing I needed was to get sucked into a vortex of responsibilities toward other people. Added to the responsibilities were the difficulties inherent in the itineracy system, the Methodist method of placement of pastors. The system developed in the eighteenth century when both Methodism and the United States were infants. The Revolutionary War had created a shortage of ministers in this country. The Church of England had been sending ministers to this side of the Atlantic for years, but those priests weren't safe with the outbreak of hostilities. England has a state church, so its ministers were viewed, naturally enough, as allies of the Crown. Those who didn't high-tail it back to England went into hiding.

The shortage created a gap. Who was going to offer the sacraments? Who was going to preach?

John Wesley answered the questions. He had a corps of traveling preachers, had already sent some of them to America, and now realized they were going to have to be ordained. The Church of England wouldn't do it, so Wesley got on with it. Thus our ordination system was born in irregularity, a fact that has some denominations still turning up their noses at us. Those denominations take great pride in their line of apostolic succession—"Look, we were there from the beginning; we trace the lineage of our ordinations all the way back to Saint Peter the Apostle"—but we Methodists are a pragmatic people. We were here, in this country, when nobody else was available, and we did the work that needed to be done. Our ministers went out on horses, their saddlebags packed with books to read, and they kept going until they reached the Pacific Ocean. The colophon of our publishing company commemorates these dedicated, lonely men: it shows a preacher on horseback, his left hand holding the reins and his head bowed toward the open book in his right hand.

▲   ▲   ▲

The itineracy system is still part of our polity. Churches don't hire pastors, nor do pastors interview churches to see which they'd prefer to serve. Instead, the bishop and the cabinet decide who is going where. Fifty years ago, ministers didn't learn of a new appointment until the names and churches were read out at Annual Conference. More recently, the church has allowed for introductory meetings between pastor and congregations, but neither side is interviewing; they're simply looking each other over. I was suspicious of the system. It reminded me too much of the army during the sixties: promises that turn into lies, institutions indifferent to the needs of the institutionalized.

I didn't want to play—and I assumed the feeling was mutual.

Joe Bethea changed my mind.

I ran into the bishop at a meeting. I saw him down a hallway and approached him to introduce myself. When we shook hands, he grinned at me and said, "Hey, I'm Joe Bethea. It's good to meet you."

"Well, hello, Joe Bethea. It's nice to meet you, too."

I don't know what I thought a bishop would be, but Joe wasn't it. Instead of formality, I found friendliness. Instead of distance, I found connection. Instead of reserve, I found warmth.

The next Sunday, I was sitting in a pew at the back of the small church. I'd started the morning by having a conversation with the older woman next to me about hot flashes, brought on by the wild fanning I was doing with my bulletin. It took me some time to settle down and focus on the proceedings at the front of the church. Christine had finished her sermon and said she was now going to accept new members into the church.

A woman, thin, with frilly light brown hair, came forward with her two children. She knelt at the altar to be baptized. I watched, thoughts drifting, as Christine read the baptismal passages, pronounced the invocation over the water, and then dipped her hand into the water and began to recite the baptismal formula: "I baptize you in the name of . . ." Somewhere between the words "Father" and "Son" I thought, *Well, you know, if my buddy Joe wants me to serve a church in the lower part of the state, I guess that would be all right with me.*

I considered the thought from many angles over the next few days, and it stayed constant. Yes, itinerating would be a pain in the ass, but I was all right with that. A day or two later I was at another church meeting, and somewhere in the middle of whatever discussions were going on, I thought, *I'm supposed to go into the ordained ministry.*

I went home to tell Fred. He was sitting in his grandfather's chair, recently reupholstered in hunter green. I sat down in front of him on the matching hassock and put my hands on his knees.

"I have to go to divinity school now," I said.

"What did you say?"

"I have to go to divinity school now."

A slow smile of satisfaction stretched across his face. "Finally."

"What do you mean 'finally'?"

"Eileen and I knew this a long time ago. This is wonderful."

"No, Fred, it isn't."

"Yes, it is."

"Well, if you think so, why don't you do it instead?"

"Because I'm not supposed to. You're the one called to the ministry."

"How are we going to pay for it?"

Fred shook his head in disbelief. "Mary Jo? When have you ever made a decision based on money?" He started laughing, and I started crying.

I could not imagine anything worse. Me in divinity school? How was I going to get through? I'd never read the whole Bible, let alone had a class in religion. I couldn't quote chapter and verse the way ordinary religious people did. I got the punch lines of dirty jokes. Could I really be the kind of the person the church wanted?

chapter seven

DECISIONS ON ORDINATION DON'T BELONG TO THE individual; they belong to the church community. Within Methodism, that means both your local congregation and various denominational boards have to confirm and approve your candidacy. My first required step was to prepare a written request for approval from the Staff-Parish Relations Committee in my congregation. I said in my letter that going into the ministry was not in my plans. I said I already had a calling—to write—and the freedom to pursue that avenue as far as it might take me. I said my candidacy request arose because, first, "numerous people of deep faith have remarked that my sense of God's call and of the Holy Spirit's abiding and directive presence in my life are not the norm but are different, 'set apart.' Secondly, I have no inward sense of culmination. I have great gifts of communication, exuberance, and faith. I believe the work I've done to date has been preparation, and that only in the ordained ministry will I learn and understand the fullness of God's intention for me."

Once the committee approved me, I met with a specially called session of my congregation's Charge Conference. One member stood to speak.

"We need to be very clear what we're doing here. We've already sent one woman into the ministry. If we accept Mary Jo's candidacy, it means we have to support her with our prayers and our gifts, and it also means that someday we're going to have to let a woman come here as pastor. We need to think long and hard before we take this vote."

I didn't know if he was affirming or refuting my candidacy, but Fred, who'd known the speaker for more than twenty years, was clear on the point. "I never did like that son of a bitch," he said.

The Charge Conference approved my candidacy, but the district-wide committee on ordained ministry was a tougher sell. I felt the tension when I walked into the room. The chair barely bothered to shake my hand before he gestured me to sit, then scuttled through a few questions before opening the conversation to the rest of the committee. One member asked about my book. I hit the high points, primarily that it was a friendly look at the wicked women of the Bible.

"So are you judging these people?"

"I don't think it's my place to judge them."

"Well, you're wrong. That's part of your job." The questioner's tone was surly, if not downright rude.

My job? When did it become my job to pass judgment? Dismayed by the confrontational tone, I looked around the room for response. Frozen faces looked back at me or off into the distance. I was dismissed. Back home, I phoned the person I knew best on the committee and asked, "So did you throw my application in the trash when I left?"

"Of course not. Why would you think that?"

"Because the meeting was horrible."

She explained there were power struggles going on within the committee, and some people resented my application, not only because I had a book in print (apparently half of the clergy in the country either have a half-finished manuscript in a desk drawer, or think they would if they had a bit more time to write one) but I was (am) a woman to boot. Just because our denomination ordained women in the 1950s doesn't mean all the gender issues are settled. Some clergymen are concerned about the feminization of the ministry, and that salaries, already low compared to other professions, will drop further if too many women are ordained, in the same way that other predominantly female professions— teaching, social services—are lower-paid than other, male-dominated professions.

Deciding which divinity school to attend didn't take up a lot of my time. I looked through a brochure about Methodist-related seminaries and thought, *Ah, I'm supposed to go to Duke.* Despite the fact that I didn't fit the profile of Duke divinity students—I was much too old—I applied and was accepted.

Before school began, I met with a pastor appointed to supervise my progress. We would continue to meet over the next three years, and each time he encouraged me to think of ministry in terms other than as the pastor of a congregation. He insisted I interview a college chaplain and meet with other people doing ministry in creative ways. He laughed the day he got back the results from a required test I took that covered my interest areas in ministry.

He said, "I don't think I've ever seen such a lopsided score. In the academic-interest area you're in the ninety-fifth percentile. In all the other ones you're around ten percent."

"What does that mean?"

"It means you're going to stagnate as pastor of a congregation. You won't find the intellectual stimulation you need."

"But the Church needs pastors. That's what I'm going into the ministry to do." How else was I going to help fill the gap when all those ministers retired in the next eight years?

"So what does that mean?" I asked again, waiting for him to tell me I was disqualified for the ministry.

"It means we're going to get you through this process as fast as we can before the Church figures out what we've got in you."

He was excited about my candidacy and yet insistent that I camouflage my problematic intellect. That was to create a tension I wouldn't resolve for five years.

▲   ▲   ▲

Fred insisted I begin divinity school in January, so I did. I don't know exactly how we sort through this kind of decision-making—with fear and trembling as often as not. We are both fairly strong personalities, and Fred perhaps more so because he was the oldest child in his family. He started bossing his siblings around at an early age, and his skills expanded over the years. I, unfortunately, am not an apt recipient for bossiness. I was concerned when he retired that we might have some problems in this regard. I got the chance to set the record straight a week after he stopped working, when he came into the kitchen with two of his business suits draped over his arm.

"Go get your clothes together, and I'll take them to the dry cleaners along with mine," he said.

It was the imperatives "go" and "get" that caught my attention. I don't care for imperatives.

"You know what, Fred? You've been bossing people around for thirty years. I know you're really good at it, and I understand that you might want to keep on doing it. But if that's the case, you need to go hire someone to boss around, because it's not going to be me."

Fred stared at me with that look he gets sometimes when my response to his statements turns out to be wildly different from his intention. Then he smiled. "Let me rephrase the statement. I'm going to the dry cleaners. Have you got anything you'd like me to drop off for you while I'm there?"

I grinned at him. "I think so. Let me go check."

When it comes to issues like his taking my clothing to the dry cleaners, I'm in charge. When it came to when to begin divinity school, I ceded to Fred's judgment of the timing. We sorted through details quickly. Because I was entering in the winter term, no financial aid was available, so we took out a home-equity loan to cover tuition, books, and a cheap apartment in Durham. We had enough transitions going on because of Fred's retirement; we weren't going to sell our house and relocate at the same time. Instead I'd commute the four hours each way each week. We were daffy enough to think splitting residences and long car rides would be fun, or at least interesting. Logistically it worked out all right. I'd come home on weekends with a laundry basket in the trunk of the car and the backseat full of books. Fred would have supper waiting (his meat loaf is especially good, and the man can bake a cake with the best of them). While I looked through the week's accumulation of mail, he'd get the laundry basket from the car and put the first load of clothes in the wash. On Monday afternoons or Tuesday mornings, depending on my class schedule, he'd put the basket back in the trunk, tell me he was proud of me, tell me to be careful, and kiss me good-bye. For three years he did all the grocery shopping, all the laundry, and all the cooking. I did all the driving, all the studying, and all the preaching. He was happy with the arrangement. Something elemental had clicked into place for him when I'd told him I had to go to divinity school. It's as though his life had gained an added dimension of meaning.

I had more trouble than Fred working through the meaning of it all. I spent the first year and a half wondering what a nice feminist like me was doing in a school that prided itself on its Gothic, phallic splendor. I snorted when I noticed the LADIES signs posted on the doors to the women's rest rooms. The rest of the world had switched to the word "Women" decades before; apparently the theological academy was a little behind the times.

I was altogether unprepared for the atmosphere in the divinity school. The student profile was very young, very male, and very Caucasian. Most of the students arrived directly out of college. Only about 30 percent of the students were women, compared to about 50 percent in other Methodist-related seminaries. There were only a few African-American, Native American, or Hispanic students. In some of my classes, all the students were white. The idea of an inclusive church got a lot of attention, but physical evidence of its inclusivity was in short supply.

Behind those obvious shortcomings was a more threatening reality. In 1990 some outspoken students had made clear, in classroom settings and otherwise, their commitment to the rights of women, of people of non-European descent, of people with disabilities, of gays, lesbians, bisexuals, and transsexuals. As a result, five or six of them received a series of notes in their school mailboxes warning them that they'd better watch their backs if they knew what was good for them. (One woman told me she received rape threats as well.) Nobody doubted that the authors of the threats were other students in the divinity school.

Now who would have thought such a thing? Students in divinity school, studying to preach and teach the gospel of Jesus Christ, the prince of peace, threatening to attack people with whom they disagreed. It's enough to make you swear off Christianity.

▲   ▲   ▲

If you're going to attend seminary, it probably works out better if you've taken a religion class or two beforehand. Since I hadn't, I was at a disadvantage. My undergraduate degree was in English, and I have a fairly large vocabulary, but meanings of words were slippery. Take the words *the Church,* for instance. The phrase could mean, depending on who said it in which context, a particular building in which people worship; the people on the membership roll for that building; an entire denomination; all of the denominations, from Roman Catholic to Foursquare Gospel Holiness; every single individual believer in the world, whether or not they're officially members of a denomination; and/or every single person, living and dead, who's ever been baptized or received Holy Communion. If I was confused by *the Church,* I was positively buffaloed by the *-ologies:* soteriology, eschatology, ecclesiology, christology, pneumatology, and beyond. Some days all I could do was write down everything I heard and trust it would make sense in the future.

The *-ology* I had the most trouble with was christology: not in understanding it but in caring about it. My theology had been a bit lop-sided from the beginning. Christians believe in a God in three persons (God, Jesus Christ, and the Holy Spirit), but most people, when you get down to it, don't have well-balanced concepts of the trinity. If you think of it as a tripod, for most people, especially those influenced by the evangelical traditions so deeply a part of southern theology, the Jesus leg is six feet high while the God leg and the Holy Spirit leg are about two inches high. For lots of people, God and Jesus are strong legs in the tripod, but the Holy Spirit leg is missing entirely. I, on the other hand, was clear on God and the Holy Spirit, but my Jesus leg was a spindly thing carrying hardly any weight. I thought this made me a suspect Christian until I learned enough doctrinal language to say of myself, "I have a low christology."

My favorite study topic in my first year or two in seminary was heresy, the arguments about what was and was not sound doctrine. My favorite heresy was docetism. Many early believers rejected the idea that God was born in the same way every other human being is born and that God lived in a human body. The shorthand rendition of this belief is "body, bad; soul, good." Docetists may grant that Jesus had a body, but they think either it wasn't a real body (the kind with sweat glands, pubic hair, and a digestive system) or that Jesus didn't exactly live within a body but just sort of borrowed it while he was on earth. Docetism is like racism; we all have a bit of it, whether we acknowledge it or not. I was forced to acknowledge mine when I had to watch the movie *The Last Temptation of Christ* for theology class. In one scene in the Martin Scorsese film, Jesus dances at a wedding. I was irate when I watched the scene—not because Jesus was dancing, but because he was gawky doing it. His arms flailed so wildly, I expected him to blacken someone's eye. His legs seemed unconnected to his body, his feet didn't know where they should go next, and he had no discernible sense of rhythm.

That's ridiculous, I thought. *Jesus wouldn't have danced like that. He'd have danced like Gene Kelly, or like Michael Jackson in his early music videos. With grace. Ease. A pleasure to behold. That's how Jesus would have danced.*

Sirens blared in my head, and strobe lights pounded.

Damn. I was a heretic. And not just any kind of heretic: I was a docetist. I didn't want Jesus to have a regular body. I wanted his body to be like Gene Kelly's when Kelly sang and danced in the rain, like

Martina Navratilova's when she was still competing in international tennis competitions in her forties, like Mark McGwire's when he broke the home run record, like Baryshnikov's. If Jesus could also leap tall buildings with a single bound, that was okay with me, and while he was at it could he please crush a beer can in one hand, lift a Volkswagen Beetle with the other, and whistle "Dixie"?

I didn't want a Jesus who was embodied the same way the rest of us are. Theologically speaking, though, that's the Jesus we're stuck with, because the Christian claim is that he was both fully divine and fully human.

▲   ▲   ▲

My hardest class my first semester was Christian Theology, in which students were taught the boundaries for what is and is not sound Christian doctrine. Where I came from, *dogma* was a dirty word, denoting a rigid structure of thinking used to control and limit freedom of thought. I nearly gagged the day I was told that one of the tasks of ministry is to pass on the Church's dogma. I was even more ground down by a statement the theology professor repeated throughout the semester. A student would pose a question, the professor would think things over, and then he'd say, "You can't ask that question."

I almost asked for a refund of my tuition.

I kept finding more evidence of rigidity and antiwoman views. I overheard one male student warn another male student not to take classes from female professors with two last names. "They aren't really Christians" is the way he phrased the explanation. Male colleagues explained to me, as though I would appreciate their visionary stance, that God was only calling women into the ministry because not enough men were responding to the call—as though women were God's second-string team, only privileged to be on the field because the first-string players got drunk the night before and were too hung over to play.

I was so often angry that finally I shut down to shield myself. Passivity was a new skill for me, and it is not one I recall with pride. One day my New Testament professor was pointing out passages that "proved"—to his thinking—that homosexuality is a sin against God. A young woman in the class countered the professor, citing other texts and other interpretations in which homosexuality is understood to be no greater a sin than is being nonmale or nonwhite.

After class, she was furious with several of us. "Why was I the only one talking? Why weren't any of the rest of you participating? Why didn't you contribute?"

I had no answer, except that by then I'd given up. I was sick of the one-sidedness of the lectures; annoyed with the self-righteousness; and repulsed by the mean-spiritedness. I would have quit, except when I did my check-in, moving into the interior space where I connect to God, I was certain I was where God intended me to be.

Ministry as a profession gave few models for living. The majority of clergy I met, and most of the students around me, seemed to have lost the ability to feel, if they ever had such an ability. It was like living in a Volkswagen bus filled with clowns. What anybody was thinking or feeling (if they were thinking or feeling) was hidden within a tightly controlled package, behavior that ran counter to everything I knew about healthy emotional functioning. If you're doing God's work, wouldn't emotional health be an asset?

My new spike-haired friend Lisa and I confronted the questions head-on one night in our class in the spiritual disciplines. We asked, "What do you do when you're angry at God about having to be in the ministry?"

"Your anger's fine. Keep raging at God," the professor said. And then he chuckled.

After class, four of us talked about the professor's response. One said, "Anger is an important question. None of the church liturgies ever address this topic. They're sterile in that they don't touch deep feelings. Everything we do and say seems to be intentionally benign, as though God can't take our anger or disappointment."

Maybe we'd discovered the reason many of our colleagues seemed flat emotionally. If you think God can't contend with anger or disappointment, and consequently you close off those feelings in yourself, you're bound to have to close off other feelings as well.

A few weeks later, I stood for my oral examination with the Board of Ordained Ministry. The meeting went smoothly, except for the matter of my conversion experience, which wasn't exactly proper, technically speaking. It turns out I should have had the experience in a church—preferably at the altar—rather than in my Chevette.

"What did you do after the experience?" one member of the Board of Ordained Ministry asked me.

"I started going to church."

"Is that all?"

"Well, yeah. I decided that if there was a God—and after what happened in my car I was sure there was—then I ought to be in church. So I started going."

"Did you tell the pastor what had happened to you?"

"No."

My questioner scowled. "Why not?"

"I don't know. I didn't know I was supposed to."

My examiner started to ask another question but was interrupted by another member of the Board saying, "She did enough. She went to church."

"She should have told the pastor."

"I didn't know that," I said again, but neither of them heard. They were glaring at each other as one insisted, "She should have told him" and the other snapped, "How was she to know that?"

The chair of the Board interrupted their argument. "Does anyone have any more questions?" he asked. Nobody did.

Several weeks later I received a letter in the mail telling me I'd been approved for ordination as a deacon and a probationary membership in the Annual Conference.

▲   ▲   ▲

I was ordained on June 1, 1993. That status—ordained deacon—no longer exists in United Methodism, superseded by a new church law passed in 1996. When I was in the pipeline, though, the Church had a two-step ordination process. The first ordination took place after candidates completed half of divinity school and fulfilled the rest of the requirements set forth in *The Book of Discipline.* Later, after graduating from divinity school, pastoring a congregation for two years, and completing a second set of documentation, candidates were eligible for election as full members of Annual Conference (akin to being granted tenure by a university) and ordination as elders.

I was ordained in the basketball arena where I'd heard Leontine Kelly preach three years earlier. Bishop Joseph Bethea—the man who'd stuck out his hand and welcomed me so warmly years before, a man who would later be stabbed in the abdomen by a car thief and nearly die from the wounds but survive to die in his sleep of heart failure a few years later; a man who expected heaven to be as chaotic and argumentative as Annual Conference; a man who, when an earnest classmate of mine asked when he first wanted to be bishop, replied, "The first time I ever heard the word"—that same Joe Bethea laid his hands on my head and said, "Lord, pour upon Mary Joanna Cartledgehayes the Holy Spirit for the office and work of a deacon, in the name of the Father, and of the Son, and of the Holy Spirit." A few minutes later he presented each ordinand with a Bible. I still have the card from which he read, before handing mine to me, "Take authority as a deacon in the Church to preach the Word of God, and to serve all God's people."

A month after my ordination, my parents, who'd celebrated their fiftieth wedding anniversary in February, threw an anniversary bash on the island.

My father introduced me proudly.

"I'd like you to meet my daughter. She was recently ordained a minister."

"Oh, really? It's nice to meet you," people said.

"She's a Jehovah's Witness" was my dad's follow-up comment. Then he'd laugh and walk away, leaving me looking into the face of people wishing they were anywhere other than in front of me.

"No, really, I'm United Methodist," I'd assure them.

The party guests were consistent in their response to me.

"Are you really a minister?"

I'd nod.

"You don't look like a minister."

I was wearing shorts and a T-shirt, my hair was curling wildly from the lake air, and I was hauling trays of food out to the picnic table, taking photos, and grinning—in other words, being a human being. Their comments made me a bit queasy, because I didn't want to look glum and grim, and I didn't want to appear, if not less than human, then at least no fun to be around.

Or maybe their statement had to do with my gender. God knows enough other people had trouble with it. I'd be at friends' or relatives' houses and it would be time for somebody to say grace before the meal. Was I asked to do the blessing? Why, no. These were people who would have asked any snot-nosed eighteen-year-old boy who ever wanted to be a minister to say grace, but would they ask a grown woman? Hell, no. Luckily I had grown so much spiritually that it hardly pissed me off at all.

When I got home from Ohio, Terry and I decided to replace the orange-flowered wallpaper left in her kitchen by the previous owner with something lighter and brighter. We'd never actually wallpapered before, but I think one of us got a book from the public library telling how to do so, or maybe we simply read the instructions that came with the wallpaper. Terry's arthritis was still more or less okay at that point, so we alternated the jobs of hanging and cutting. One day while I was there, Terry's sister Maureen dropped by. We got to talking about their parents, and their parents' death. Terry remarked that she thought she hadn't yet processed the loss of her mother.

Maureen nudged me. "You're a minister now. Fix it."

"What?"

"Fix it. Fix Terry."

I shook my head. "Ministers can't fix things. They're only allowed to be there."

I already hated that part of ministry. It felt like cheating. Surely we're supposed to be fixing things? But no. Not much that we encounter can be fixed.

I spent a lot of time that summer and fall working with things that couldn't be fixed. I was doing a required field-education unit with the Resource Center for Women and Ministry in the South. South Carolina has one of the highest murder rates involving domestic violence in the United States. The county I lived in had the highest rate in the state. As part of my field education, I was working with a task force putting together a conference on domestic violence and hearing a lot of horror stories, like the one about the man who staked his wife out naked in their backyard and shot into the ground all around her; and about how unless he was charged with and convicted of attempted murder, the maximum penalty would be a $235 fine. I ended up chairing the task force. Early on, I had a serious conversation with the director of the local women's shelter. I asked her if she ever wanted to form a posse or a vigilante group. "I'm only asking in case I want to join," I explained.

She smiled, and I would swear there was a look of longing in her eyes, but then she shook her head. "We all have moments of wanting to do that, but we can't. We can't use violence to end violence."

I knew killing people was counter to Christian tradition, but I still didn't know if she was right. I'd read a newspaper article that summer about a Florida community where a serial rapist was on the loose. In response, thousands of women bought guns, and the rape rate dropped by 85 percent. Although an armed and shooting citizenry doesn't serve the interests of justice and mercy, I suspected once a posse gunned down a dozen or so rapists and wife beaters, the rest of the men in town might settle down and behave themselves.

And then I thought, *Good God. I've just made an argument for the death penalty.* Which took me back to my acquaintance's point: we can't use violence to end violence.

I got a call the second week of August asking me to help with a march and rally to call attention to the violence in the county. Five people—four women and a ten-year-old girl—had been killed between June 21 and August 1. I met with the sponsoring groups the next day, and we laid out strategy, time and place, speakers, publicity, and a list of the things we wanted to have done differently by judicial authorities. After vetting the list with a staff member of a domestic-violence organization, I went with another woman to city hall to get a parade permit. I had a list of things to do for the march the next day, but I had to ask somebody else to fulfill them, because at 6:30 in the morning my daughter Jennifer called. She was in the hospital having a baby.

Jennifer and her family lived in Charlotte, an hour and a half away.

When we arrived at eleven A.M., Jennifer was in the middle of a labor pain. Her husband and her little boy Bradley were in the room with her. When Jennifer's contraction ended, she chatted a little with us, even though her face was gray with pain. Bradley sat on my lap for a while. When he got engrossed in a coloring book, I approached the machine that was documenting the duration and strength of her contractions.

"Look, Fred. This is really interesting."

Together we figured out what the numbers meant, and from then on we provided Jennifer with updates on her body. One or the other of us would say, "Hang on, Jenn. There's a big one on its way."

Jennifer, who was clutching the bars on the headboard of the hospital bed and glaring, said, "I know that."

The baby dawdled until 2:01 in the afternoon. As soon as he was delivered, the doctor came to find me. He said, "The cord was wrapped around the baby's neck, so I had to use forceps. The baby's fine, and so is Jennifer."

At 2:31 they let us in to see Jennifer and the baby, who was swaddled in a thick white blanket with his hands anchored in for warmth. Devin's face was nicely pink. We peeked under the blankets: his arms and feet were still cadaverously pale. He felt good, though; at eight pounds and thirteen ounces, he had the solidity of a brick. Holding him in those first few minutes, I heard a sound I'd only heard three other times in my life, at the births of my daughters and my first grandson. It was the song of the newborn, that series of little piggy snorty noises that babies make for only a few minutes—an hour, an hour and a half?—after they're born. I breathed in the smell of his head, that infant earthy odor like a plowed field as you drive past in the late winter.

A nurse came to take the baby to the nursery. We watched Devin get weighed and measured and have his reflexes checked. I stepped down the hall to tell Jennifer he seemed to be fine. When I came back he'd had his footprints stamped on a form, and the nurse was diapering and undershirting him. It was when she drew his arm through the undershirt that I finally relaxed. An undershirt on a newborn is a certain sign there's nothing to fear.

▲   ▲   ▲

The march and rally were two days later. The contrast between the sight of the new baby and the sight of a woman missing four fingers because her husband got mad and cut them off was almost overwhelming. There were about ninety people present, plus two newspapers and the local television station. Two other ministers were there: a United Methodist who did the closing ritual and the head of a coalition called Concerned Citizens against Crime. Of the three of us, only the latter, who was the only one of us who was male, was introduced as "the Reverend."

I barely noticed.

▲   ▲   ▲

A week later two more people were murdered in Spartanburg: a sixteen-year-old, killed by a former boyfriend, and a twenty-year-old neighbor who tried to help. The former boyfriend then committed suicide.

When I heard the news, I wished I'd never become involved with the domestic-violence movement, and then I thought, *Where do you get off being so damned delicate? It's not as though you're on the front lines.* And then I thought, *Bullshit. We're all on the front lines. It's about women not having power, and the best way to hang on to power is to keep women out. And a corpse is the epitome of powerlessness.*

About that time the phone rang. A reporter from a local newspaper wanted comments on the murders from me, because I was leading the task force for the conference in the fall. Near the end of the conversation, though, he said he'd seen the demands that were posted at the rally.

"'Demands' is a strong word. It puts people's backs up," he informed me.

I thought the top of my head was going to explode from anger. "Maybe it's time we made demands. Seven people have been murdered here in less than two months. Maybe it's time somebody demands that the safety of women and children be treated as a public-safety issue so the killing can stop."

I was angry with the legislative system, the judicial system, and the police, but most of all I was angry with the Church. In the book *Surviving Crisis,* Annie Dillard wrote in her essay "An Expedition to the Pole," "On the whole, I do not find Christians . . . sufficiently sensible of conditions. Does anyone have the foggiest idea what sort of power we so blithely invoke? Or, as I suspect, does no one believe a word of it? The churches are children playing on the floor with their chemistry sets, making up a batch of TNT to kill a Sunday morning. It is madness to wear ladies' straw hats and velvet hats to church; we should all be wearing crash helmets. Ushers should issue life preservers and signal flares; they should lash us to our pews. For the sleeping god may wake someday and take offense, or the waking god may draw us out to where we can never return."

The Church has the power, and the responsibility if every human being really is *imago dei,* made in the image of God, to be a flying wedge in the battle against domestic violence. Instead it presents to the world folded hands and genteel silence. The waking god had put me where I now stood, but I was beginning to wonder if Dillard was right and that nobody believed a word of it.

chapter eight

ORIGINAL SIN—THE TENET THAT WE ARE ALL STAINED
from birth by Adam's sin—was on my mind during my fourth semester
at divinity school. It wasn't my classes that raised the question; it was
the violence, racism, and sexism I was encountering. To go deep into any
of the three might change you; to wrestle with the three simultaneously
transformed my sense of myself. Oh, and there were the babies, too. The
babies were part of the transformation, too.

My questions about original sin actually began with Devin. Fred
and I were in the car on the way to see him and Bradley. I'd been reading
John Wesley's sermons, and I said, "I think the whole concept of original
sin is stupid. I just don't believe that human beings are born sinful."

Fred, as usual, took the statement under advisement. We rode in
silence for forty miles or so, Fred driving, me fiddling with the radio station and highlighting my book of sermons. He must have been thinking
our conversation through the whole time, because just before we reached
our destination, he said, "I cannot look at Devin and believe in original
sin." When we got to Jennifer's, it was the first thing out of his mouth:
"Hey, Jenn, did you know your boys are sinners?"

She started laughing, and kept on laughing, and so did Fred. When
my daughter Tara called us later that week, he told her, too, and she
laughed, too. She was seven months pregnant. There was no way she was
going to give birth to a sinner.

Original sin would be such a useful concept if I believed in it.
Without it, it's tough to explain the evil people do to other people. At
the fall conference on domestic violence, the state attorney general was
one of the speakers. When he stated that 70 to 75 percent of violence in
South Carolina is domestic, the audience gasped. He grimaced when he
said, "The figure surprised me, too." During a break, an attendee told
me that six years earlier, she and her husband had appeared before one of

the family-court judges on the panel. The couple was legally separated and seeking a divorce. She told me that not only had the judge refused to accept into the proceedings the evidence of seventy-two police reports and emergency-room visits, but when the husband said his wife was dating, the judge turned to her and said, "I'd beat you, too, if you were my wife and committing adultery."

Later that afternoon a group of us reviewed the day's work. One member of the committee leaned back in her chair and said, "For months now I've been doing research on violence on television, but listening to those speakers today, it struck me how little impact television violence has compared to seeing your dad beat your mother's head against the wall."

My hardest conversation that day was with a woman who said to me, "I just don't understand, Mary Jo. If you value women's lives, how can you be part of the Church?"

"What do you mean?"

"The churches don't care. They make a big deal about things like gambling and homosexuality, but when it comes to women's lives, they don't have anything to say. I don't know how you can be part of that."

I shrugged. "I don't know, either, except that the Church has to care. There's no way it can *not* care."

"Then why are you the only religious official I've ever known who thinks it's important?"

I had no answer. In classes I was hearing all sorts of talk about the power of the Christian community and about how it had an ethical stance lacking in the secular world, but who are the heathens when you've got magistrates who think citizens are rude for protesting a $235 bond for a man who stakes his wife, naked, out on the ground and shoots around her, and an attorney general whose state-of-the-state report a few months earlier had not even a single sentence on the topic of family violence?

That fall I worked with another bunch of Christians, or at least a bunch of people who went to church on Sunday mornings. I was an appointee to a county commission that held oversight responsibilities for a local public college. The group had done no harm until the college needed a new chancellor and the prime candidate was a black man. I knew I was in for trouble when the chair of the group called to tell me of a meeting scheduled to interview the candidate. "He's not the kind of man we need," said the chair.

"Mmmm," I said, figuring I could draw my own conclusion during the interview. I'd been on the committee for two years, which wasn't long enough to prepare me for the interview. The candidate, who was president of a midwestern college, was a demonstrated genius in fund-raising and student recruitment.

I did what I could, which wasn't much. First I listened to the questions of five or six of the white men on the board with me. Each of them prefaced his questions by saying, "I am not a racist, but . . . ," filling in the statement with a query about how could the candidate expect to be effective in a predominantly white setting. When my turn arrived, I pointed out that the candidate had increased state appropriations by 43 percent (a goal of our group for the previous five years had been such an increase). I then said to the candidate, "It will be a horrible shock to this community when an African American is named chancellor of any of the institutes of higher education. I'm sure it was a shock in Indiana as well. Could you talk about the transition?" I felt the person next to me twitch, but I kept my eyes focused on the candidate, who nodded (before the meeting convened, I'd alerted him to the question I would ask) and then answered.

The board voted against him. A reporter who called to get a statement from me quoted the chair as saying, "We need a chancellor from South Carolina. This man doesn't know this state. We need someone from the Southeast."

"The candidate's from Arkansas," I told the reporter. "Last time I checked it's in the Southeast."

Another reporter phoned and said, "Other board members have said repeatedly that race has nothing to do with their decision. Do you agree?"

"Of course the vote was about race. Whether he was elected or not, race was going to be an issue."

So there's that to say for the concept of original sin: it explains why otherwise decent people, American and Christian, lawmakers, judges, and committee members insult other people publicly, or deny evidence as plain as the skin on their hands, or overlook evidence of diligence, accomplishment, and dignity while claiming they're only doing their job. In one of my classes, a renowned ethics professor insisted that Christians are a set-apart community and must operate differently from the dominant American culture. Maybe so, but Christians who take literally the biblical call for justice are watching the courts make it happen, not the Church.

I wanted—I hoped—but did I ever imagine that my ordination and my service as a pastor could change people? Probably not. I wasn't proceeding because I thought my work could stimulate more effective legislation or transform racists into decent human beings. I was proceeding because it was what I was called to do.

▲   ▲   ▲

With the fall conference on domestic violence successfully completed, I decided to go to Minnesota. An advertisement for Re-Imagining: A Global Theological Conference had come into my hands. I knew the moment I read about it that I was going to Minneapolis to attend. Who wouldn't want to go? It was to be a global gathering of theologians. Presenters would include "theologians, writers, preachers, artists, and educators" from a dozen nations. Participants would include "dreamers, organizers, activists, visionaries, question askers, mediators, messengers, educators, writers, dancers, musicians, and artists." Its intent was to move women and men "beyond their own experience, expanding and bridging their geographical, cultural, and theological boundaries."

The list of speakers included Chung Hyun Kyung, the Korean theologian I'd admired at the seminar in Ohio before I entered the ministry pipeline; Kwok Pui-Lan, author of *Chinese Women and Christianity;* Mercy Amba Oduyoye of Ghana, deputy general secretary of the World Council of Churches and editor of *With Passion and Compassion;* Ada María Isasi-Díaz, born in Cuba, now a professor of ethics and theology and author of *Hispanic Women: Prophetic Voice in the Church;* and other theologians from Costa Rica, India, Zimbabwe, and the United States, including my old friend Johanna van Wijk-Bos.

From the time I'd started seminary, I'd been lectured to about the way Christianity has been tainted by American culture. This gathering, with its cluster of theologians from around the world, might clarify the essence of Christianity by shedding light on its American accretions. Besides, it was the most interesting and energizing event I'd heard of since I'd come home from Nairobi.

The conference was exactly what it billed itself to be: a global theological conference where women and men could reimagine God and Jesus, creation and community, spirituality and sexuality, arts and ethics, language and work. On the second day, I spoke with some of the women at the conference about their concerns. Some of them answered cautiously because they had a lot to lose, especially the Presbyterian women, who expected repercussions from their attendance because the conservative element in their denomination had sent people to the conference to take names and photographs for follow-up inquiries.

At the time, I suspected the women were a bit paranoid. Later, when the uproar began and at least one person, Mary Ann Lundy, the highest-ranking woman in the Presbyterian Church (U.S.A.), was forced to resign, I regretted my naïveté. The Church—the Church in its largest sense, Protestant, Catholic, Orthodox—has been slow to acknowledge that women can speak, lead, and think. Now here was a conference where women were claiming their theological authority, stepping up to the plate to aver and investigate the very nature of God.

Cutting-edge theology makes people nervous. When women are doing it, some people's nervousness turns to anger; "How dare you?" seems to be their attitude. How dare you mess with God—as though only men of the Church should think and formulate.

Some members of an ecumenical group called CLOUT—Christian Lesbians Out Together—attended the conference. Just before lunch on Saturday, Melanie Morrison, the co-convener of the group, approached the dais, asked permission to speak, and said, "We are keenly aware that the world is not safe for lesbian women, and often the least safe place is the Church." She then invited any lesbian, bisexual, or transsexual woman who was willing, able, and free to do so to form a circle in the room, "because here in this place it's safe to be who we are."

It was a curious statement, given the fears of repercussions. Watching women step forward, some in tears, and listening to the applause that erupted from many of the spectators was so moving I could hardly stand it. Later one woman who'd joined the circle told me of the weird scene when she returned to her table. Although her table mates were all on their feet applauding the action, none of them said a word directly to her. As soon as they sat down, they began talking about something else.

I said, "Nobody spoke to you? Or touched you? Nobody took your hand?" and she said no. I hugged her, because I wanted to and nobody had, and off we went on our separate ways.

For me, the most important aspect of the conference was that I, too, felt safe and free. I hadn't realized until then how straitjacketed I felt in seminary. Perhaps it was the threats my colleagues had received, or the LADIES sign on the women's rest room, or the male students who thought we had no business being there, or the ineffectiveness of the lighting in the divinity-school parking lot, or the time I walked past undergraduate dorms and saw, spray-painted on benches, the words "Bitch," "I'd fuck her," and "Dyke" (an effort, it was explained to me, to make an outward and visible sign of the rating system with which male undergraduate students audibly graded female students who walked past). Or perhaps it was no one thing but the general climate that left me wondering what in the hell I was doing in the Church.

▲   ▲   ▲

By the time I got back to school, the shit was already hitting the fan.

They said the Re-Imagining conference was paganism.

They said it was a mockery of the name of our Lord and Savior Jesus Christ, of the Church, and of Christianity.

They said any woman who attended the conference should be thrown out of the Church.

They—editors of, writers for, and readers of various denominational magazines and newspapers—were horrified by the statements and actions of "those women" who attended. The controversy went on, and on, and on. Come May, a *New York Times* piece by Peter Steinfels was headlined "Female Concept of God Is Shaking Protestants: Churches Accused of Goddess Worship." A few weeks later, delegates to my Annual Conference condemned Re-Imagining as "heresy of the worse kind." Following the vote, someone did ask politely if we could amend the phrase to read "heresy of the worst kind." The Conference agreed, although few delegates seemed to care one way or the other about either the grammatical correction or the reality that Christians, even the ones without penises, are free to ask "What if?" regarding both God and the Church. The delegates, perturbed by the creative rituals at Re-Imagining, such as the one in which milk and honey were served to the attendees, called upon "United Methodists and their employees everywhere to monitor carefully all conferences and gatherings in which they participate or promote to be reassured . . . that their perspective is rooted in the heritage of a positive proclamation of the Gospel of Jesus Christ as it is best understood in the Christian tradition and Wesleyan theology." I sat silent through it all, intimidated, and certain no action of mine could stay the rage.

Where did all that rage come from? I think the tinder was the conference's underlying theme, which was that women are made in the image of God. The statement is sound Christian doctrine, but there's a gap between believing it intellectually and incorporating it. Most women don't. We have trouble believing that our physicality—these breasts, these menstrual cycles, these hormones—has anything to do with God. Our souls? Oh, sure. This body? Oh, come now. The rituals at Re-Imagining prodded us to think about *imago dei,* the conviction embedded in the book of Genesis that we are created in the image of God, and that creation includes women as well as men, and that the creation is good. A radical idea, indeed. And that's what I think caused the uproar: women taking the authority to claim for themselves the same idea of creation and goodness that men in the Church claim.

The controversy was annoying, and invigorating, and frightening. By the time I'd been back at school a month, I concluded men were right to resist women coming into the ministry. It is true that not a rock of this temple will stand. We don't bleed the preferred blood. We bleed messy normal blood and it gets all over us and the sheets if it starts early, in the middle of the night, say, and we do this bleeding regularly, month in and month out, and it's not pretty and "pure" like the martyrs' blood and Jesus' blood are romanticized into being. It's ordinary blood, and it's happening at the altar, and the altar is going to be changed. Women know varieties of blood: bright red and pulsing, dark and flowing, brownish and seeping, clots and globs and lumps sometimes. Christianity has known only one sort of blood, has made obeisance to sterile blood, drinkable blood, and it isn't enough. Sterile blood, sanctified blood permits us to ignore the ordinary blood: periods, spontaneous abortions, the blood of childbirth, the blood spurting from the hands of a woman whose fingers have been chopped off by her husband.

If there were 2,200 women at the conference and most cycles last five days and there are thirty days in a month, and thus one-sixth of women have their periods at any given time, then (What's 6 into 2,200?) 366 women had their periods, and if we take off another 10 percent for those who are menopausal like me, or the ones pregnant or lactating, then 330 women had their periods, and another 330 were aware of theirs because they had just ended, and another 330 were aware theirs should be starting, so we had 990 women with one form of blood on their minds or in their underpants in one way or another and the subject didn't come up. But it will. I don't know when, but it will.

▲   ▲   ▲

A week after Re-Imagining, I was in my favorite haunt, the smoking area at the divinity school, when a male student pastor said he'd been forced to go to the altar to pray one Sunday because, just before the worship service began, a young, beautiful blond woman walked into the sanctuary wearing a sheer dress, and, when the light fell just right through the windows, it was as though she had nothing on. Another male student pastor said the woman probably knew that would happen; there was a fifty-fifty chance she was guilty of trying to turn his attention from the sacred to the sexual.

I said, sweetly, pastorally, "She was coming to the church on a Sunday morning to worship. I find it highly unlikely that when she got dressed she asked herself what she could wear so that if she walked through the door just at the right time the preacher could see through her dress. Our assumption must be that she came to worship God, not to have someone look through her dress."

The conversation pivoted. One of the men asked if I'd begun my work toward ordination. I said I'd completed it, and I told him about singing "Standing on the Promises" on my way to the Board interview and being asked about my conversion experience, and I told him how the bishop's hands felt on my head and how being told to "take authority" grounded me and mandated some things that I wouldn't have done otherwise. His face changed as I talked, and I saw him walk through a state of cognitive dissonance because what else are you going to experience when a woman you're pretty sure is a feminist and suspect might be one of those castrating bitches tells you about the power of the Holy Spirit in her life?

▲   ▲   ▲

Tara, finally in the third trimester of pregnancy, came to visit the next weekend, and so did Jennifer and her boys. While the girls and Fred talked, Bradley and I took the baby into the living room to play. Devin, now three months old, was next door to learning how to roll over. He'd crank his head around, arch his back, and stomp the air with his right foot. Bradley and I tipped him over, just so he'd know what it is he was trying to do. I changed his clothes (I perpetually change babies' clothes, for the fun of it) and, between doffing and donning, rattled his ribs to make him laugh.

What tactile creatures we are. Waves of love passed through me when I touched his skin, when I felt the communion between my palm and his chest and plump knees and round feet. Family, the sense of kinship, doesn't come through blood but through touch, I decided. And that's why it mattered to Fred and to me when Bradley paused long enough in his stroll through life (rolling in the grass with the dog, saying he's hungry, telling his mother he doesn't need a nap because he's not tired) to climb up beside Fred or me and lean against us for a while. We stay connected to each other through our bodies.

▲   ▲   ▲

Tara's due date was December 12. Waiting was onerous. I studied for final exams while Fred wrapped Christmas presents. He didn't do it right. He picked up whatever roll of paper was handy and used it until it was all gone. It was bad enough when he wrapped a present for Mary Flowers's little girl Jessica in purple and gold stripes rather than Santa paper, but then he wrapped four presents in a row with wedding paper, gray with white doves on it. I wanted to clobber him.

Tara had contractions; then a hospital stay; then she went back home. The days crawled by.

Jennifer's boys came to spend the night. When it was time to dress Devin for bed, I laid him on the couch in the living room. He was on his back with just a diaper on in the moment between wearing his daytime Christmas outfit and his nightgown. Between looking at me and looking at the lights on the Christmas tree, he had a lot of things to discuss. He warbled, kicked, and waved his arms when his hands weren't in his drooly mouth. Bradley came in to help me teach Devin how to play peekaboo.

Later that night I went to check on the sleeping boys and noticed, not for the first time, that a baby in a nightgown is a fine thing. Devin was thoroughly covered except for his feet, which were out from under the cover and crossed at the ankles, with his toes burrowing into the mattress.

At ten the next morning the phone rang: "We're having a baby."

Tara's water had broken, she was having contractions, they were in the hospital, the doctor had just left the room: we're having a baby.

▲   ▲   ▲

It was a girl, Elizabeth Grace, eight pounds exactly, twenty and a half inches long, a mop of dark hair down almost to her shoulders. We peeked, and then she got whisked into the nursery. Through the long window we watched her bellow through being measured, getting a shot of vitamin K in her thigh and a poke in her heel, being footprinted. We watched her hands and feet, which were purple at first, pinken more and more as she yelled.

On the way home I thought about what big a step it was from "Tara's baby" to "Elizabeth." It was the space between the generic baby Tara had carried and the particular person Elizabeth, who discovered at an hour old that a fist is a glorious thing to have in her mouth. And that hair! And those ears. I've been accused of fixating on babies' ears. It's because when Tara was a newborn I noticed her ears were miraculous miniature intricacies.

▲   ▲   ▲

On Christmas Eve I served communion at my home church's eleven o'clock service. The bread was a round loaf with immense crumbling powers. The officiating minister gave me the option of serving the bread or the wine (juice, really, because we're Methodists). I chose the bread. He then asked if I wanted to carry it in a napkin or bare-handed. Another seminarian, also home for Christmas, trilled in the background, "And how do you understand this theologically?"

I left the napkin on the table. My theological thinking: the napkin emphasizes the preciousness of the bread while bare hands emphasize that it's real bread—and the latter is what people forget.

I served with crumbs flying, catching on people's collars and in their hair, scattered bits on the altar and on the floor. Bread: we were receiving the bread of life. I was struck again by the hilarity of it all, especially the moment when a hunk came loose the size of my palm and the communicant and I looked into each other's eyes, both envisioning her chewing half the night, so I broke the piece in half.

I'd never dreamed the ritual could be fun. Most people serve somberly. I am not somber. Theologically I believe the bread to be real bread, and that flying crumbs are required, and that this sacrament is a celebration—solemn, yes, but festive, too. And it is also so incredibly intimate that you learn volumes about each person in the few seconds of connection. There was the guy in the green sweater with his head drooped low; the couple who I think must not be Methodist because they each looked me full in the face, expectantly, when I said, "The body of Christ . . ."; the woman who left her mink in the pew when she came to the communion rail.

The day after Christmas I started wallpapering the dining room in a Jack-and-the-Beanstalk, minus Jack, pattern. I loved wallpapering. The rhythms of the movement—measure, wet, book, hang, straighten, rinse—were regenerative. The physical action, concrete, with immediate results, revitalized me.

When I wasn't wallpapering, I read Fred B. Craddock's book *Preaching* in preparation for my first preaching class, which was scheduled for the spring term. Craddock said sermons contain an inevitable humor because they include the requisite ingredients: concrete and specific references, concern for the significant and sacred, and a sense of freedom. Humor, he says, is a genuine response to grace; grace gives us gratitude; and (I loved this next statement) the grateful person acknowledges that there is usually a small party going on in the back of the mind. I realized that the small party going on in the back of my mind was a crowd of seventy-year-old women sitting around a picnic table under some oak trees with shadow and sunlight falling on them, whooping with laughter.

By New Year's Day, Devin had learned to eat cereal, and Elizabeth Grace had grown a second chin. I gave her a bath a few days before I went back to school, and when I dried her hair (rub, rub, rub), it erupted into curls. Occasionally her dad petted her head like she was a puppy. Occasionally I did, too.

Sometimes when babies get cranky, you suspect they want a pacifier. You stick it in their mouths. They're too upset to realize it's there, so they keep wailing. What you do then is you cluck at them. Or, not quite cluck. You go "tsk, tsk, tsk," staccato. Immediately they begin to suck. I believe it reminds them of their mother's heartbeat in utero.

It had worked every time since Devin was born, every time, until the week before I went back to school. He'd grown up, our nearly five-month-old, no-kneed, wide-mouthed grinner with slobber dripping off his chin. He'd forgotten that his mother's heartbeat is the most certain sound in the world.

chapter nine

AS BEST I CAN RECONSTRUCT, IT WAS THE BABIES THAT made me do it, and the blood, the stupidity, and the cruelty. How else can you explain standing up in public in mixed company—a crowd of preachers, no less—and talking about a woman who was having her period?

There was, of course, more to it than that. When I got back to school after Christmas break in January 1994, one friend who'd had a miscarriage in the spring was four months pregnant. Another, who'd had four miscarriages the prior year, was not. Mightily depressed, she was having trouble leaving her apartment to go to class and had resigned all her campus-leadership positions. I'd listen to her grieve, and once in a while I could cajole her to come out to supper with me. I thought it was odd that I knew how to converse with the pain of miscarrying a wanted baby. The women in my family had never confronted such a shock; our lot had always been the shock of unexpected pregnancy. And it's not as though I consider an eight-week fetus a baby. I think what I was able to converse with was the despair.

Some people, it seems to me, have the luxury of living on the outskirts of life. Never shackled by trauma, they believe that if you just live right—work hard, pay your bills, obey the posted speed limit, teach your children to say "please" and "thank you"—then nothing bad happens. The corollary is that when you struggle—in poverty, for instance—it's because you didn't work hard, pay your bills, etc. And many, if not most, people's lives are ordinary: they get born, they go to school, get a spouse and a job, get pregnant about the time they decide to do so. Simple. Easy to know how things work and to tell others how, if they lived right, they wouldn't have these irritating problems. People can stay on the outskirts of life only until they run headlong into forces beyond their control. Only then do they learn that they, too, are powerless.

Why did I know these things? Ah—because I'd come to terms with my own powerlessness three times in my late teens and early twenties. My first pregnancy was unexpected. My second pregnancy was, too, although in a different way. My husband and I hadn't made any plans to have a second child, but I'd been having mildly suspicious Pap tests for three years. One day my gynecologist looked over my medical records and said, "If you want to have a second child, you should go ahead and get pregnant now, because we don't know what's developing here." A week later I went off the birth control pill. Within six weeks I was pregnant. The baby was born in January of 1973. My Pap smear results descended from moderate to severe dysplasia, and the procedures enlisted to clear them up all failed. Finally, after four years of watching for cancer, I had a hysterectomy in 1974. I was in the hospital for a week, and a month later when I ventured out to the grocery store for the first time, husband and two children in tow, I had to sit on the floor of the first aisle to keep from fainting.

This body, my body, was not something over which I had control. Oh, yes, there were things I could do with it—add weight, lose weight, carry a pregnancy to term, run, walk, turn somersaults, have orgasms— but before I was twenty-five, I'd lost the innocence of believing my energy or strength of will or sunny nature or desire were enough to hold me harmless from disaster. I had no control over disease. I had no control over my life, its duration or expectations. No matter what I did, no matter how well I felt, something capable of felling me might be developing at any time.

Maybe that's where my sense of urgency originates, my conviction that all we have is this moment. And maybe that's the reason that when push came to shove, I stood my ground, no matter whether the tension came from outside myself or was self-inflicted.

I can't pretend that I wasn't also mentally challenging the Church. I was afraid the institution was an intellectual mausoleum. I didn't know if it wanted, or needed, a thinking priesthood, or if it would be better served by people who gave lip service to the vitality of the gospel but spent their Sundays re-creating the tones, rhythms, and sermons they'd listened to their whole lives. Maybe sermons were supposed to be like bedtime stories, repetitive, soothing, no surprises.

Then again, maybe not.

The only way I could find out was by trial and error. The best place to experiment was in the classroom. I could try things that might not be appropriate later in front of a congregation—which is why, in spite of my misgivings, in my first preaching class I talked about that unclean woman.

The assignment was simple: tell a Bible story; tell how the story connects to your life or to the life of someone you know; and do both as dramatically as you can. I was drawn to the story in Mark 5 of a woman who'd been hemorrhaging for twelve years, who tracked Jesus down and touched his cloak. She had no business doing such a thing; because she was bleeding, she was unclean under the codes of Leviticus. Therefore, she defiled anyone she came into contact with. When he felt her hand on his garment, Jesus turned to ask who was touching him. She told him the truth, and Jesus healed her.

My primary question was *How on earth can a woman hemorrhage for twelve years without bleeding to death?* The answer was self-evident: *She can't. It doesn't take anywhere near twelve years for a hemorrhaging person to bleed to death. It doesn't even take twelve hours.*

In that case, what medical problem was the text referring to? In what situation can a woman bleed for twelve years? *Ah—the answer is obvious. She had her period.*

With that realization, I nearly gave up on the text. The divinity school had a very young, very male student body. A number of the people in my group were in their early twenties, many of them unmarried and, at least theoretically, virgins. It would be unseemly to speak to them from the pulpit about a woman's period.

Yet I was also being taught that, if we're going to preach the gospel, we must preach the entire gospel, not pick and choose the texts that are comfortable and easy for us. The bleeding-woman text was a tough and tricky one to contend with. Was there a way to talk about it without being offensive?

I decided the safest approach was to make the story personal, to humanize it. The way to do so was to tell it in the first person.

I was comfortable with my decision until two hours before my presentation, when I dissolved into nervous frenzy. What was I thinking? I must be crazy. We'd been told not to do research for this assignment, but I took myself to the library anyhow, under the theory that researching the background of the passage might engage my mind and disengage my concerns.

I looked up *blood* in one commentary and learned that a woman with breakthrough bleeding was permanently unclean and conveyed uncleanness to whatever she touched. I kept reading, following intertwined paths from subject to subject and reference book to reference book until I got to a paragraph about the "universal rite" of circumcision. The writer stated matter-of-factly that circumcision was understood "primarily as a manifestation of the desire to eliminate any traces of feminization in the male."

The statement is outlandish, but at the time I took it as gospel. A bolt of heat slammed through my body. Circumcision exists to eliminate any trace of feminization? *Good God,* I thought. *Men hate women so much they'll cut off part of their dicks to keep from being like us. And we all know how precious their dicks are to them.*

My next thought was *Why the hell should women bother with men when they hate us that much?*

By the time I had to speak, I'd sequestered my rage in a deep psychic pocket. I took my place at the front of the room, gathered myself, took a careful breath, and began speaking, slowly, slowly.

Twelve years. I bled for twelve years. If it embarrasses you to hear about my period, think what it was like to live it. I was unclean. I wasn't fit to be around other human beings. I wasn't like the people who could smell their neighbor's bread baking and stop in to say how lovely the smell was. I wasn't like the people who could sit and chatter about the children playing in the dust. I wasn't like anybody else—because I was unclean.

I kept on with the story, and the more I talked, the more I identified with the woman in her isolation and misery. I moved into the intensity of her pain and then backed off a fraction, just enough to speak through it rather than have it come howling out of me. To connect the biblical story to real life, I told the true story of a woman who was pastoring her first church in the lower part of South Carolina. She came home early from vacation and went by the church. Seeing lights on in a Sunday-school classroom, she stepped in to see what the congregation was up to. What she found was a Ku Klux Klan meeting in progress.

I don't know what I'd do if that ever happened to me, but I know what this woman did. She stepped to the front of the room and said firmly and clearly, "Under the *Book of Discipline* of the United Methodist Church, this meeting is out of order. It is adjourned."

I said, I can't imagine being in that woman's position, seeing those faces in the congregation the next Sunday and having to tell them of the grace and peace God offered to them. I hate those people, detest them, want them to fall off the face of the earth, because they are [pause, pause, pause] unclean. The heart of the story of the unclean woman is that change can come, and that means those people can reach out to touch the robe of Jesus Christ—and when they do, my hand better already be there.

I sat down to silence in the room, and then a great exhalation, and then a softer sigh. We sat together in that windowless room for a moment, or two, breathing in unison, and then the air shifted and people began to speak.

They said words I hadn't expected, words like "dramatic" and "powerful" and "suspense-filled story" and "gifted storyteller." One young man said that when I uttered the first sentence he thought, *Oh, no, I can't believe she's going to talk about this passage,* but then he couldn't stop listening, and it was okay, he was okay, he was safe listening to me. My professor said he couldn't figure out where I was going with the Bible story, that he expected the meeting was about replacing the female pastor, so there was a jolt when I said the words Ku Klux Klan. He said he couldn't figure out my hermeneutic, how these stories could speak to each other, until I got to the sentence that both shocked and pulled it all together: "I despise these people because they are [pause, pause, pause] unclean."

"How did you do that?" he asked.

"I don't know."

I still don't know. There were Christmas programs when I was in grade school, drama groups in high school, poetry readings after college, the speeches I'd presented post-Nairobi, but none of them were like this. Nothing had prepared me for how I now felt.

I think what happened to me, what transformed me, is that in those moments of speaking I was, for once, certain that the things I was saying needed to be said, and that I was the person who needed to say them.

Later I watched a video of Episcopal priest Barbara Brown Taylor preaching. In her sermon she said, "Take the sunroom at the nursing home where you stand by the piano. . . . Say 'resurrection' in [those people's] presence. Say 'life everlasting.' Say 'remember.' Just let those words loose in the room, just utter them in the light and trust them to do their work." I think what I did that day in preaching class was to utter the story of the unclean woman in the light and to trust the story to do its job. When I did so, the story became both true and free. And I was the one who'd unloosed it, who'd cast it into the air and let it live.

The experience, while wonderful, was also horribly unsettling. I spoke with someone who'd once taught preaching and told her how hard it was for me because of the risks I took.

She said, "I don't think I've ever done that."

"Done what?"

"Taken risks when I preach."

I was puzzled then, and I still am. I don't understand how a preacher can avoid risks, and I understand even less clearly why they'd avoid them. The risk itself forms a connection between the preacher and the congregation. Some days the tension is an epoxy binding speaker and listeners. Other days it's as though it lays out a gravel path between preacher and hearer, a straight short path with sunlight glistening on its pale gravel, the kind of gravel that doesn't hurt your feet when you walk on it barefoot.

Over the next few weeks I listened to other people's presentations and felt as though someone had taken a potato peeler to my skin. Life, death; dying, birth; boat rides, camel rides; fear, conflict; wild humor, living grief, despair, hope, power, hopelessness: we touched on it all. Our professor said he'd never seen anything like our class, that together we were powerful, and risk-taking, and trusting, and kind. It was glorious, exciting, empowering, and I felt vibrant, and alive, and peaceful about my place in the Church.

Like all such moments, it was fleeting.

The day after the professor's comment, some members of my Board of Ordained Ministry paid a campus visit. It was a biennial event, Duke graduates returning to campus to spend time with the ministerial candidates, check on their progress, and take them out to dinner. This time the group got into a conversation with me about the particular stresses for women in the ministry. I said I'd talked with a number of ordained women and I knew there were extra challenges for us. I said I thought I'd be able to handle them.

At that point one of the members of the Board (all of them happened to be male and white that day) leaned closer to me and said, "There are going to be problems, all right. Don't think there won't be. When I was a district superintendent, people used to tell me they'd rather have a nigger pastoring their church than a woman."

I sat there, speechless. I hadn't heard the n-word in years, and never in the divinity school. The speaker must have wanted to emphasize the point, because he repeated himself.

"Yes, I had lots of people telling me they'd rather have a nigger than a woman."

Part of my undertaking in divinity school and in my preparations for ordination was to construct a vision of the Church. I'd accepted the premise that Christianity is lived in community and that the Church is the solid ground upon which we stand. I needed to believe it in order to continue, and yet it was, and is, unfathomable that good and true church people can be offended by phrases like "goddamn it" and yet don't see blasphemy in the slurs they use against other people.

I felt as though I'd stepped into an open elevator shaft.

▲   ▲   ▲

If my first realization in preaching class was that I'm good at preaching, my second was that there's a glitch in my mental processes. In all the Sundays I'd spent in church, I watched the other people seated in the pews, concentrating on the sermons. Not me. I couldn't sit still. I'd twitch. I'd wonder what on earth the preacher was talking about and when or if he or she would ever stop talking. I'd write mental grocery lists and compose letters to friends in the white spaces on the bulletin.

I don't have problems with my hearing, and yet I just plain can't hang on to what the preacher is saying, to what it means or why it might be important. The difficulty in preaching class was that students had to fill out evaluations on each other, and we couldn't take notes during the sermon. We were to give the student preacher our full attention. The questions were straightforward: What was the theme of the sermon? What were the major movements? Was the student faithful to the text?

Damned if I knew. Week after week, while the rest of the class discussed the responses they'd written on their evaluation forms, I sat silent, humiliated, pondering questions of my own: *How on earth do they do that? How do they remember what the person preaching said? What's wrong with me that I can't remember anything anybody says?*

I now know I have a specific, aural learning disability, and that flat deliveries—presentations where the speaker seems to have no wild party going on, no fascination with the subject matter or with God, with life—are death to my concentration. Out of that flaw springs my greatest strength as a preacher: my commitment to vitality in the pulpit.

▲   ▲   ▲

That fourth semester, all of my questions—the ones about domestic violence, the frenzy over Re-Imagining, the trustworthiness of institutions—localized into one big question: *Can I survive in the institution?* It came to a head the day an acquaintance overheard one of the deans at the divinity school say, on learning I'd attended the Re-Imagining conference, that I'd never be able to pastor a church in South Carolina. I was stunned at first, and then my shock transmuted into active paranoia. Was I disqualifying myself from the ministry? If a theological conference could disqualify me, then what else should I not be doing? Was any conference of religious women suspect? What about raising money for a women's center? What activities exactly made me unclean, unfit to serve the Church?

This is one way the Church kills people's spirits: it subsumes them under the question of *what other people will think.* Truth, and the sense of where the Holy Spirit might be leading, get blocked, not so much out of fear as out of confusion over where the danger lies. In the end you paralyze yourself; you clip your own wings once, and once more, and once more until not only can you not fly, but you can't flutter, and then you can't flap your wings, and then you stop bothering.

I decided if I was going down in flames, I'd go down for things I said, not for things other people said at a conference. My next sermon was to be on Romans 5:12–21, an incredibly convoluted passage about sin and grace. I decided to go for broke, to see if the Church, as represented by the men and women in my preaching class, could handle the hard, real-life stuff. I decided to begin with the question I'd been wrestling with since the conference on domestic violence: "If you value women's lives, how can you be part of the Church?"

I fought with questions all through my exegetical research, questions like "Could I say this to a pregnant woman who's just been punched in the belly? Would it still be true?" and "What if there's someone in the class who beats his wife? Am I going to rile him up so much that he goes home and punches her?" I told myself that preaching about domestic violence doesn't cause domestic violence any more than burnt pork chops or a messy house cause domestic violence. Silence—neither my silence nor the institutional Church's—was not the answer.

A few days later I stood in the classroom facing a congregation of peers and talked about my struggle. I started first by telling them about the passage, about how in it Paul laid out salvation history, beginning with Adam. Adam broke a commandment, and sin came into the world, and with sin came death. Back then God didn't hold sin against people.

Then came the law and, according to Paul, life took a turn for the worse. First, God began holding sin against people, counting sin as transgression. That would be bad enough, but a second thing happened: the law brought forth more sin. If the situation sounds hopeless to you, that was Paul's point: the situation was hopeless.

Then came Jesus Christ. Through the obedience of this particular person, the power of grace came into the world and into all of humanity. Grace and sin were opposed, and grace wins.

That's the outline through which Paul is talking about sin and abundant grace, about Adam and Jesus Christ.

I read the passage out loud, ending with "where sin increased, grace abounded all the more, so that, just as sin exercised dominion in death, so grace might also exercise dominion through justification leading to eternal life through Jesus Christ our Lord." I looked around the room, steadying myself for what was to come. And then I spoke the words out loud:

If you value women's lives, how can you be part of the Church?

I repeated myself, just in case they thought they'd heard me wrong:

If you value women's lives, how can you be part of the Church?

And then I told them where I'd heard the question, and about how the summer I was ordained a deacon, eight women were murdered in my hometown by men who claimed to love them.

To us inside the Church, it appears we differentiate very clearly between sin and death, between grace and life. We are called to manifest the difference, and in many ways the Church does so. And yet my friend could ask me, "If you value women's lives, how can you be part of the Church?"

What can she be thinking, that she believes that valuing women's lives and being part of the Church are mutually exclusive?

I couldn't find grace, or the exercise of Christ's dominion, when I listened to a friend tell about the preacher in a fast-growing church near my home. Last summer he preached on Paul. "Wives, be submissive," he said. "Husbands," he said, "this means you need to beat your wives weekly, or her salvation and yours will be in peril." I don't want to believe a religious leader could say such a thing, but the person who told me is an honest woman.

I can't find grace, or the exercise of Christ's dominion, when I think of conversations I've had with women who grew up in the Church and tell me they'll never go back. Somewhere along the way, ministers looked at their black eyes or their bruises and told them, in one way or another, that God wanted it this way. "You're to be a suffering servant like Christ," the ministers said. "This is your cross to bear," or "Divorce is a sin; you'll burn in hell if you leave."

I can't find grace or the exercise of Christ's dominion when I think of a conversation I had with the Board of Ordained Ministry when I was up for deacon's orders. They asked me about my conversion experience. They were concerned that I might expect everybody to have experienced what I'd experienced. "Heavens, no," I responded. "I just figured I was so thick-headed that God had to use a baseball bat to get through to me." Today I name my statement as blasphemy, the imaging of God as One who will take a baseball bat to a person's head out of love.

In the Christian tradition, such language has not been considered blasphemous. In one of his poems John Donne used the phrase "Batter my heart, three-person'd God," and we have continued to use the image of God as beating us, battering us, all for our own good. But in this century we have seen too many instances of God's name being used to justify sin and death. Think of Germany under Hitler. Think of the stockpiles of nuclear weapons around the world. Think of the reality that the leading cause of death for women between the ages of twenty-five and forty is violence at the hands of men who claim to love them.

I said when I think about things like this, I want magic dust. I want a nice story about a woman who was battered but knew grace in her life anyhow.

Paul doesn't allow me to tell those stories. Paul is discussing sin, and death, and grace, and Paul isn't sprinkling magic dust. Sin is sin, and neither magic dust nor a tidy story can lighten that truth for us. That same situation, according to Paul, was the situation under the law: we, humanity, were dying under the reign of sin.

And then comes the second half of the story, the part that tells us sin did not win. Adam lost the battle. Adam was a paltry opponent who never had a chance against sin. Jesus Christ was born, lived, died on the cross, and was resurrected. Jesus Christ reigns, and a sign of the power of that reign is that death held dominion alone, but with Jesus we share in the reign. The power of Christ is so immense that it is shared with us. We hold the power to reign with Christ.

What does that look like? Picture this with me. Say I'd brought my bathroom scales along with me and set them down in the middle of the aisle. Say we all got together and tried to bundle up sin and put it on the scale. It would be a tough task, but if we got it on there, sin would register. Now say we tried to bundle up grace to weigh it.

And at this moment I somehow began to grow in the pulpit. As the sentences emerged my gestures grew larger, larger, larger, until they were huge, superabundant, taking up acres of space in that small room.

First of all, we couldn't bundle grace. Grace is too big. But say we were granted superabundant arms and could. The needle on the scale would fly off the top and ricochet into the universe.

The air began to ricochet, the energy bouncing from me through the listeners, off the walls, around and around the room in a spiral of dancing grace. And out of that spiral I spoke these words:

My central message today—the good news that I bring—is that we live in the power of superabundant grace. We share the power, and the responsibility, and the joy of embodying the difference between sin and grace.

I slowed down to turn the sermon back toward its beginning, to my presenting question. I said when it comes to family violence, death still exercises dominion. The Church is changing, but only slowly, and women and children are dying while we pretend it has nothing to do with us. I said the United Methodist Church has in its *Book of Resolutions* a list of fourteen ways to address violence, and one of the steps is for seminaries to offer a mandatory class on family violence. I suggested my listeners stop the dean in the hall and ask him where our mandatory class was, because when the world looks at the Church, it sees no grace in this area.

We must face the sin. We must name the sin. In doing so, we are also naming the reality that we are a people in whom the superabundant grace of Jesus Christ lives and reigns. Claim the grace. Amen.

In the discussion afterward I could feel my colleagues' excitement, their engagement. Later, I preached the sermon again in front of a video camera. I was competing for the school's annual preaching award. Seven friends came to listen. I felt on fire and knew for the first time that if adrenaline is my drug of choice, preaching is my ultimate fix.

I read an article once about the painter Willem de Kooning. In discussing one of his paintings, he said, "It is a picture about absorption, and absorption is the last happiness." The absorption of preaching was the last happiness for me because it demanded every aspect of my being: mind and heart and soul.

That spring, though, Devin and Elizabeth were proving to me that absorption is the first happiness, too. Whatever they did—laughing at Grandpa, picking up a Cheerio with pincer-finger and thumb, trying to mobilize their bodies, crying in hunger—they did entirely. Elizabeth by then was turning over, and the week before Easter Devin got up on his elbows and knees and crawled.

The children were at my house that Sunday afternoon. When Elizabeth was born, Tara was firm that the baby was to have no nicknames. And what did she call the baby? Elizabeth, Lizzy, Liza, Bet, Lizbet, Silly

Little Thing, Sweet Baby, Mama's Girl. She's filled with so much love that one name isn't enough. It's like the God-thing.

Devin's two front teeth were ready to pop through. One point on his gums showed a tiny edge of white, and another point looked bruised. Within the last week he'd fallen out of his walker and off his parents' bed, and he'd raked the roof of his mouth with his spoon hard enough to draw blood. He was taking life in stride; Jennifer was beside herself with the idea that he was getting bigger, and that meant he would tumble, would bleed. While Jennifer played with the babies, Tara watched me dissect an ivory silk bridesmaid's gown she'd worn for a friend's wedding. From the silk we constructed a baptismal gown for Elizabeth, and then I brought out my collection of handmade antique lace. We chose a piece with deep points, and I tacked the lace onto the dress for a collar.

That was the last quiet time for months. Before I could catch up with myself, Easter was over, I'd won the preaching award, Elizabeth had been baptized, and I was doing a student internship with three different pastors and three different sets of churches. I visited nursing homes and hospitals, studied forms, helped give communion to someone in a hospital bed, performed my first wedding, taught at two vacation bible schools, and preached a four-night revival. That was also the summer Beth Flynn died, and the summer I was exposed to the most deadening aspect of pastoring, which is the interminable meetings required to keep churches operational. I went to dozens of those meetings, and there I watched people be kind to each other and rude to each other in equal measure. All the time I was pondering the question of whether I could stand life as a pastor. One night I was sitting in a folding metal chair at a meeting where the pastor and the committee members launched charges and countercharges at each other over an issue so trivial I've forgotten what it was. I was trying to get them to lower the volume, if not the toxicity, of their vitriol when I thought, *I don't have to do this. I can resign my ordination tonight and not have to contend with any of this church stupidity ever again.*

Maybe I should have done just that, gone home and resigned. It would have saved me a fair amount of suffering. But I'd have missed so much—of grace, of heartbreak, of life. Besides, how could I have known time was in short supply?

chapter ten

———————

AS PART OF A FIELD-EDUCATION ASSIGNMENT, I ONCE LED
an arts group at the local shelter for battered women and their children.
Before the first of the half dozen sessions, I called Nancy Hardesty, the
friend who'd encouraged me to write *To Love Delilah,* to talk through the
art activities.

"I may wear my clergy collar when I do the group," I said.

"That's a good idea."

"I think so, too. I think it'll create a good subterranean tension."
What I hoped to do was to contradict, tacitly, the bad theology that says
God wants women to remain in abusive relationships.

On the other end of the phone, there was a long pause before Nancy
spoke. "Mary Jo? Did you know most people don't try to create tension?"

Although her tone was admiring, her information was disconcerting. "They don't?"

"No."

"Oh. Why not?"

"Because it makes most people uncomfortable."

"But the tension is where the learning happens."

Nancy sighed. "You're right. I just thought you might want to
make things easier on yourself."

"But easy is so boring, isn't it?"

Off I went, and over the next several weeks the women and I made
jewelry and drew mandalas and wrote our name in large oval letters and
colored in the spaces. The subject of God never came up directly, which
was fine with me; my collar was speaking clearly.

▲   ▲   ▲

I got to play God my last semester. The event was a healing service for
people who'd been physically or sexually abused, and I was asked to read

the ritualized Words of Assurance. Easy enough, but every time I rehearsed the few sentences, I wept. I thought it was a bad thing, what with me speaking as the voice of God, but I concluded there is no heresy in depicting God with tears in God's voice. And then I read theologian Howard Thurman's book *For the Inward Journey* and found this passage:

> You must go through some things, crying all the way, perhaps, if you are ever to live with them without crying. This is an important law of living. There are many experiences which we face that are . . . too terrible even to contemplate. And yet we must face them and deal with them directly. We chide ourselves because at first we tend to go to pieces. Go to pieces, then. Weep all the way through the first terrible impact, if need be. This may be the only way that you will ever be able to deal with the problem without emotional up-heaval [which] is necessary if you are ever going to be able to manage it at all.

That night, after the songs and the taped recordings of two survivors, one male, one female; after the litany in which candles were lit in honor of people who died from abuse, people who survived it, people who chose to talk about it, people who chose not to talk about it, and others; after the sixty or seventy people there had approached the altar to light candles of their own (white, pink, burgundy, or purple), after a poem and a haunting solo about the Holy Spirit, I spoke my assigned words: "I the God of Strength heal you who are broken in spirit. I bind up your wounds. I am turning your laments into dancing. You are precious to me; you are honored in my sight, and I love you." The tears in my voice reflected the tears in the eyes of some of the attendees.

If God had been talking, perhaps God would have spoken with a tear-filled voice about loving us in the face of our suffering. Maybe that's even a way of understanding Jesus, as the tears in God's voice made physical.

▲   ▲   ▲

As the weeks of seminary dwindled away, somebody asked if it was scary knowing I'd be finished so soon.

"No," I said. "It's delightful."

One of the delights was that, because I'd won the preaching award,

I was invited to preach in York Chapel, the divinity school chapel. My sermon was geared toward first-year students, but for me personally it was a valedictory address, a warning and promise to myself about what lay ahead, a benediction. The passage I chose, from the book of James, had to do with "works righteousness," the mistaken notion that people can earn their way into heaven. I said,

God has called us together in this place, and those of you who are new have begun to notice you aren't in Kansas anymore. You've begun participating in the rituals of the school, rituals of worship, rituals of the classroom, rituals of registration and of the search for a parking space. If you're feeling nervous about them, relax. You'll figure them out. You're capable, or you wouldn't be here. And the same God who called you here will sustain you here.

The rituals are relatively easy. What's tough is remaining unstained by the world. What's tough is remembering that our priority has nothing to do with succeeding at Duke. Because we profess Jesus Christ as our Lord and Savior, our priority is being servants. Our priority is loving God and loving our neighbors as ourselves. I thought that would be a breeze here. I thought I was entering the Holy of Holies, a community of saints. What I found here instead were human beings. Go figure.

Think again of the reading from James. The communities James wrote his letter to thought themselves virtuous, faithful Christians. Some scholars think the communities were overeducated on one aspect of faith, the dangers of works righteousness. They knew their actions couldn't earn God's grace, that grace is a gift freely given. The people heard the word, took the sacraments, and praised God. They received the gift of free grace; said, "What a pretty bow!"; unwrapped the package; said thank you; and then sat quietly, holding the present on their laps. Hearing did not prompt them to action; it merely prompted them to more listening. As a result they were double-minded. Double-minded people are those who profess a complete commitment to Christ but live by the world's standards rather than by God's standards. In rejecting works righteousness, they went overboard, rejecting action of any kind.

What does that have to do with us? We're in danger of being double-minded, too. Duke University is a fine academic institution, but we risk forgetting that following Jesus has nothing to do with power or privilege. Jesus did not say, "Follow me and the world will be impressed." The academy did not applaud Jesus. On the cross he wore no academic hood.

A second temptation here is that you will come to believe that knowing about God is the same as knowing God. We suffer from righteousness of the left brain here. You know about the left brain. It controls the processes of language, of sequencing and systematizing, or analysis. You'll need to use all those functions here. That's good. The Church needs your brain. But the very process of learning puts you at risk of forgetting God. Both the effort to learn and the passion we feel about what we learn are so intense that sometimes we get hateful. Church history teaches us that Christians have regularly slaughtered each other in Jesus' name. We aren't that bad here. We just fly into rages or get sullen. And the rest of the community walks on tiptoe, afraid if they do more than utter the Apostles' Creed, they'll get caught in the crossfire. Our convictions become a shroud, and we are dead to the people around us.

How are we to resist the temptations of the world, of our own striving for education? James says if we don't act, we won't be able to retain what we hear and learn. It's like looking at our faces in the mirror. Carl Sandburg wrote about love in a poem called "Honey and Salt." The poem speaks about what happens when we love somebody deeply, over time, about the impact of the dailiness of living together. Poets care about verbs, and one of the verbs Sandburg used in the poem is "winding." He says that over time, with dailiness, "the winding of it gets into your walk, your hands, your face and eyes."

For us to live together faithfully, holiness—the love of God and the love of our neighbor—must wind into our lives. And the way for that to happen is for us to act.

Act. Seek what God is calling you do to, and take time away from studying to do it. Care for widows and orphans. Write a poem, or a song, or a book. Chop onions in a soup kitchen. Visit someone in prison. Watercolor. Read about the struggles of gays and lesbians in the Church. Protest a state execution. Sit down and talk to someone who doesn't look like you. Better yet, don't talk: listen. Sculpt an eagle.

As you do, slowly, over time, God's righteousness will wind into your walk, your hands, your face and eyes. And when you leave here, you will go out as a servant of Christ.

Amen.

▲   ▲   ▲

I was as ready as I was going to be. I turned in the last of my term papers and packed my car. All the way home I listened to "Lida Rose" from *The Music Man*. When I burst into the kitchen, I discovered Fred frosting a celebratory chocolate cake, and I serenaded him with "I'm home again, Rose, to put the sun back in your smile."

It was December 1994. I had six months until Moving Day, the day I would begin my first pastorate. Time enough to relax, regenerate, and catch up with myself and with Fred. I sent a rousing thank-you to God that I never, ever had to drive to Durham again.

▲   ▲   ▲

Three weeks later I was back in Durham. In my excitement, I'd forgotten that Clinical Pastoral Education is required for ordination as an elder in South Carolina. Clinical Pastoral Education is group therapy with a vengeance for people who are working as pastors or chaplains or in service agencies. Although some clergy believe God will fix all their problems, my denomination recognizes that therapy is as beneficial to clergy as to lay people.

Under the leadership of poor or average directors, the weekly meetings are brutal. Group dynamics are adversarial, and the students rip each other to shreds. Under the leadership of a good director, the students rip themselves to shreds, and the director offers a spool of thread, a sharp needle, and a sanctuary in which to mend. Perry Miller, the director I worked with, was a good one. A large man with shaggy white hair that usually looks like he meant to get a haircut two weeks ago, Perry is a master of eye contact, knowing when to focus in on you and when to look out the window or toward the floor to give you space. Perry's goal for me was to get in touch with the suffering in my life.

I thought him silly. "Compared to what some other people endure, my life's been a day at the beach with free hot dogs and a cute lifeguard. Suffering comes with life."

While that's true, Perry was right that there's more to be said. I once took an art class where the instructor told the students about her first charcoal class in art school. "The professor never came to class. All he did was open the door once or twice each session, stick his head in, shout 'Go darker,' and go on his way." In Clinical Pastoral Education I learned how to go darker within myself and how to sit gently with other people in their darkness. I gave my theological questions a name, "road-kill theology," and by the end of the unit, I had new questions: How do we claim suffering without allowing suffering to own us? How do we live fully, creatively, and hopefully inside lives touched by, shaped by, pain, agony, betrayal? And how do we do so without sounding pious and naive?

▲   ▲   ▲

It was late April when my district superintendent phoned to tell me what my appointment was. I was to pastor one of the three churches at which I'd interned the previous summer, the one where Beth Flynn had died of the aneurysm.

"The congregation is very proud of their parsonage. If you have a problem with living there, we'll place you somewhere else," he cautioned me.

"That's not a problem," I assured him. If the rules meant Fred and I had to move out of our spacious, airy house, so be it.

My district superintendent spoke honestly about the health of the congregation. He said, "The church is trying to decide if they want to live or die. They tell me they want to live. I'm sending you there to see if they mean it."

I was delighted. I already knew these people, and *of course* they meant it.

▲   ▲   ▲

Moving Day was the second Wednesday in June. I thought I'd devote the next few weeks to packing, but instead I went to see my grandmother, who'd recently had three strokes.

Aunt Mary picked me up at the airport in Manchester, England. She took me to her house in Blackwell-in-the-Peak, a few miles and twisted curves from Daddy's hometown of Tideswell, where she fed me tea and biscuits and sent me to bed for a nap.

The next morning, Mary cautioned me about Grandma. "The strokes didn't cause much damage, but she won't recognize you. She doesn't recognize anyone. She's very sweet, though, to everyone who visits, except me. She's vile to me. She calls me names and hisses."

Grandma, who was wedged into a plastic-covered armchair near a high window when we arrived, looked very much herself, although a bit more frail. She didn't recognize me, exactly, or maybe she did. Mary had given her a chocolate bar and asked, when Grandma had unwrapped it and begun to eat, "Mother, will you share some of your chocolate with Mary Jo?"

Grandma turned to me, scowled, and sniffed. "I'd rather shove it up me arse than give any to her."

I laughed, which must have been the wrong thing to do. She patted the arm of her chair and smiled malevolently. "Put your hand here," she instructed me.

"I beg your pardon?"

"Put your hand here, right here."

"Why, Grandma?"

In an imperious, why-am-I-surrounded-by-fools tone: "So I can scratch you."

I laughed. "No, you can't scratch me, Grandma."

Mary and I were in the elevator before I could ask how my upright grandmother had learned such words.

"Her early life was harsh. When she grew up, she left the roughness behind, but it stayed in memory."

Then my eyes began to water. "Mary, she recognized me. If she's only hateful toward you, and now toward me, then it means she recognizes something in us that she doesn't in other people. Somewhere in her confusion there's a spark of connection. She can't recognize the difference between love and hate, but something in her is still responding. She knew me."

Mary nodded. "Yes. Yes, she did."

Is that kind of thinking a vice or a virtue? Which is it when you look into someone's face and see not who they are in a moment of bluster and threats and mean-spiritedness but who they are really, truly, who they have been over time, who they would or could be again if the pain, illness, and fear disappeared? Is it blindness to reality or a greater vision of reality? Or can it be both?

Late that afternoon Aunt Mary spread thin slices of bread with butter, draped them with tomato slices, and poured tea into a thermos bottle. We followed a footpath through a neighboring farm, and Mary pointed out a glen once inhabited by badgers, "great, hulking beasts," she said. We passed through sheep enclosures on our way to the river

Wye, where we picked watercress for sandwiches. On the way home we sat on an outcropping of rock to have our picnic.

In a photograph from that day, I'm stepping up onto a turnstile, the low area in a drystone wall that allows the farmer and afternoon strollers, but not sheep, access from one enclosure to another. I'm dressed in blue jeans and a dark fleece overshirt, a white turtleneck peeking out from underneath. Smiling slightly at the camera, I look determined, and vibrantly alive. The metaphoric load may be too much for a photograph to carry, but it matches my excitement as I stepped into my new role as shepherd of a congregation.

chapter eleven

IT'S NOT LIKE I EXPECTED IT TO BE EASY. THE DROPOUT rates don't allow such a supposition. Ten years after ordination, according to a survey conducted by United Methodist pastor Rolf Memming, 40 percent of ordained men and more than 50 percent of ordained women are no long serving full-time appointments as pastors. The statistics, though, failed to alert me to just how grueling the job is in the best of circumstances—and the church to which I was appointed was not the best of circumstances.

Congregations go through stages in life. At birth they're vigorous, filled with energy, and resilient. In adolescence they tend to struggle with the question of who they are and with whom they want to be identified. As they age and mature, they sometimes get tired; they sometimes get sick; and sometimes they die. The church to which I was appointed was mature, organized in 1948. Recently, however, the major nearby employer had shut down. The neighborhood, stable for decades, was in flux; its sense of unity had dissipated. Both the community and the congregation were grieving over the changes.

Transition combined with deep grief has killed off more than one congregation. No wonder mine was struggling, as the district superintendent had told me, with the tension between life and death.

A more experienced pastor might have allowed the church to work out its own decision. Not me, boy. Let the church perish when there might be something I could do to keep it alive? Not bloody likely.

The thing is, your first church is like your first baby: It's the most adorable thing you've ever seen. You want to dress it in cute clothes and take pictures to send to all your friends. You worry whether it's getting enough to eat. You peek into its crib at night and stand very still until you can see its chest moving and know it's still breathing. Some moments you love it so much you can hardly breathe yourself.

I was breathless the first Sunday I emerged from the church office with a four-page sermon manuscript—thirty-five hours worth of researching and writing—clutched in my hand. I was headed for the bathroom to apply a fresh coat of lipstick when I heard a familiar song emanating from behind the closed door of the choir room.

I walked down the hall, opened the choir-room door, and asked the director, "You're not going to sing that hymn, are you?"

That hymn was "Here I Am, Lord," written by Daniel L. Schutte in 1981. The hymn, which has a quietly lilting rhythm, is based on a story in the Bible in which God asked, "Whom shall I send, and who will go for us?" and in reply a man named Isaiah said, "Here am I; send me." It was a signature hymn for me, guaranteed to make me laugh and cry. I expect I was pale when the choir director turned toward me. She hesitated before she confessed. Fred had called her the week before to ask if, as a gift on my first Sunday, the choir would surprise me by singing "Here I Am, Lord." They'd learned it just for me. They sang it as the anthem, and I sat listening, lost in wonder that I was here, in clerical garb. *All right, God. This is it. I'm where you want me to be.* And then I stood up to preach.

A wiser person might have chosen a different text. The third chapter of Galatians is a classic text for defining the United Methodist Church's stand against discrimination, whether the object is minorities, the handicapped, homosexuals, the poor—or women. When I'd noticed it was one of the week's lectionary readings, I'd insisted to Fred, "There's no way I'm taking on that subject this Sunday."

What possessed me to change my mind? Two major issues: first, avoiding the topic of my gender would have felt like a failure of nerve; and second—and this factor gained increasing importance as the months unfolded—I resolved that when there's an elephant in the sanctuary, integrity demanded I acknowledge its existence. And then there was the minor issue of the sheer challenge of it all, the search for a way to talk about the issue of my gender without sending the congregation to their telephones to insist that the district superintendent get that feminist bitch out of their pulpit.

I read the passage, which says, in part, "You are all children of God through faith. . . . There is no longer Jew or Greek, there is no longer slave or free, there is no longer male and female; for all of you are one in Christ Jesus." I talked a bit about Fred and me and the five children, and

a bit about the new things going on in the church—a wedding I'd performed the day before, the new dishwasher and storage shed at the parsonage, the new grocery store Fred and I were using. I said, *You're
adjusting, too. You have a new pastor. And, then, your pastor is a woman, which
is an old story for Methodism, but a brand-new experience for this church.*

I said I was learning a new language, that I'd studied American Sign
Language years earlier but was so rusty as to be incoherent. I asked those
who knew some ASL—more than a dozen people, thanks to the sign-
language classes held after a person who was deaf joined the congregation—
to demonstrate how to sign the letter *J*. Then I held up my hand and
showed them how I couldn't do *J* because I can't raise my little finger
into the air. I said, *I've rediscovered that in sign language I have a lisp. That
could get frustrating for me, because I could be signing, thinking I'm communi-
cating clearly, and then later I might find out I'm not being understood.*

I said Paul had run into communication problems with the church
in Galatia, and I laid out the whole story of the false preachers who'd
come after him. I detoured from a description of Paul's anger, and its
basis, to mention that I'd resisted preaching on the text so often quoted
in conversations about the ordination of women. *I was concerned that if I
preached on this text you might think I'm trying to justify my presence in this
pulpit. I have nothing to justify. It is not my choice to be here. I'm here by the
grace of God.*

"Amen!"

Startled, I looked to my right. There I saw, in the third row back,
an elderly woman with snowy white hair. Her hands were in the air and
a grin was on her face.

"Amen!" she repeated, staring straight into my eyes.

I grinned back at her. I'd learn later that her name was Mrs. Beasley,
and that she didn't waste "amen's" on just any old thing a preacher might
utter. She reserved them for the few times that she heard something important.

A retired Methodist minister, visiting with a member of the congregation, introduced himself to me after the service. "Good sermon," he
said. "You said the one thing that needs to be said: God loves you. The
trouble is going to be figuring out a way to say the same thing every
Sunday."

I nodded, smiled, and turned to the next person in line. The man
meant well, but I wasn't sure his take on the matter was broad enough.

Some people know entirely too well that God loves them; they need to be told that God loves the rest of us, too.

The summer of 1995 is a blur of sermon preparation, of visiting shut-ins and people in the hospital, of making phone calls to get committees together for meetings, of searching the rolls to identify members and searching the _Book of Discipline_ to learn what to do with them, and of heat. The church's central air-conditioning was turned on only long enough to cool the building for Sunday's activities and for choir practice on Wednesday nights. The church office, as a result, was a sweltering habitation throughout the week. I'd unlock the door, hit the button on the window air-conditioning unit, sweat for an hour or so, and, usually just as the temperature in the room dropped into the nineties, turn off the unit as I left the building. I tried leaving it running when I knew I'd be returning shortly, but most often on return I'd find it turned off. Everybody in the world seemed to have a key to the church, and most of those people also knew the location of the hook on which the spare key to my office hung.

More than once I was told the church couldn't afford to cool the place off when nobody was there. I decided I could live with a little sweat.

Everything was new, critical, exciting, and frightening. The most difficult part was sermon preparation. I'd say "amen" at the end of the Sunday service, and by the time I blinked twice, the church secretary was demanding the title of the next sermon. I felt as if a freight train were constantly bearing down on me.

I tried different things all summer, searching for my stride, testing both myself and the congregation, growing accustomed to their breathing patterns. I finally hit my stride in August. The lectionary reading was from Luke, chapter 12. Jesus, in telling his followers not to worry about the future, says, "Be dressed for action and have your lamps lit; be like those who are waiting for their master to return from the wedding banquet. . . . You also must be ready, for the Son of Man is coming at an unexpected hour."

The passage was germane to all sorts of conversations in the South, where cars wear bumper stickers proclaiming, "In case of the Rapture this car will be unmanned." The statement emerges from a fundamentalist theology that developed in America early in the twentieth century. Some Christian leaders blamed Charles Darwin and evolutionary theory for what they thought to be the moral degeneration of society. They espoused the conviction that the Bible is literally the word of God and, therefore, every text from the creation story in Genesis through the apocalyptic visions of Revelation must be taken literally. Heaven and hell are real, physical locations. Jesus is going to make a return trip to earth and, while here, separate who belongs where. On that day of the Second Coming, true believers will be whisked to heaven, and the rest of us will be left behind wailing and flailing in torment. Some people believe these events are going to happen very soon: next week, maybe, or the day after tomorrow.

I don't see how you can believe such things if you take the Bible literally. The Luke passage I was getting ready to preach on is a case in point. In it, Jesus himself said he didn't know when he was coming back. Now I ask you: if Jesus didn't know, what are the chances anybody else does?

The theological concept is important, and I needed to make the point, but not at the cost of a holy war. How could I avoid a head-on collision with the congregation's extant theologies?

I started by explaining the historical context for Luke's gospel, a time decades after Jesus' death when Christians were struggling. Their leader had died as a common criminal, and it wasn't safe to admit you were a disciple of such a man. Also, Jesus was supposed to be on his way back. At first his followers looked for his return on a daily basis, but after fifty years they were a little less certain of the time frame. Most of the people who'd known him personally were dead, and he still hadn't come back. Luke knew people were fearful because of the time lag; that's why he chose to include this parable.

I told the congregation,

This parable is about slaves and masters. My imagination isn't big enough to grasp what it would be like to be either one. I can't imagine being owned by anyone else. I can't imagine being careful at the tasks set for me because if I'm not I may be beaten. I can't imagine being seen not as a person but as a possession, a possession with no voice, no life, no freedom of my own.

They couldn't see me taking off my shoes behind the pulpit, although they might have noticed that I'd suddenly lost two inches in height.

But I can't imagine being a master, either.

I clasped the zipper of my preaching robe, pulled it down, and shrugged the robe off my shoulders.

I can't imagine handing money to someone else to purchase a human being. I can't imagine owning someone, or having them jump at my bidding, or having them live in fear of me.

I laid my robe across the pulpit chair and picked up the coated rubber band I'd placed on the pulpit.

I don't understand much about masters and slaves.

With one hand I pulled my hair back.

But I understand this parable.

With the other hand I slipped the band into my hair, creating an awkward ponytail with renegade strands of hair intentionally left poking up and out.

Because it's about watchfulness and about faithfulness and about waiting. It's about hope and trust. It's about a revolution, a time when poverty and powerlessness and all the social boundaries we know no longer exist.

I stepped down from the pulpit area and stood in front of the first pew, allowing everyone a moment to see the black jeans and T-shirt I was wearing and to make the connection that I was taking the role of a slave.

The story goes something like this, *I said.*
You're not going to believe what happened to me. I wouldn't believe it if I hadn't been here myself. You know my master went to a wedding banquet last night, that big wedding that people came for from miles around. And we were left here waiting for him to come back. Oh, my, it was a long night. We were up for hours and hours. We prepared the food, because we knew he'd be hungry again by the time he got home. We

made sure there was enough oil in the lamps so that we could light them whenever he arrived. We made sure everything was in order for his return.

And he still wasn't back. And then we waited for him. We thought he might come at ten o'clock, but he didn't. We thought he might come at midnight, but he didn't. He didn't come until way on in the night, till almost dawn.

It was a long night, but it was a good night. We talked among our-selves. We told stories from back when we were young, and we told stories about what it might be like when we're old. We sang songs together, songs we'd learned when we were children, songs our parents had learned when they were children, songs I'll bet even Moses learned as a child. Some of them, the words had gotten away from us, so we kind of hummed in the middle.

We had a really good time together, singing and listening to each other's stories and talking about festivals we'd been to or might go to some-day. All the time we were talking, though, a part of our attention was some-where else. We were glancing outside to see if a light was coming our way down the road, or listening to see if we heard a rustling at the door, or a knocking.

You know how Mark is, he's got that little bit of a lazy streak. Some-time way in the night, Mark tried to convince us it was stupid to wait up any longer. Mark said, "Well, maybe he's not coming back tonight after all. Maybe he's decided to stay where he is, at the wedding banquet, and sleep there. It's so late. Maybe he's not going to come at all tonight. Let's blow out the lamps and go on to bed. It won't matter that we're not up waiting for him, because he's not coming."

I gave him one good look, and he shut up. Why, we never even thought about going to bed. He said he'd be back, and we knew we could trust him, and we wanted to be ready when he got here. It didn't matter to us what time that might be. We knew that he WAS coming, and that was enough. Enough that we'd be sure we got the work done that needed to be done.

So we waited. Oh, it was late when he got here. Really late. It got to be the third watch, heading for dawn. And then, long into the night, one of us glanced out the window and said, "Look! I see something. Way off down yonder. I see something."

We all hurried to look. At first it was just a shape, and the night was so dark . . . we weren't sure if we were really seeing something or if the dark was playing tricks on us. But slowly it took form. And it was our master! He was coming!

When he knocked, we were right there, ready to pull the door open for him.

Then the strangest thing happened.

Our master came in, and he looked around at us all and got this look on his face, like he hadn't known for sure if we'd be waiting up, ready for him to return. And it was like it meant everything to him that we were.

He said, "Sit down!" so we did. You know how he is; he's the master; we do what we're told. So even though we had things we needed to be doing—we needed to set out the food for him to eat; we had chores to do for him—when he said, "Sit down," we sat down.

We didn't know what was coming next. We looked around the table at each other, and then we looked over where he was to see what he was doing. Our master, our *master,* had put the food on a platter. With his own hands, he put the food on the platter. And as we, the servants, sat, he came over to us, with that platter in his hands.

He served Rebecca. He served Timothy. He served Anna. He served Mark. And then he served me.

And then he got the drink, our master. He served Rebecca. He served Timothy. He served Anna. He served Mark. And then he served me.

I never would have dreamed it could happen. If I hadn't been there, I wouldn't believe it now. But our master served us. Our master, in whose presence we stand. Our master, whom we are duty-bound to obey. Our master, whose voice we hear with fear and trembling. Our master . . . became our servant.

And then our master—and I think he did this because he was so happy to find us ready, and waiting, when he came back—our master told us that we, *we,* are blessed. Imagine that. Me. You. All of us. Blessed.

I was exhausted when I finished, but it was worth it. The congregation had been mesmerized. That sermon was a watershed. From then on, I knew I had determination enough and skill enough to develop even the most sensitive passages into an effective sermon. Equally important, I had learned that the congregation could flow—willingly—into unexpected developments from the pulpit.

Preparation for worship—researching and writing sermons, laying out the order of worship, choosing hymns, studying books on liturgy—

took thirty hours, sometimes more, each week. Before the first Sunday I officiated at Holy Communion, Fred and I spent a morning in the sanctuary with me reading the service and practicing my movements while he watched and commented from the back pew. Before my first baptism (baptisms, actually, of my grandsons, Bradley and Devin) I spent more hours in the sanctuary, ascertaining that I could pour the water into the baptismal bowl without drenching myself and the altar. Even with all the practice, baptizing the boys almost undid me. By then Devin was walking. He and Bradley, dressed in matching khaki pants and striped shirts, came up to the altar with their parents. I was steady until I'd filled the bowl with water. I stood staring into the water, immersed in the moment. Through the water I would soon cup in my hands, my grandsons were going to become part of the body of Christ. This was what ordination meant: that I was the vehicle for this extraordinary moment. I didn't seem able to move.

The lay leader, standing beside me to assist with the baptisms, stirred.

"Are you all right?" he whispered.

I shook my head to clear the tears. "I'm all right."

I turned and beckoned my grandsons, one at a time, to kneel and be baptized in the name of the Father, the Son, and the Holy Spirit.

▲   ▲   ▲

A cardinal rule for pastors is to make no changes the first year at a new appointment. You must go slowly because congregations are resistant to change.

Such rules are fine, but a church on its deathbed doesn't have that luxury. Church leaders repeatedly told me they were exhausted from carrying the administrative weight of service on three or four committees. It simplified life, because they could schedule all the meetings on the same night, but it taxed their time. From my perspective, it vested congregational power in too few hands, so I was as committed as they were to recruiting additional committee members.

A second priority was stabilizing the church's finances. Together, the treasurer and I devised a method for producing an accurate budget and for normalizing the counting of the Sunday offering. When I arrived, the treasurer was doing the job, contrary to a denominational requirement that two people must do the counting, and that neither of them can be the treasurer. The finance committee members didn't care when he'd told them so, and they weren't a bit more impressed when I told them so.

"I trust the treasurer," said one person, mistakenly assuming I was questioning the treasurer's honesty.

"There's no reason for anyone else to know how much people give to the church. People will stop contributing if they think everybody knows their business," said another.

I repeated what I'd already said. "This isn't personal. It has nothing to do with the treasurer. It's about the rules of sound financial practice."

The treasurer spoke up. "She's right. This is the way we have to do things."

The committee members weren't appeased. Why did I insist on fixing something that wasn't broken? And who did I think could do the job instead? Nobody else had time. Besides, they were a small church; those rules were made for churches with more resources.

The sensibility of their arguments didn't permit me to alleviate their anger. "We're going to have to come up with an alternative. We have no choice. The rules are clear: the treasurer cannot touch the money."

My first meeting with the trustees didn't go much better. To begin with, they didn't know why we were meeting at all. As in many small churches, the two trustees handled day-to-day needs of the church's physical plant. When the grass needed mowing, when the toilets needed plunging, or when rain poured down the parsonage chimney, they addressed the problem. They glared when I said the committee also had a planning function and that we'd need to expand the committee and meet more often to be in accord with the *Book of Discipline*.

Everything I did that first year was part of a great personal test. I was soon to present myself for permanent ordination, where I would again be asked John Wesley's historic questions, including *Have you studied our form of Church discipline and polity?; Do you approve our Church government and polity?; Will you support and maintain them?*

Before I answered yes, I was going to test everything and try everything so that I could gauge whether I was able to do the job right.

At first it was all a challenge, and invigorating, and fun, and then it wasn't. Pastors aren't pressed out of cookie cutters any more than congregations are. We are different people with different theologies, different personalities, different goals, which means in every church a third of the congregation doesn't like what the pastor's doing. I can't date the end of my innocence, but I know I was still happy when I celebrated my forty-sixth birthday in September, and I know by the time I got to Charge Conference a month later, my relationship with the church leaders had deteriorated and I was miserable.

My definitive sin, I think, was in telling the administrative board that one of my goals was the purchase of new hymnals for the church. The congregation sang out of the 1964 edition of the denominational hymnal. A new edition, published in 1989, contained some more recent, dynamic hymns, including "Here I Am, Lord," a wide selection of congregational prayers, a more contemporary translation of the psalms for use in responsive readings, and options for communion services in less archaic language. Three members of the core leadership had told me in private that they wanted the new hymnals. I thought I was on solid ground, especially since one of the church's goals was a more vibrant worship service.

You'd have thought from the cold waves of anger rolling toward me that I'd suggested we skin, chop, and deep-fry their cats to serve up at the next church dinner. The feedback was harsh: we had more important things to spend money on; the old ones were just fine; the congregation didn't need more participatory liturgies; who cared about a Methodist hymnal when they weren't especially Methodist in the first place? People weren't just resistant; they were heels-dug-in, no-way-in-hell resistant.

The depth of anger I encountered suggests that the issue was not the hymnal so much as the speed of change.

The group responsible for padding relationships between a pastor and a congregation is called The Pastor-Parish Relations Committee, but there wasn't much padding. When we met in September, their feedback was tepid. I was doing a good job, so far. On my performance evaluation, they rated me "average" in a number of areas, including my knowledge of scripture and religious writing.

It was the moment of my first fury with them. I had studied scripture, church history, theology, and devotional writings for years. I had published both poetry and fiction about people in the Bible, not to mention an entire book. I had not only attended a highly respected divinity school but had graduated with honors. And these people thought I was average?

"Compared to whom?" I might have asked. Previous pastors with twenty years of experience and file cabinets full of exegetical notes and sermons from which to draw? Other preachers whose sermons were interlocking chains of scripture quotations? Televangelists?

The moment passed. The evaluation form had fifteen more points for them to comment on, and it was hot, and I wasn't going to argue over my capabilities.

Relationships declined even further a few weeks later when I rearranged the church office to make it more welcoming. I shoved my heavy oak desk, the lighter metal secretary's desk, and the towering photocopy machine from place to place, searching out angles that opened up the most floor space. Then I substituted new fabric I'd bought, light turquoise cotton printed with clouds and hot-air balloons in primary colors, for the textured beige-and-brown at the windows.

One volunteer church secretary didn't take kindly to my efforts. Whether it was me or my decorating skills she detested I can't say, but the next day she resigned, and when she left she took with her all of the paper clips, pens, staples, and notepads in the church office. The items belonged to her—she'd purchased them with her own money—but the pettiness made me crazy. To top things off, several members of the personnel committee, annoyed that I'd upset the secretary, stopped speaking to me.

All of this would have been bad enough if nobody around me had been dying, but people were. One of the people was Fred's mother, Ethel. The other was a twenty-year-old man named Greg who started attending the day after his wife moved to Idaho, leaving him alone with his two-month-old daughter Phoebe. He and the baby were in church every week for months, and then they weren't. When I investigated, I learned he'd collapsed during his shift at a local bakery. The diagnosis was a brain tumor. The prognosis was death. Both Greg's parents were dead. His siblings fled the hospital when they heard the diagnosis, but the next day they returned with plans in hand. Greg and a hospital bed would move into one brother's house. The baby would move into a sister's house. The other siblings would be backup caregivers and also be in charge of driving the baby the thirty miles every day so that, for as long as he was able, Greg could hold her, feed her, sing to her.

I saw a lot of Greg in the three months before he died. We chatted for hours about cowboy boots and motorcycles (about which I knew nothing but had great curiosity). Sometimes we'd confer about the great beyond. I told him I expected that in heaven he'd be riding a Harley-Davidson cycle with the wind blowing against his face; told him, too, to plan on giving me a ride when I arrived.

As the illness progressed and the dosage of painkillers increased, Greg spent a lot of time watching the angels who sat on the windowsills in his bedroom.

"They scare me," he said.

"There's nobody there," I responded firmly.

"Isn't there? Oh. Good."

One day I mentioned that Fred's mother had Alzheimer's and was dying.

Greg surprised me by saying, "Tell Fred that if he or his mother ever needs anything, I'll be there waiting for them."

"What?" Surely I'd heard wrong. How did Fred's name fit into that statement?

"Tell Fred if he or his mother ever needs anything, I'll be there waiting."

I gave Fred the message when I got home.

"Me? He said if *I* ever need anything?"

"Yes."

"I wonder where that came from. I can't imagine needing anything."

▲   ▲   ▲

Charge Conference was on October 24 that year. At such meetings, chaired by the district superintendent, every major committee files a written report; the pastor gives an account of the state of the church and of his or her pastoral ministry, and the church budget for the next year is approved. I was content with my accomplishments in four months. We had two people counting money each Sunday, neither of whom was the treasurer; we had weekly meetings of the youth group; we had 180 members on the church roll and a budget of $65,197 for the upcoming year. I thought I'd made a good start.

The next week I learned that a conservative couple was refusing to return to church until "that woman" was gone from the pulpit. I dropped in to visit Mrs. Beasley, the woman who *amen*ed me my first Sunday in the pulpit, and she told me that every week since the news of my appointment was announced—nearly five months' worth of Sundays—her Sunday-school class had endured a lecture on how everyone in the church was going to hell because a woman was pastoring.

"Don't worry about them. I was tired of listening to them anyhow," said Mrs. Beasley.

Easier said than done. My gender was both a given and an issue. I am a woman, and it's not my fault God called me into the ministry. When I entered the sanctuary on Sunday mornings with my shoulder-length hair, with my breasts no preaching robe could hide, and with a shade of lipstick dark enough that people who were hard of hearing could read my lips, I looked like no other preacher who'd preceded me. Because of my embodiment, the ritualistic words and statements of faith I offered were received differently.

Back in the eighteenth century, John Wesley had authorized women to expound from the pulpit, to handle finances, and to evaluate the gifts of male preachers. The man had no interest in political correctness; his interest was God. If God chose to call and empower women, then Wesley was going to do everything possible to equip women to do the job. The United Methodist Church is committed to women's ministry; people with theological objections need to find a denomination that shares their prejudice.

In November I paid a pastoral call on a couple who'd visited the church several times. I'd written them my usual note after their first visit, and I'd phoned once or twice to say hello. After their third visit I went to see them. She belonged to a Lutheran church. Her husband, a Baptist, hadn't been to church since the late 1940s.

"How'd the two of you get to our church?" I asked.

It seems he took long walks through the neighborhood every day. One Saturday he came home from a walk and said, "We ought to go visit that white church tomorrow morning." (He was referring to the color of the siding, not to the congregation's ethnicity.)

"All right," his wife replied.

Counting back on the day they joined the church, I noticed that their first visit had coincided with the departure of the couple who hated having a woman in the pulpit. You might call it coincidence. If you're like me, you call it the Holy Spirit.

One preparatory member of the congregation kept the gender

issues in perspective. A first-grader wandered into my office after the bell rang at the end of the Sunday-school hour. She planted herself directly in front of me so that she could see straight up into my eyes, and she announced, "Our last preacher was a man."

I looked down at her and thought things over.

"Was he?" I replied.

"Yes."

Neither she nor I knew what else to say, so we looked at each other in a friendly fashion for a little while longer, and then she went on her way.

The conversation became a ritual between us, occurring at odd intervals over my first two years at the church. She'd appear in front of me and state once more, "Our last preacher was a man." If it took that long for a child to sort through the questions—none of which she could articulate—raised by my gender, surely it must take longer for adults, even adults who welcome women's ministry.

▲   ▲   ▲

Some days it seemed people gave me hell for the sheer pleasure of it. The size of a piece of communion bread and the history of a hymn aren't enough to excoriate a person over, are they?

Methodists have four liturgies for Holy Communion, six if you count the two in the old hymnal. Over time I wanted to use each of the liturgies and to offer communion in its traditional guise, with the bread and juice offered separately, and also by intinction, where the communicants dip bread into a single, shared chalice. The congregation was accustomed to receiving minuscule slivers of bread cut from slices of a loaf of white bread. It looked puny and suggested communion was a pill to swallow rather than a meal. Prior to my second communion service, I asked someone to bake a loaf of bread, and I offered from it serious chunks, the kind with crumbs, and right behind me the lay leader offered the common cup for dipping the bread.

Heads rolled at the next worship-committee meeting.

Let me rephrase that. One head rolled. It was mine.

One committee member said people were opposed to the common cup to the point where they would accept the bread but wouldn't dip. How dare I interfere with someone's ability to take communion? Other people were disgusted that I'd broken the communion loaf with my bare hands. The sanest committee member, who was trying to find a middle ground, suggested I wear latex gloves like the ones used in doctors' offices.

"I can't do that," I said flatly.

That's when somebody raised the issue of "The Battle Hymn of the Republic."

"I'm just warning you for your own good. Some people don't like that hymn. In fact, we used to have a member who stood up and walked out if it was played."

Not sing "The Battle Hymn of the Republic"? When had we sung it in the first place? And why would anybody not like it? And what was the appropriate response from me, as the spiritual leader of the congregation, to the complaint? If people thought they had authority over the choice of hymns, would they next decide they wanted authority over my preaching?

I learned later that "The Battle Hymn of the Republic" is anathema to some southerners; they think it a Yankee hymn because it originated in the Civil War. The tones, though, indicated that neither intinction nor "The Battle Hymn of the Republic" was the real issue.

Eventually I staggered home.

"I'm not believing everything I've done that's made people mad," I told Fred.

"You were at a worship-committee meeting. What could they have to complain about at a worship-committee meeting? You're the best worship leader I've ever seen."

Fred's deep experience in management didn't extrapolate to church mechanics. His interpretation of events was also clouded by his conviction that the denomination should have made me a bishop the day I finished seminary. More to the point, his professional life was spent in the corporate world, where the paramount question is "Is this person doing the job?"

I was doing my job. The worship service had vitality; my sermons were bang-on exegetically and spiritually; I was officiating at the sacraments; attendance at worship was up; the youth group was meeting every Sunday night; the bills were being paid; I was scouting for leadership for the men's group; I was visiting people at an unprecedented rate;

and more and more people were agreeing to take on leadership responsibilities. What, then, was the problem? Why were such trivial issues demanding this level of attention and energy?

I contemplated leaving the ministry. I talked it over with my old friend Eileen, the one who'd kept asking me if I'd noticed I'd been called into the ministry.

"I know, I know," she said when I exploded to her over the bread controversy. "That's just how churches are. You're doing a fine job. Just keep on."

Did I really need to contend with all this? Would it matter a hundred years from now that I once stood in a pulpit?

Fred recognized my frustration, but still he urged me to stay. "I've never seen anyone as alive in my whole life as you are when you stand in that pulpit, and I've never seen a congregation as alive at the end of a worship service. How can you think you don't belong here?"

chapter twelve

I DID MY FIRST TWO FUNERALS WITHIN WEEKS OF EACH other in February 1996. The first was that of an elderly woman. I'd been called to the nursing home as she lay dying. Her breathing was harsh when I arrived, and then harsher. That phase endured for what felt like hours, and then gradually the harsh breaths came farther and farther apart, and she breathed more slowly, and more slowly, and more slowly still. Dying looked to be hard work, but not unpleasant work, more like a tidying up, just a bit of breathing still to do, and another bit, and after a while another bit, and after a longer while another bit, until finally there weren't any more breaths left to take.

The next few days were filled with visits, conversations with family members, plates of food at their tables, and then the funeral. It was Fred's sixty-first birthday, so I worked on my funeral homily to the smell of cake baking and the sound of Fred saying, "Keep it short. Twenty minutes door to door is the most a family can stand."

The question I pondered as I wrote was what happens to love when someone dies. Where does the love go? What are we to do with it? How do we stop the habit of a lifetime? How do we bear the idea of stopping? I stared into space, frosted the cake, wrote the order of worship for the coming Sunday, and waited for answers.

I didn't know where to go, and then three hours before the service I knew. At the funeral I spoke of the dead woman's feistiness, and her love, and of God, and I said, "Many people loved her. The task now in front of you, her family and friends, is not to stop loving her. It's to learn to love her differently."

Fred attended the funeral. Afterward he said, "I never heard any-body say that before, but you're right."

That aspect of ministry is what I love most: facing questions of ulti-mate meaning and contemplating, meditating, weighing, and waiting until language arrives, often a new and simple language I didn't know I knew until the words formed, and then discovering the words are true. It made the pettiness endurable.

▴   ▴   ▴

My second funeral was for Fred's mother. We got the call at eight o'clock on a Friday night. We drove to North Carolina the next morning, made the arrangements, planned the service, and then went to one of Fred's brothers' houses where we sat outside in rocking chairs in the February sun and paged through a hymnal to choose the hymns. People kept coming and going, the way they do, some to drop off a meal, others to sit and talk and remember.

I'd thought we'd stay the night in North Carolina, that I would call a guest preacher to fill in for me, but Fred said, "I need to hear you preach," and so sometime after midnight we drove home, and the next morning I stood in the pulpit, announced Ethel's death right along with the schedule of meetings for the week, and then moved numbly through the service until Fred and I could escape during the singing of the last hymn.

The next morning I dressed in my serious black suit with the double-breasted jacket and the box-pleated skirt to conduct the funeral, along with one of Fred's relatives who was a Baptist minister. At the grave I read from a prayer in our book of worship: *For all that Ethel has given us to make us what we are, for that of her which lives and grows in each of us, and for her life that in your love will never end, we give you thanks.*

We were nearly home when Fred made a wildly uncharacteristic statement. We'd decided to stop at a fast-food restaurant for supper and were pulling into the parking lot when he said, "Nobody better give me any trouble, or I'm going to start throwing chairs."

Trouble? At a fast-food restaurant? What kind of trouble could there be? And throwing chairs? Fred was going to throw chairs? My Fred?

Here's the thing about death: it makes people mad—even people as level as Fred. It goes to show that Dylan Thomas nailed the human condition when he wrote, "Rage, rage, at the dying of the light."

▴   ▴   ▴

No doubt the funeral food brought forth my Transfiguration Sunday sermon. I told the congregation about Jesus taking three of his disciples—

Peter, James, and John—up to the top of a mountain with him, and, while they were there, changing in front of their eyes. His clothes turned sparkling white, and he glowed from within with the power of God, and two prophets of Israel who'd been dead for centuries, Moses and Elijah, appeared.

It must have been amazing, but what did Peter do? He changed the subject. He started jabbering about what he could do for the Jesus, Moses, and Elijah, how he'd build something to honor the three of them. On the one hand, Peter got it. On the other hand, he missed the point completely.

I told the congregation it all reminded me of potato salad. I've been thinking about potato salad since last weekend, at my brother-in-law's house in North Carolina. People brought food in each day, and one of the most successful dishes was potato salad. We had two schools of thought on potato salad. Fred's of the school that says any potato salad is good potato salad. I'm of the school that says there is only one way to make good potato salad. The first day's offering had all the requirements: potatoes and onions and celery and hard-boiled eggs and mayonnaise and a bit of mustard. But it had something else, too: something green, like maybe somebody tossed in a couple of tablespoons of relish. The second day's version was just right: all the proper ingredients, no relish, and just enough yellow to show the hint of mustard that was there.

I told them I'd gone to my file cabinet to find a copy of a poem Jo Carson included in her 1989 book *Stories I Ain't Told Nobody Yet.* In the poem, a mother is giving advice to her daughter, who's getting married. The mother says, "Don't make good potato salad / . . . Just cook up beans; people eat them, too." Later the poem continues, "What my mother might and could have said is:/Choose carefully what you get good at/'cause you'll spend the rest of your life doing it."

The mother was saying sometimes we choose our tasks in life, and sometimes our tasks choose us. Sometimes our talents—the things we're good at, the things we do well—keep us from noticing that something else may be desired for us, something else may be the task to which we're called. Like Peter. Peter stood in the middle of the mystery of God and thought he was supposed to be an architect, or an engineer, building things. Jesus told him to shut up, and then the voice of God came from the clouds: "This is my Son. Listen to him." Even Peter couldn't help but notice that voice. Even Peter stopped what he was doing.

The concern the passage pulls us to see is that we may come face to face with the living God but be too busy making potato salad to notice. Or maybe making banana pudding, or building houses, or studying, or digging ditches, or planting gardens. We do those tasks because we find out we're good at them, and people reward us for doing them. Or maybe it's less-positive tasks we're good at: partying, or wheeling and dealing, or getting our own way. And in either case we get locked in. Before we know it, we're locked into patterns of life that keep us from seeing God, that keep us from sensing the greater tasks for which we're gifted and needed.

The disciples didn't have a clue to what they were doing when they agreed to follow Jesus. He invited them on his journey, and in all their ignorance they joined up. Along the way they learned a few things and saw enough, trusted enough, and believed enough to do what was asked, because the One who was transfigured was the only One who could save them.

I was finally articulating my own essential question: Was this the place, the best place, the necessary place for me? Was this God's intent? Surely, surely the Church—not just this local congregation, but the institutional Church—needed the peculiar gifts of a person who can make the connection between potato salad and salvation? Surely, surely I needed to be in a place where I could make such connections?

▲   ▲   ▲

Of all the things that look different from the far side of the pulpit, the Ash Wednesday service is the most different of all.

I had to plan the service, type the order of worship (the secretarial situation was still a bit touchy), write a short sermon, and prepare the ashes. It took me an hour to find the dead palm leaves from the Palm Sunday service the year before. I took the palm leaves back to the parsonage with me and burned them in the driveway, catching them in a black and brown, rough-edged earthenware bowl from which I'd once eaten rice at a seminary fund-raiser. I added water and Wesson oil to the accumulated ashes in order to create a sloppy, stinking mess. The whiff of smoke carried me back to the filth and ruin of our home after our house fire; smelling the wet ashes re-created the emotions. I grumbled to myself, *Ash Wednesday makes no sense. As though we need to set aside a day to focus on misery. As though we need to look for grief and despair. As though they don't come to us quickly enough as it is.*

That evening, when it came time for the imposition of ashes, I lifted the earthenware bowl from its position on the altar and, holding it aloft, I read a prayer.

Almighty God, you have created us out of the dust of the earth. Grant that these ashes may be to us a sign of our mortality and penitence, so that we may remember that only by your gracious gift are we given everlasting life; through Jesus Christ our Savior. Amen.

Then I invited the congregation, only twenty or so for this special service, to the altar. They came and knelt. As I approached each of them, I plunged my thumb into the bowl of ashes so I could mark a fat cross on each forehead as I said the words, "Remember that you are dust, and to dust you shall return."

When they rose to return to their pews, I turned away, replaced the bowl of ashes on the altar, climbed the steps to the pulpit, checked my order of worship to see what came next in the service, and looked out across the congregation.

I blinked, looked down again at my order of worship, and looked up again, fighting to keep my facial muscles under control. If a muscle twitched, I knew I was going to break out laughing.

All I could see before me were black crosses. I knew there were bodies beneath the crosses, but I couldn't distinguish them. I couldn't distinguish faces, either, not even Fred's. They were a group of anonymous human beings, dear and vulnerable human beings, with fragile bodies and pale faces beneath the strident black marks. I coughed and bowed my head as though I were praying, fighting not to point and laugh, fighting for composure so that my merriment wouldn't offend anyone.

For that one moment, that instant, I could see what God sees. For that speck of time each year, I knew that God doesn't see us as we are, a bunch of irascible, sometimes irrational, often obnoxious individuals. Instead, God sees us in our reality, which is the whole lot of us, heads bowed from the weight of ashes, and we sit behind our cross scarred and dear, vulnerable and beautiful. For that speck, that mote of time, I knew God loves us with that same impossible joy I feel with a newborn baby nestled against my chin. In that fleeting moment, everything false fell away, and I could see who we are in the eyes of God: cherished, adored, loved without limits, a flock of lambs of Christ's own redeeming.

How can you walk away from a sight so precious?

▲   ▲   ▲

Lent bloomed its way into Easter and Easter into Pentecost. The motorcycle-riding father of the two-year-old died, and so did Mary Flowers's mother, Evelyn, my old friend who'd taken me to the church where the woman spoke in tongues. I tried to think my way through Evelyn's death, through all the deaths, but it didn't work. Mary's eight-year-old daughter Jessica seemed to be onto something when she suggested we not bury Evelyn. Her idea was that, instead of burying the body, we keep her at the funeral home in her coffin.

"That way we could go visit her on the way home from school every day."

I thought it was a great idea. I nearly said so, but reality interrupted me too soon.

"We can't really do that, Jessie. Life would interfere. We might go visit every day for the first week or two, but then things would happen, and pretty soon we'd be going only once a week, and then once a month, and then not at all. It wouldn't be fair to leave your grandma where she is."

That's the trouble: Once someone is dead, they stay dead, and the job of the living is to continue to live. And so we buried Evelyn.

▲   ▲   ▲

After Evelyn's funeral I gave up on trying to fix death. Instead I started searching for ways to banish grief. My logic was unassailable: if you don't love people, you're not going to grieve when they die. More than once I swore to Fred I'd never fall in love again, but then something would happen—a baby was born or, odd as it seems, a man I barely knew volunteered to throw up in my pocket—and I'd forget and once again be caught up in affection.

It's just as well, because banishing grief is even more dangerous than it is difficult. Pastors who inure themselves to affection are like squirrels starving to death in January even though the nuts they buried in October are waiting for them. You can recognize pastors who are starving to death by their blank expressions and their slick responses. I got so I could smell these automated salvation dispensers when I shared a hospital elevator or a gravesite with them. They emanated an air of certainty and eagerness to respond to any spiritual need, which, for them, meant reducing people to silence by turning powerful statements of faith to platitudes: "God is good"; "Look to the hills"; "Give your heart to Jesus."

I'm tempted to make fun of ministers who work that way—they're such easy targets—but I know why they are the way they are. Like the squirrels with nuts, those people have buried their feelings, and they refuse to dig them up because they can't bear to see any more suffering or, perhaps, to suffer any more themselves.

▲   ▲   ▲

There were avenues I could have taken around the pain, training that might have thickened my hide. Therapists, I know, are trained to leave other people's problems at the office. I like to pretend it's tidier for them; after all, their clients come to their offices and write checks on the way out. Pastors, on the other hand, engage in messy spiritual transactions. And what, after all, constitutes a pastor's office? We see people in emergency rooms, in hospital beds, in waiting rooms, in their living rooms, in the church office, on the church porch steps, in the grocery store, and in the living room of the parsonage. We meet people's wives and husbands, their mothers and grandparents, their brothers-in-law and cousins, their friends, dogs, hamsters, and goldfish. We see people at midnight, at noon, at dawn. We see them eating, swimming, throwing up, bowling, praying, and ranting. We see them wearing suits and jeans, sweats and softball uniforms and footed pink pajamas decorated with blue and yellow bunnies. We see people live. We see them die. We plan their funerals. We name their lives. We speak their benedictions.

People told me to detach, that I couldn't fall in love because it was too costly. They said people will die, or you'll be appointed to a different church, and there you'll be, starting over, falling in love again, your emotions scraped raw. It's too hard a life.

Those people were right, and yet what does it mean if a person chooses the certain spiritual death of detachment? The Bible tells us to love the Lord our God with all our heart and mind and soul and strength, and to love our neighbor as ourselves. Loving our neighbor suggests, at a bare minimum, some outlay of affection, of respect, of acknowledgment that each of us exists *imago dei,* in the image of God.

It's hard to live a spiritual life if you're closed off from relationships. At least, I couldn't do it. Maybe if I'd been someone else, someone less intense, I might have handled the love aspect of pastoring differently. But I wasn't someone else. I exist in my own form of gawky goofiness, of goofy gawkiness, of celebration and pain. If being a pastor meant I had to kill off aspects of myself, I wasn't going to do it, not even for Christ's sake.

▲   ▲   ▲

All through the spring, I deliberated the question of ordination. Did I want to move from probationary status to permanent status? The meaningful aspects energized me, but the triviality sucked me dry, like the day I left someone gravely ill at the hospital and ran into a church member on my way home.

"There you are! You need to do something about the bulletins. The type is too small."

The type is too small? Why, yes, it is. But if we enlarge the type, we'll need more pages for the bulletin and people will complain about the expense. Besides, I don't even know who's doing the bulletin this week, and I still haven't made it to the office-supply store to buy frigging paper clips.

John Wesley's question regarding candidates for the ministry was, "Have they fruits?" God seemed to want me ordained, because the fruits were in front of me. New members were joining, the committees were focused, the financial picture was improving. Was it enough? Not really. But then one afternoon I listened to Mrs. Beasley demanding that my title "the Reverend" be included with my name in the bulletin because I'd worked hard to earn that honorific, and I knew there were people who understood a bit of what I was enduring, and then one Sunday during communion I looked at the people kneeling at the altar and saw person after person whose hospital beds I'd sat beside or with whom I'd prayed in waiting rooms or their living rooms, and I felt a surge of love so strong I knew I couldn't leave.

I began the paperwork for final orders. I had to provide documentation of my sanity and my physical and financial health. I had to write a Bible study. I had to preach and record a sermon. I had to answer a list of what are called disciplinary questions regarding theology and Methodist polity.

I'd nearly finished my documents when, at the end of August, I had to meet with the congregation's personnel committee. I should have known disaster was at hand when a committee member began passing photocopies around the room and explaining that members of the congregation had been asked what they thought of me, and their answers had been transcribed so that I'd know what they really thought. "Of course everybody agrees you're a great preacher, so I didn't bother putting that on the list. You can see some people have real problems with you."

The evidence was in my hand. Members of the congregation had stated I was insincere, demanding, bossy, operating under the pretense that I was in charge, not working hard enough, not making enough altar calls, lacking interpersonal skills, rude, and obnoxious.

One of the disciplinary questions I'd just answered was "What effect has the practice of ministry had on your understanding of humanity and the need for divine grace?" My response had been *The practice of ministry has given me deeper insight into the reality that while humanity is made in the image of God, we are not God. We fall short; we fail; we are, in the end, powerless in the face of sin and of death.* I mentioned a colleague describing to me a scene from the movie *The Lion in Winter.*

Eleanor of Aquitane is speaking with her two sons. One son yelled for his mother to watch out because his brother had a knife. Eleanor replied, "Of course he has a knife. We all have knives." I've learned in the practice of ministry that *we all have knives.*

Reading the list, I felt the knife of every member of the congregation. I felt as though I were bleeding to death in front of the committee's eyes. For my own self-protection I had to hide the wounds, so I set the document aside and endured yet another conversation about my ineptitude.

I saw the committee members to the door. Before their headlights faded from the driveway, I was rancid with frustration and hurt.

"What's the matter?" Fred asked.

I handed him the list. He scanned it quickly. "Who said these things?"

"How should I know? They're all anonymous."

"You can't pay attention to things people say anonymously. The people probably had no idea they were going to be quoted."

"That doesn't help."

"Well, look, there are four or five positive statements on here. Couldn't you just pay attention to them and ignore the negative ones?"

No, I couldn't. The next morning I visited the new district superintendent, Clark Jenkins.

"How are you doing?" he asked.

"I'm pissed off."

He laughed. "What are you pissed off about?"

"That damned congregation."

I ran him through recent events. "I'd feel better if I could just kill a few of these people," I said.

"Mary Jo, you can't kill them."

"Why not?"

He leaned back in his swivel chair and looked thoughtful. "I don't know. But I know it's true, because Joe Bethea told me so."

Oh. Well, then. If Bishop Bethea had said it, it must be true. I changed my approach. "I want out of this church," I said.

"We need you there, this year and for at least one more year after this one."

"I don't care."

"That church needs you."

"They don't need me, and they don't want me."

"They'd have to be crazy not to want you."

"Apparently they are exactly that."

The district superintendent was amused by my attitude. He was also helpful. He told me to schedule state-of-the-church meetings, get-togethers for people to name their goals and dreams for the church. With goals formed out of the group's desires, I was then to use the power of the pulpit to focus their eyes on the prize.

▲   ▲   ▲

A few weeks later Bertha Flynn drove into the parsonage driveway. Bertha was the mother of Beth, the young woman who'd died of the aneurysm in 1994.

I walked over to the driver's side of the car.

"Hey, Bertha. How are you?"

"I came to tell you Chris is in the hospital and to see if there's a way the church can help us with these forms."

"Chris? Your son Chris is in the hospital?"

"Yes. We just found out he has acute leukemia. He and Kathy moved into their new house last weekend, and he got really worn out, so he went to the doctor today because he thought he had a virus or something, and the doctor sent him straight over to the oncologist, and the oncologist sent him straight to the hospital."

"Your son Chris has acute leukemia?"

"Yes. He's already had one blood transfusion, and they've started chemotherapy."

Oh, sweet Jesus. Beth had an aneurysm, and now Chris had leukemia.

Bertha showed me the forms from the hospital telling where, when, and how people could donate the blood and plasma Chris needed. Shadows from the sun behind the crepe myrtle tree danced across the form, light and dark, light and dark, light and dark.

Fred joined us, and I shared Bertha's news. I saw the shock I felt replicated on his face. It may have been harder for him to hear the news than it was for me. Fred knew Chris better than I did, knew he worked for a major bank in the area, that he'd been traveling out of town to install new computer systems in various branches of the bank, and that he was annoyed at how job and home-purchase responsibilities were interrupting his golf game. He'd also heard Alva, Chris's father, say, "Chris is a third child who never took anything off anyone."

Fred was waiting for me in the parsonage kitchen when I finally hugged Bertha good-bye and watched her leave. "Oh, my God," I said when I saw his wet eyes.

"I can't believe this is happening to them," he said.

I stepped up to him, leaned my body against his, and put my nose against the indentation just above his collarbone. I inhaled him, part Chanel for men, part October sun, part pure earthy Fred.

"You know what, Fred?" I asked into his collarbone.

"What?"

"I know life isn't fair, but this is so fucking unfair I can't stand it."

They say God never gives people more than they can handle. They're wrong. The death of one of your children followed, sixteen months later, by the diagnosis of leukemia in another of your children is unbearable. And the worst of it is that you, the parent, don't get to die instead of, or as well as, your child. You're stuck with living.

I visited Chris that day, and the next, and the next. Information dribbled in, a dribble being the operative speed for medical crises. The human body is too strong and too fragile, medical science too much science and too much art, for quick answers. It's hell for the patient and the family because they want a tidal wave, but all they get is sea spray.

▲   ▲   ▲

Chris has a rare strain of acute leukemia. He's only the eighth case diagnosed in the United States in twenty years.

Nothing can be done. He will die.

One potential treatment is available: arsenic.

Yes, arsenic. It's been tested in China.

Well, not exactly the same cancer as Chris's. It's a leukemia like his, but his chromosomes are different from the test patients.

Survival rates? We don't have that information.

Survival rates? They're all dead.

▲   ▲   ▲

Oh fuck fuck fuck fuck fuck. Fuck me fuck you fuck the world fuck a duck Jesus fucking Christ what a fucking nightmare. Chris's family could hardly stand it, I could hardly stand it, the church could hardly stand it. In fact, the only person who seemed able to stand it was Chris, who was certain his leukemia was treatable and he would be fine.

I fell in love with the man one day when his hospital room was filled with friends, family, and church members. I'd barely stepped in the door when I heard Chris yell, "Bucket!"

His wife, Kathy, leaped up from her chair, grabbed a plastic bucket, and got it under Chris's chin before he began heaving. I ducked out of the room and waited in the hallway until Alva came out to say Chris was once more settled.

I went back in to say good-bye and to ask Chris if I could say a prayer before I left. He, Kathy, and I clasped hands. The other people in the room gathered around the bed and bowed their heads.

I paused, waiting for words to pray, when I remembered how oddly people sometimes behave when there's a minister around. I lifted my head.

"Chris?" I said.

He lifted his bowed head and opened his eyes.

"If you decide you have to throw up, I don't want you to wait for me to say 'amen.' Interrupt me. Yell 'Bucket.' And, Kathy, if he does, you grab the bucket and hand it to him."

Chris looked directly into my eyes, and said, "Oh, that won't be necessary. You just keep praying, and I'll throw up in your pocket."

Pocket? He'd throw up in my pocket? Oh, Lord: a man who can joke on one of the worst days of his life is a man worth loving.

▲   ▲   ▲

On another visit, Alva and Kathy were the only people there. Alva drew me off to the side. "Chris wants to talk to you alone," he whispered.

"Okay," I said, wondering what Chris might have to ask me, or tell me.

A few minutes later, Alva said to Kathy, "The preacher wants to talk to Chris alone."

Did I miss something? I wondered as I watched the two of them walk out of the room together, Alva tall and thin, Kathy tiny beside him.

God only knows what Alva wants us to do, I decided. I scooted a chair close enough to Chris's bed to prop my feet on the rails. We considered each other gravely while I waited to see what words came into my mind.

Suddenly Chris burst out with, "I'm going to live." He sank back against the bed pillows, scowling. "Now tell me what you think of that."

I regarded him carefully. He was going to live? He had a rare form of acute leukemia, and he was going to live?

Hot diggity dog and thank you, Jesus. I know how to do life. It was the prospect of death that rattled me, especially in this case because Chris was exactly the age of my daughter Tara. (Have I already used the word "unfuckingbearable"?)

I said to Chris, "The doctors have told you you can die from this?"

"Yes."

"And Beth died, so you know death happens."

A jerk of his head in the affirmative.

"And you're not going to."

"That's right. I'm not going to."

I studied his face for a moment, waiting. *Praying,* I suppose you could call it, although the word feels too formal for the space I was in. I said, "Well, good. I'm glad. I don't want you to die, and the one thing I'm absolutely sure of is that God wants you to be healthy, happy, and whole."

Chris was staring at me blankly, so I repeated myself. "God wants you to be healthy and happy and whole. And you're claiming life even though suffering and grief are part of it. That's a wonderful thing."

Actually, I was being far more abstract than Chris. When he was growing up, the Flynns had a family friend with leukemia of a type that could be controlled with medication. Chris assumed his would turn out to be the same.

Before leaving, I asked Chris if he wanted me to say a prayer.

"It's okay with me," he said.

"What would you like me to pray for?"

"That I get well," he said.

So I did.

▲   ▲   ▲

Meanwhile, back at the church, I conducted three state-of-the-church meetings where the fifteen or twenty attendees prepared a vision statement and a list of what the congregation did well. I'd had the trustees begin preparing a list of everything that needed to be done to the church's physical plant. We also needed new sewer lines and new electrical wiring here and there, and a handicapped-accessible rest room, and if we didn't get the children's Sunday-school classrooms painted pretty soon, we might as well give up on ever having young families join.

I got a call one afternoon from a clergyman at a nearby Lutheran church. He'd resigned, he told me, and his parting, prayerful recommendation to me was "Mary Jo, you need to find another church. The community is too fragmented; there's too much enmity."

A second departing clergyman, this one Baptist, agreed. "Bail out. If you have any desire to continue serving in the local church, bail out now. This experience is going to destroy you for further pastoring," he warned.

I had an obligation to stay, but learning that some of my difficulties were situational allowed me to conserve my emotional energy. At my next evaluation by the personnel committee, my stoicism wavered only once, when somebody said it was obvious that I loved the work I was doing. I laughed, probably harshly, and said, "I have mixed feelings. I love it, and I hate it. This isn't an easy church."

A long silence.

"I'm sure that's true of all of them," somebody offered delicately.

"Actually, it's not. This church had long-term problems when I got here. The committees weren't functioning; the youth group and men's group weren't functioning; the people who got mad at each other thirty years ago were still throwing bricks at each other; and half the time I was the one getting my brains bashed out by the bricks, and this committee told me they thought the church was dying. That's a tougher situation to walk into than in a lot of churches."

Come Charge Conference on November 11, 1996, I'd documented every inch of my life over the previous year. The numbers shocked me: 244 pastoral visits, 138 meetings, 4 baptisms, 3 weddings, 5 funerals, 2 meditations and 2 sermons published, 2 guest preaching events, 2 lectures at a retreat sponsored by the bishop for people interested in entering the ministry. My report was positive and forward-looking, because we really *were* looking ahead, new leadership really *was* coming on board, we *were* accomplishing the things that needed to be done—but I felt no pleasure in the accounting.

As though numbers are a magnifying glass revealing the condition of a pastor's soul. All those visits, all those meetings . . . for what? None of them gave me a sense of peace, a sense of happiness, or of satisfaction. Accomplishment, yes, but that pleasure wasn't sufficient.

Had I done anything in all these months that mattered? Not if you count the things that mattered before I got there, things like violence against women and people being denied employment because of their race. And yet . . . Ah. One Sunday when I was to preach on the perfidy of Peter, I'd sewn together a stole with roosters printed on it, symbolizing the cock crowing three times. Ah. One Sunday I'd heard our deaf member preach, with his wife beside him interpreting, on how he found God in this place. I'd preached some fine and satisfying sermons myself. I'd taken the youth to a communion service at an African-American church.

I'd taken an art course to learn a bit about using water colors. I'd had some great sex with Fred. I'd fed Joe, my newest grandson, cereal on a spoon for the first time in his life, and I was the one who discovered his first tooth.

The numbers on my pastoral report left out more than they revealed. The numbers didn't say I was weary, didn't say the constant nitpicking was beating me into the ground, didn't say I no longer trusted the congregation. There was, for me, no alternative but to continue.

chapter thirteen

FOR THE NEXT TWO MONTHS, WHILE CHRIS FLYNN AND his family were in and out of New York for the arsenic treatments, the congregation exhibited love and generosity at a level I'd never seen before. *Praxis* is the theological term for their response. *Praxis:* "faith in action." People donated blood and plasma. They held a yard sale, a church dinner, and a spaghetti supper and gospel concert to help fund travel expenses. They sent cards and letters. They prayed, some of them without ceasing, which isn't as difficult as you might think. It's like when you wash your car and sing simultaneously, except in my case the song had only three words: *God* and *Chris* and *please.*

Every Sunday they were in town, Chris and Kathy came to church. They were always ten minutes late, an attempt to preserve Chris, with his weakened immune system, from the bacteria and viruses that we, the most devout of Christians, carried on our hands and expelled in our sneezes. Even if I was in the pulpit, focused on reading the first scripture lesson out loud, I could gauge their arrival. The first tremor would be behind my back in the choir loft. The second one surfaced when the people in the pew nearest the door noticed Chris and Kathy. The tremor would ripple forward in slow time with their steps to the fourth pew from the rear where they'd sit with Bertha and Alva and, often, Chris's brother, Jimmy, Jimmy's wife, Candy, and their three children.

One Sunday morning I was scheduled to baptize a baby, and I constructed my sermon around the question, "Why would we do such a thing to such a nice baby, and to ourselves, when being a Christian puts such demands on each of us?" Around eight-thirty that morning, the baby's mother called to say she'd been up all night with the flu, and now her husband had the flu, too, and they couldn't make it to church. I had less than two hours to write a new sermon. And then Chris's niece told me Chris and Kathy were coming to church that morning.

Did my sermon have anything to say to a person with arsenic in his bloodstream? Probably not, but it was all I had. I talked about the processes we undergo in the three stages of life, youth, middle age, and old age. Exploring our talents at each stage is difficult work; what sustains us are the promises of God: the promise that we're made in God's image and God wants us to be happy and healthy and whole; the promise that Christ broke the boundaries in his resurrection; the promise that we can claim God's loving presence; the promise that we are a people of hope. We ended by singing an old hymn of hope, "Standing on the Promises."

During all the hymns and the prayers and the sermon, people's eyes were red with tears, and a lot of nose-blowing was going on. Love, grief, and fear made the service as intense as a funeral.

Chris was supposed to leave the sanctuary during the last hymn to reduce his potential for exposure to infection from colds, flu, or the ordinary germs people carry around that can kill someone with a compromised immune system. He never left early. Instead he'd walk out onto the porch, just one of the crowd, and make his way down the steep front steps.

No, thank you, he didn't need to ride the elevator down.

No, thank you, nobody needed to hold his arm to steady him.

He could do it, he said. He would do it.

▲   ▲   ▲

The congregation and I watched him do it, week after week, month after month. We watched him adjust the blue face mask over his nose and mouth. We watched his skin tone change shades: yellow to yellower to white, to gray, grayer, and back to yellow, depending on his blood levels and his medications. We watched his hair fall out. We watched him get puffy and palsied from the steroids. We measured his well-being by the vigor of his trembling.

▲   ▲   ▲

Come January, the church was in good shape. I'd worked with the new leader of the youth group in planning a fund-raiser so that the teenagers could afford an upcoming spiritual-life retreat at the beach. I'd also recruited someone to lead mission projects; she'd put together five projects for the coming year. I'd contacted a retired clergyperson to lead a stewardship campaign that would shore up finances. Unfortunately, these achievements hadn't eased any of the tension between me and the original church leadership.

I met with Clark Jenkins, the district superintendent, to ask about my options for the next conference year. He told me I had none except to stay where I was. There was a shortage of pastors, so my only possible appointment was to a congregation. No other concept of ordained ministry was acceptable.

"Then give me the church up the road. I hear they're getting a new pastor."

"They don't want a woman."

"What if I pursue deaf ministries? What if I go back to school and get the courses I need to be a campus minister or teach at a college?"

"Gifted pastors need to be in local churches, and you are a gifted pastor," Clark insisted. "Besides, you can't be burned out after only two years."

"This isn't burnout, Clark."

"I need you there. I need you to do it for me."

"I can't. It isn't just the congregation. I've got this sense of urgency, like I'm being pulled somewhere else."

"I can't help you. There aren't any other options."

Given the percentages of clergy who, ten years after ordination, are doing work other than pastoring, I knew two things: I had options, and I had to invent what I was going to do. The simplest step was to request a leave of absence, which could start as early as June; so I started drafting my formal request.

I was heading out the door to visit Chris and Kathy one afternoon when Clark phoned.

"It's not that I thought you were making things up, but I understand better now what you're up against. A member of your church was in to see me." Clark had instructed the person to arrange a meeting with me. "Are you going to be all right?" he asked.

"Sure. I'm focused on June. I'm fine."

And then I learned that Chris's arsenic chemotherapy hadn't worked. His only remaining option was a bone-marrow transplant.

By Sunday, a schedule was in place. The next day, Chris would enter Richland Memorial Hospital in Columbia, South Carolina, for a mismatched bone-marrow transplant. He'd first undergo high-dose chemotherapy and full-body radiation to destroy his blood system. On Friday, Alva would have a hundred or so holes drilled into his bones and the marrow extracted. The marrow would be transfused into Chris that same day. If the procedure was successful, Chris's cancerous cells would be gone and his father's bone marrow would start manufacturing healthy new replacement cells.

Sunday morning I was robing when a member of the choir stuck her head in the door. "Do you have time for me to reintroduce you to someone?"

I didn't, really. I was mentally restructuring my sermon, a little game I played with myself every Sunday once I realized the worship service was about to begin and the sermon I'd written was incoherent and lacked a conclusion. I don't know how my sermons managed to transmogrify themselves into senseless, lifeless blobs every Sunday between the parsonage and the church, but they did.

Team player that I am, I smiled. "Sure, I have time. Is it somebody special?"

"Yes, my friend Brian. He's going to play the piano for the offertory again today."

Preoccupied, I didn't pay much attention when I shook hands except to note that Brian was young—twentyish—and eminently presentable in khaki pants, a white button-down shirt, a subdued tie, and brown wavy hair pushed back behind his ears.

I observed the formalities. "Nice to meet you, Brian. You're going to play the piano. Great. I'm looking forward to it."

I was lying. I didn't care who played the offertory or what was played. I need music with words attached. Otherwise I can't hold the sound. I blank it out the same way I blank out droning politicians, whining children, and boring preachers. While Brian played, I'd be thinking through my sermon one last time, strengthening its transitions and perhaps altering its nature in response to events in the worship service. I love that part of preaching free-style, where you write out the sermon but don't consult the manuscript once you're in the pulpit. You have the freedom to change as you go and to maintain a level of eye contact that lets you know when you need to linger a while, or move into fast-forward, or shut up and let everybody go home for lunch.

Brian turned to leave the room, and I noticed his hair was clasped back into a ponytail that hung far below his shoulders. I remembered then the first time we'd met. He'd played the piano, and afterward I'd asked if his hair was naturally curly, like mine, and he'd said yes, and that he had a terrible time keeping it under control.

▲   ▲   ▲

Early in the service I baptized two little girls—sisters, one dressed in purple velvet, the other in blue. Then came the time for prayer requests. I asked Chris if he wanted me to update the congregation for him. He nodded.

When I finished, he raised his hand. "Can I add something?"

"You certainly can."

Chris rose shakily and thanked the congregation for all their support, and he also thanked his father, who "gave me life once already, and now he's giving me life again." Chris started to sit down and then seemed to change his mind. He stood again and squared his shoulders. "The doctors told me most people have a thirty percent chance of surviving this procedure," he said. Then his voice cracked. "But they say I've only got a twenty percent chance." He fell silent, head down, shoulders shaking. We waited, alarmed. When he spoke again, he said, "And I'm afraid."

He sank into the pew and buried his head in his hands. Kathy put her right arm around his shaking shoulders and held his upper arm with her left hand. Beside her, Bertha and Alva were trembling. The rest of the congregation was a blur of rigid bodies, stricken faces, and held breath. I could smell wails of grief hiding just under their skin, and my own.

I had no idea what to do. I was still inexperienced, only eighteen months on the job, and seminary training didn't cover a time such as this. I looked to Fred for a vote of confidence that I could handle the situation. I didn't get one; he, too, looked shaken and at a loss. I said the only words that came to mind: "Our love and prayers go with you." Then I had no place to hide except in the words "Let us pray." As heads bowed, I put my elbows on the pulpit, leaned my forehead into my open hands, and thought, *Oh, my God. Somebody needs to do something, or none of us is going to make it through this service.*

Silence, broken only by choked-back sobs, one from the choir loft, one from the near front, one from the far right back. I waited. Eventually words came. I took a lung-filling breath and said, "Oh, God, pour out your blessings on Chris and Kathy and Bertha and Alva and everyone who loves them. We know they are so very tired."

Memory toys with you after an experience like this, so I can't be sure of what I said next. Most likely I began in the neighborhood of "Oh, God, we are joined this morning in fear and sorrow" and ended in the vicinity of "We ask for your grace whatever may come," but the truth is that, for all I can remember, I publicly took God to task for not giving me the blue bicycle with chrome fenders I wanted for my sixth birthday.

Whatever I said, we were all still so shaken that the ushers, when they came forward to receive the offering plates from my hand, couldn't make eye contact with me. I sent them on their way and sat down in the oak pulpit chair. Chris's head was still in his hands. Kathy looked bewildered and terrified. In the other pews, people wiped their eyes or noses or stared fixedly at nonexistent spots on the wall or floor.

My nose was running. I whispered into the choir loft, "Have you got any Kleenexes back there?"

"No."

Right at that moment I didn't want to be myself. I wanted to be the kind of preacher who owns a storehouse full of truisms to pull out, sayings like "Give your heart to Jesus" or "The Lord will provide" or "God doesn't give us anything we can't handle." Truisms are handy. They distance you from the pain, keep you from getting involved. Distance was an attractive alternative given that my cheeks were adorned with tears and my upper lip with snot.

A moment of clarity: *I'm going to have to blow my nose before I can preach.* A second moment of clarity: *I am not going to blow my nose on the hem of my robe.*

Deliverance came after the ushers returned the offering plates to me and I saw the guest pianist rise and approach the piano. He walked as though his knees were made of marshmallows. No wonder: it was hardly the kind of crowd a guest pianist wants to play into.

As Brian sat down, I made my escape. In the rest room, I grabbed a roll of toilet paper, ripped off the cover, wiped my eyes, blew my nose, considered the situation, and blew my nose again. *Sweet Jesus. The congregation is ready to implode. Somebody needs to do something.* I was halfway back to the sanctuary when it struck me that the person responsible for doing something was me, and that all I had to work with was my perfectly ordinary sermon. Well. Then. So be it. If I was all we had, I had to be enough.

I returned to the pulpit chair, leaned back, closed my eyes, and listened to the sniffles, which hadn't abated in my absence. If anything, they'd increased. I wished I'd brought an armload of toilet-paper rolls with me from the bathroom. I could have lobbed them in any direction, and the recipients would have been grateful.

Maybe I should go get more toilet-paper rolls?

No. The tears were not my responsibility. My responsibility was to figure out how to rescue us. I was brooding over the question when the notes from the piano nudged their way into my consciousness. At first I thought I was getting ready to throw up, because something was quivering in my midsection. I took a deep breath, settled myself, and paid attention to my body. No, I wasn't ill. Something was plucking at me.

It was the music. The music was rich and pulsating, airy and alive, and it was whispering to me. *Listen,* it said. *Listen.*

I didn't have time to listen. I had a poor, piddling, miserable excuse for a sermon, and in moments I had to preach it into a despairing congregation.

Wait, said the notes. *Listen.*

Puzzled, I turned my head toward the piano. Its back faced me. Above its lid I could see Brian's face, the beads of sweat on his forehead, and the undulations of his shoulder muscles under his shirt as his arms moved up and down the keyboard.

I turned away, still puzzled. *What's happening here?*

Listen, said the music.

I placed my hands, palms up, on the arms of the pulpit chair, closed my eyes, leaned back, and let the music touch me. It took me up, hung me over a precipice with my fingernails clutching at a boulder, caught me as I plunged, set me firmly onto my feet, stroked my hair, spoke softly into my ear, promised me I was safe.

Later I read a short story by George W. Bagby, published in 1891 in the second volume of *Half Hours with the Best Humorous Authors.* Bagby describes a performance by Anton Rubinstein, a great Russian pianist who performed in New York in the 1870s:

Then the moonlight came, without any sunset, and shone on the graveyards . . . and between the black, sharp-top trees marble houses rose up, with fine ladies in the lit-up windows, and men that loved 'em, but could never get anigh 'em, who played on guitars under the trees, and made me that miserable I could have cried, because I wanted to love somebody, I don't know who, better than the men with the guitars did.

Then the sun went down, it got dark, the wind moaned and wept like a lost child for its dead mother, and I could 'a' got up then and there and preached a better sermon than any I ever listened to. There wasn't a thing in the world left to live for, not a blame thing, and yet I didn't want the music to stop one bit. It was happier to be miserable than to be happy without being miserable.

Brian played, and I didn't want the music to stop one bit. There wasn't a thing in the world left to live for, and yet it was happy to be miserable. That day I got up and preached a better sermon than any I ever listened to. My sniveling little sermon grew and grew until it became large enough to grab up the shadow of death and toss it out the sanctuary door. I began with a reference to that morning's baptism and said,

We call it a sacrament because we believe that in the action God is right here in this sanctuary doing something.

I said how different the notion is from the Greek and Roman gods and goddesses I studied in high school.

Zeus, Athena, Mercury: they were thought to be entirely engaged in their own loves and conspiracies. From their distance they'd occasionally take a look below at the petty little creatures with their petty little concerns. The God we worship—Yahweh, rock of ages, almighty king—chooses to be in our midst, chooses to pull up a chair and sit down with us. God doing so is recorded, persistently, in the Bible.

I reminded the congregation of Moses, who'd pitch a tent far away from the people he was leading through the wilderness, and the people would see a pillar of cloud at the tent's entrance and know God was speaking with Moses face to face. I told them, too, about the dedication of the Temple in Jerusalem and how I Kings 8 documented Solomon saying, "The Lord has said that he would dwell in thick darkness. I, Solomon, have built you an exalted house, a place for you to dwell in forever."

The verb in that passage is *yashab*. If you look at the Hebrew, you find that "dwell in" isn't the right translation. The right, the best translation, is "a place for you to sit down in forever." Israel believed God was there, right there, sitting down in their midst. And our story, the Christian story, takes it a step further: that in the person of Jesus, God walked, talked, ate, preached, healed, and sat down: in the Temple, in boats, on hillsides, in friends' houses.

I told the story of Edwina Gateley, a Roman Catholic laywoman from England who ran into numerous roadblocks in her work as a missionary. Finally, disgusted with both the Church and God, she resigned from the relief organization she'd founded and moved to America, to a cabin in the woods. I used my grandmother's British accent and my own fist when Edwina shook her fist at God and said, "I've had enough; I'm finished with you," and when I told how Edwina plopped down into a chair in the cabin, I plopped down into my pulpit chair, and when I said God pulled up a chair and plopped down beside her and stayed, God stayed, right there with her in her pain, right there with her in her exhaustion, right there with her in her rage, I indicated God, invisible, plopped down next to me, plopped down with every one of us sitting in our exhaustion, our rage, our terror. *God sits down beside us,* I told the congregation, *in celebration, fear, and pain. God does this.*

One of the most devout prayers is "Oh Lord, I believe; help my unbelief." Most of the time I believe what the Church teaches about the sacraments: that God is here, changing the life of the person who receives the sacrament. But I had a flash this week when I wondered, *What would it do to us if we REALLY believed God is here with us when the sacraments are performed?* And my next thought was *We would all die. Or if we wouldn't all die, we would at least draw back, huddle together, cover our eyes, hide under the pews, grab our children to our breasts.*

But that's not what we do. It isn't what we do at all.

I knew where I was going with the sermon, knew the last line I was aiming for, a variation on the last line of the closing hymn, could feel it building, and now I was on my feet, arms outstretched, feeling as though the top of my head were brushing the ceiling and my fingertips were inches from the stained-glass windows on either side of the sanctuary as I said,

The God we worship, the God who sat in our midst and sits in our midst, doesn't say, "Draw back." Our God says, "Come to me." The God we worship doesn't say, "Be in my presence and die." Our God says, "I have claimed you. You are mine. Stand up and laugh and love and live. Stand up, and laugh, and love, and live."

Let us pray.

Much later Brian described my expression when I finished that sermon as "somewhere between dying and dead. 'I've done all I can do; I'm going to curl up and die now' is how you looked."

If *dead* means a total absence of energy, I was dead. I stood in silence, elbows on the pulpit Bible, head in hands, breathing, waiting. Waiting for what? Inspiration, maybe. Courage. Some indication that life might go on after this moment. Energy enough to continue. It seemed a long time until I had the strength to fumble for the bulletin.

"Our closing hymn is 'I Would Be True.'"

I stood with the hymnal to my chest, my eyes closed, as the pianist, or maybe it was the organist, played the introduction. As we began to sing, I opened my eyes. The people were on their feet, singing. Nobody was crying, but some of them looked terribly rigid. I thought coming to the altar to kneel and pray might be nice for them, might break their rigidity and let air move, so I said, "If you want to come pray, you're welcome."

Chris immediately stood and lunged forward. His family merged around him, and other people merged around them, and all of them came together at the right side of the altar, some kneeling, the rest encircling the kneelers, and as we sang, "I would be strong, for there is much to suffer," I crouched low to lay my hand on Chris's head, and Kathy's, and Bertha's, and Alva's, and whisper, "God bless you," and we reached the last line of the song, "I would look up, and laugh and love and lift," and started again at the beginning with "I would be true, for there are those who trust me"; and we sang both verses again, and then a last time.

As I spoke the benediction, I knew people were still frightened, but it was different from the raw terror at the beginning of the service; the fear was deeper, all artifice expunged. Chris could die. No sermon, no prayer, no magical mystical healing was going to save him from the body burns of chemotherapy and radiation. He was staring into the face of a monster, and for a few minutes we'd seen it staring back at us all.

The sermon I'd written was kindling. Chris lit the match; the congregation proffered splinters to catch the bit of fire; Brian added a breath of air, I added more, and the Spirit burst it all into flame. It was an extraordinary worship service, which is why I was devastated at being told the next day that the church wanted to get rid of me.

▲   ▲   ▲

The next evening I met with a representative from the personnel committee who'd worked hard to make my ministry a success. I was optimistic that once we talked through the dynamics of change, and how threatening it is for people, we could come up with a way to ease the tensions. Instead, the conversation went like this:

"You need to call the district superintendent's office tomorrow."

"Why?" I asked.

"Because you need to get the forms we need to request a new pastor."

"The what?"

"The forms so we can request a new pastor." He explained that three or four people were insisting I be replaced. "When I met with the district superintendent, I did tell him maybe we haven't been as supportive as we could have been. There's never been a two years in a church like the two since you got here. You're abnormal in the way you get things done, and when you get overstressed, it shows. We need to schedule a meeting to decide what the congregation wants."

The words drizzled over me: "get rid of me"; "abnormal"; "overstressed." What brought on this conversation? My sermon the day before? Of course not. This had nothing to do with the day before, or the week before. The timing was due to the exigencies of the conference calendar. The date for discussions about a new pastor was at hand, and the conversation had to be engaged. I was, in a sense, immaterial to the conversation. I, who'd poured every ounce of my faith, strength, and personal power into the congregation the day before, and who'd seen it needed, and accepted, and grasped on to for dear life . . . I, who'd given the congregation the best that was within me, not just the day before but each day since I'd arrived . . . I was now being told I was a hired hand, and a not very good one at that.

I don't recall every word of the ensuing conversation, but I remember the red heat of rage and saying, as I slammed my fist down on the desk, "I will not be insulted in this church again."

We were both trembling when the meeting ended. I throttled my emotions long enough to conduct the scheduled finance-campaign meeting and to thank the consulting minister nicely for his efforts, but when I reached the parsonage, I called Clark, and my rage spilled out.

"Tomorrow. Meet with me tomorrow afternoon," he said.

"Jesus Christ couldn't satisfy these goddamn people. Get me the hell out." It was the next day and I'd just concluded a description of recent events.

"Now don't get in a hurry," Clark said. Two members of the church had been in to see him that morning. They admitted I was a pretty good pastor but said I was too sensitive and too strong-minded. He'd asked them if my being a woman had anything to do with the problems. Oh, no, they assured him, nothing at all.

Were they kidding themselves? Maybe not; maybe they would have treated a male pastor exactly the way they treated me.

I was glaring at Clark. "How the hell do they think I'm able to preach the way I preached on Sunday? Why do they think people are joining the church and we've got a mission program in place? It's because I'm sensitive and strong-minded."

Clark laughed. "You can't let these people bother you. You're too good at what you do. Every church needs you as its pastor one time," he said.

"Are you out of your mind?"

My anger was hardly surprising, nor was it surprising that I was in despair. Until that week I'd believed my difficulties were issues of adjustment—mine to the job, the congregation's to me, all of us to radical change—and that we would survive. After the meeting, though, I knew the problem went deeper, down, down, down to the heart of my existence. I am a person who learned to recognize the holy when it approaches me, who learned how to point out the holy to other people when it comes; and who learned—and, oh, this is the most difficult task of all, the task that burns me dry and withers me, leaves me parched and fragile—to hold open the door to the holy and let it radiate through me into the faces and hands and souls of other people. I did so willingly, even though it exposed the most tender portions of my soul.

But here's the thing: It's dangerous, even in the Church, an institution called to set standards for goodness and mercy, to leave yourself open and exposed.

What was to be done? Nothing, except go on. Bertha and Alva were headed for the hospital in Columbia the next day, so I paid them a pastoral visit. Friends had dropped off flowers, snacks, and reading material for the coming ordeal, and as I left, Bertha pressed on me a potted tulip, pink blooms with wavy edges. Plants aren't allowed on transplant units, and she wanted me to enjoy the flowering.

At home I placed the tulip on the desk near my computer. As I did so I noticed my quotation-a-day calendar. It said, "Trying to be what others want us to be is a form of slow torture and certain spiritual death."

I brooded on the statement as I drove to Columbia on Friday. Certainly I felt tortured, as though I was dying spiritually, as though little by little any goodness and mercy within me was eroding. Was the problem that I was trying to be what other people wanted me to be? Was I trying to conform my spirit to other people's image of what a pastor should be? I thought not. I was trying to be a disciple, to follow God's lead, but I was more and more confused over where God and I were headed. The vitality in the church indicated *something,* but, obviously, so did my misery.

My brooding ended at the anteroom to the transplant unit. Posted signs instructed me to don a pale yellow paper hospital gown and slip a pair of blue paper booties over my shoes. Other signs showed me how to stand in front of a stainless-steel machine that spun first water and then air around my hands to wash and dry them. The extensive preparations were due to the weakness of transplant patients' immune systems.

Chris was in good spirits for a man with a 20 percent chance of survival. "This part isn't hard on me. All I do is lie here while they run an IV into me. My dad's the one having the tough time today."

"This is a nightmare," Kathy whispered.

I went in search of Alva. Earlier that day he'd been given general anesthesia, and the medical team had shoved a series of needles through into his hipbones, boring through skin, fat, muscle, and bone into the bone marrow at the core. I found Alva awake and alert just down the hall. He told me, "I'm fine. All I care about is Chris. This has to work."

▲   ▲   ▲

Two weeks later, I had a ludicrous meeting with the personnel committee. They spent the first ten minutes complaining about the sermon I'd preached on Sunday (I'd tried an experiment that failed), and the next ten minutes complaining because I didn't visit enough.

"I can't read minds. If I'm not told that somebody's in the hospital, I can't visit them there."

They then turned to the form regarding my continuation as their pastor. Unanimously, they requested my return. When I filled out my section of the form, I wrote that I was exploring other forms of ministry. Their jaws dropped; this was a development they hadn't expected.

At the end of February, I had lunch with an experienced, highly respected clergyman in the district. He'd heard from Clark that I was requesting a leave of absence. "I was absolutely shocked and dumbfounded. I asked Clark if your church had beaten you up to force you out, and Clark told me no: they want you to stay."

"They've beaten me up, and they want me to stay." I told him I'd decided to request a leave of absence.

I spoke with another acquaintance who was familiar with the machinations of appointment authorities. "I'm sure the decision makers would prefer you to go on leave instead of figuring out where else to appoint you. Women are a problem for the system."

My neck muscles began to cramp. I was entering the leadership ranks of an institution that categorized me and my kind as a problem. Just how dysfunctional is that?

▲   ▲   ▲

Chris Flynn survived. He survived the radiation and chemotherapy prior to the transplant. He survived the graft-versus-host-disease that set in in response to the receipt of his father's bone marrow. He spent four weeks in the hospital and another four weeks in an apartment near the hospital. Finally he was stable enough to come home. He went back to work. He stopped wearing the face mask. His palsy waned. He ate three strawberries. His hair grew back in tight curls, which he would permit me to rub with my knuckles while he grinned and squirmed.

The congregation and I watched him heal. One day in the spring, Fred was talking to someone on the front porch of the church when Chris walked down the sidewalk in front of them.

"There goes a walking miracle," said the man.

Fred's eyes were wet when he repeated the conversation to me. Yes, Chris was our walking miracle, and we all knew it. Perhaps that's why, for a time, the tensions eased: because we had something in our lives more important than each other's frailties. As the azaleas and dogwood came into bloom and the peonies into bud, and the hosta poked up inch-high spikes of promise, we noticed that we, too, had survived the winter.

▲　　▲　　▲

Nevertheless, I was going through forty hells over the question of ordination. I'd been approved for ordination in May of 1997, and the question was settled as far as everybody was concerned, except me. I debated the question with Fred; with Molly; with Clark; with two friends who were on the Board of Ordained Ministry and three United Methodist clergywomen.

"You've come too far to stop now," they each insisted.

Fred and Clark were particularly adamant. "If anybody has gifts and graces for the ministry, it's you," they said. "Stop talking about it. Stop thinking about it. The decision has already been made."

For six weeks I fretted myself and my friends into misery. Then one day I had to meet with the executive committee of the Board of Ordained Ministry to discuss the request for personal leave I'd submitted months earlier. I'd assumed the meeting was a formality, but within moments I was pummeled with agitated statements, questions, and demands. Who was I to think God might call me elsewhere when the Church needed pastors? Did I think I was the only one who wanted to take a year off? Didn't I think some of them wanted that luxury, too? What exactly was I planning to do? I hadn't prepared for a ten-against-one confrontation.

"I don't know," I'd repeat. "The point of my leave request is to have the space and quiet to figure it out."

A few days later a committee representative phoned to say the group's sense was that I should take the leave but that if I did, I'd have to postpone ordination for a year while I sorted through my questions. Postpone ordination for a year? Where did that idea come from? While I had the person from the Board on the phone, I asked about some resistance I'd received to my idea of pursuing a doctorate. He sighed. "Some of them think a doctoral degree makes people unfit to serve as pastors of congregations."

Unfit? Education makes a person unfit? I'd never heard anything so stupid. Relaying the information to Fred, I concluded, "This is ridiculous. Ordination is not the holy grail."

"Yes, it is," he said. He had come too far, made too many sacrifices, and had seen too much evidence of my gifts to let me throw it all away now. A phone call to the committee and another to Clark, and all was resolved. I would stay one more year, and I would be ordained.

▲   ▲   ▲

The service took place at Annual Conference. We ordinands sat together in our black robes on metal folding chairs in front of a makeshift altar. We were supposed to be dignified, but I couldn't stop squirming. I had the feeling there was somebody in the crowd trying to make his or her presence known to me. I spotted Fred, who was beaming, and Tara, and Molly. Then I saw Terry, my friend with rheumatoid arthritis, and I thought I understood: Her mother, Helen's, spirit was in the arena, celebrating. Yet still I searched the crowd, certain somebody else—whether corporeal or spiritual—was wanting me to notice them.

Then I couldn't look any longer because we were up and kneeling at the altar, and then two by two we went forward for the laying on of hands. I'm told I looked radiant. I know Fred was when we found each other at the conclusion of the two-hour service. We laughed and hugged, and then he asked if I'd seen the Flynns.

"Were they here? Bertha and Alva?"

"Chris and Kathy and Alva."

"That explains it."

"Explains what?"

"I couldn't sit still—"

"I noticed."

"Because I was looking for someone. It was the Flynns."

▲   ▲   ▲

A few weeks later I asked Chris to assist me with communion. He immediately said yes. The title of my sermon was "The Banana of Life." The text was from the sixth chapter of Mark, where Jesus sends the disciples out to do God's work.

Off they went, two by two, with nothing but each other, and a staff, and a pair of sandals, and a tunic. No food, no backpacks, no money in their belts.

What do you think it took for them to do that? Courage? Trust? Faith? A desire to serve? Maybe what empowered them was the feeling we named in this morning's opening prayer: our hearts are restless until they find rest in God. Maybe the disciples were like us, with our restless hearts, our hungry hearts, hearts longing for something, and we don't even know what we're hungry for so we cast around for anything—lottery tickets, shopping, drugs—that will give us a thrill, a moment's excitement, a moment of thinking life has meaning.

And all the time God is waiting for us, patiently waiting for us to notice that it's God we're looking for.

When Jesus said, "I am the bread of life," he wasn't talking about bread as a helpful carbohydrate that builds strong bodies twelve ways. The man never used a fork. Bread was the utensil he used to get food into his mouth, and when he was finished he ate the bread. Without it, he would have starved.

That's why Christ invites everyone to the communion table, and why the United Methodist Church communion table is open. You don't have to be any certain age to take communion. You don't have to have passed any test. You don't have to be a member of this church, or a member of any church. You just have to be hungry.

I've read about a group of indigenous people in South America that doesn't eat bread. Imagine that: they have no concept of a food we consider a staple. A group sponsored a translation of the Bible into the tribe's language, but the translators ran into a big problem. How do you translate "bread of life" for people who've never eaten bread?

The staple food in the tribal diet turned out to be bananas. The people used bananas the way Jesus used bread, as a utensil and as a food. The translators had their solution. Now when those people read the Bible in their native language, the words they read are, "Jesus said, 'I am the banana of life.'"

Jesus, the bread of life. Jesus, the banana of life. They mean the same thing: that Christ is present with us, feeding us, nourishing us, sustaining us. It's a lot to expect from a bite of bread and a sip of grape juice, but it's not too much to ask of Christ, the bread of life, the banana of life, the life giver. And for this we say, "Thanks be to God." Amen.

I looked closely at Chris before I handed him the plate of bread. He was trembling a little from his medications, but he stood erect, shoulders back and squared, a look of assurance on his face.

"Are you all right?" I whispered. "We have another plate of bread if that one spills or gets dropped." When I saw the grin on Chris's face, I stopped worrying about his frailty.

In the moments when one group of people arose from the altar to return to their pews and the next group approached, I watched them watch Chris. I saw wonder in their eyes, and flickering memories: arsenic treatments; the bone-marrow transplant; the yard sale and spaghetti supper; the cards and phone calls; the prayers upon prayers without ceasing. Some people's eyes were red even before Chris leaned toward them to offer the bread and say, "The body of Christ, given for you."

His presence next to me made it all worthwhile: every mile I'd commuted to divinity school, every insult, every inanity. I knew I was in exactly the right place, doing exactly the right thing, and all was well with my soul.

chapter fourteen

HE DIED.

Chris Flynn died.

He had a rare type of acute leukemia, and he died. The suffering he endured never stood a chance of curing him. All it did was give him and Kathy, him and his family, him and all the rest of us, a little more time together.

"A little more time"—what an insignificant phrase for what we shared in those last months of his life.

▲   ▲   ▲

I think he knew it was over when he called me at about six o'clock one evening a few weeks after he'd assisted with the communion service. I was in the church office preparing to meet with the committee planning the church's fiftieth anniversary celebration when the phone rang. For a moment I didn't recognize the choked voice saying, "I need you to pray for me."

And then, "Chris? Chris, is that you?"

▲   ▲   ▲

He and Kathy were waiting outside when I got to their house. He'd had a blood test that day that showed something was not right. We walked through the garage into their kitchen. I paused just inside the doorway. Chris continued around a counter and faced me from the far side and, in one long exhalation, said, "I think the leukemia's back I was on a death penalty jury once the man deserved to die I voted for the death penalty for him if I'd known then what I know now I might not have voted the way I did."

Our eyes were locked.

I said, "Yes."

175

That day's blood test hadn't shown leukemia. Chris was to have a follow-up blood test and a bone-marrow biopsy the next week. He wasn't going to tell his parents yet; he didn't want to worry them.

I didn't tell him and Kathy that Alva, Chris's father, had been diagnosed with prostate cancer a week earlier. Alva and Bertha didn't want Chris to know. They didn't want him to worry.

The first bone-marrow biopsy was clear of leukemia. A repeat test showed not only that it was there but that it had gone ballistic. "They call them 'blasts,'" Alva told me. "Chris's blood is full of them. The doctors want him to go to the hospital in Columbia today for another bone-marrow transplant."

Chris refused. "I'm not going until Monday. I'm spending this weekend at home. We're not going to be in church on Sunday. Kathy and I just want to be home alone."

Come Sunday I was to preach for the fourth week in a row about Jesus being the bread of life. After four Sundays, I couldn't imagine what else I could find to say on the topic. But then one afternoon while I was digging in the front yard, I got to thinking about my father and the bread machine my brother Douglas gave him for Christmas one year. When Fred and I were on the island for my parents' fiftieth wedding anniversary, I'd awakened each morning to the smell of bread baking.

In memory I could still almost taste the warm slices. *Wouldn't it be something,* I thought, *if when we thought about Jesus being the bread of life we could feel the way I felt when I smelled and tasted that bread?*

Maybe we could.

I phoned a member of the congregation who owned a bread machine and had indulged me more than once in the past.

"I need you to bake some bread Sunday morning," I said.

"Sure. Do you want me to bring a loaf when I come to Sunday school?"

"Actually, no. I want the bread to be baking during the worship service."

"Oh, are we having communion?"

"Nope. We're just going to eat some bread."

The machine was under the communion table humming its little mixing tune when I arrived at the church Sunday morning. The worship service began. I was startled when Chris and Kathy walked into the

sanctuary while we were singing the first hymn. By 11:37, eight minutes into my sermon, the machine had clicked off.

I said, "We keep talking about Jesus being the bread of life, but
today I want to show you what it really means."

I walked down the three steps and crossed to the altar table. I
picked up the potholders I'd placed on the table before the service
began, crouched down, opened the lid of the bread machine, lifted the
interior bucket, and dumped the loaf inside it onto a plate. I tore the hot
bread into hunks, turned to the congregation, and held the plate aloft for
everyone to see.

"The bread of life," I said, "given for you."

I came from behind the altar and walked the center aisle of the
sanctuary, offering the filled plate to the people on my left.

"Want some?" I asked. "Do you want some bread?"

A teenager admired for his appetite took the first piece, and then
several children sitting near him reached for pieces, too. By then the
adults were grinning, and they started accepting pieces, too.

I was laughing and saying over and over, "Want some? It's the
bread of life, given for you."

I got to the back of the sanctuary, turned, and started up the aisle.
"Want some? Want some?" I was grinning as I offered the plate to Chris.
He laughed out loud, his eyes sparkling, and took a big hunk of bread.

On Monday Chris went back into the hospital. By then he knew
about his father's cancer. Bertha, his mother, was to be the bone-marrow
donor this time. She was ready.

"Nothing's going to stop me," she said. "I wanted to be the donor
the first time, and they wouldn't let me because I have some health
problems. I don't care if I have a heart attack, just as long as they get my
bone marrow out before I die."

Chris had his first round of chemotherapy Monday night. By the
next morning his temperature had started to climb. The doctors thought
it was pneumonia.

He couldn't have more chemotherapy until the infection was gone,
but there wasn't time, there just wasn't time for him to get well. I saw
him in the hospital in Columbia on Thursday and again on Friday. Fred
and I drove down again early Saturday afternoon.

We were on the outskirts of Columbia when he asked, "How are you going to do this? Tomorrow's Sunday. What are you going to preach on if he dies today?"

I turned to face Fred. I knew the answer and was surprised it wasn't obvious to him. "Lazarus. I'm going to tell the congregation about Lazarus."

"Lazarus? What does Lazarus have to do with Chris?"

I created my sermon right then and calmly spoke it to Fred. He looked confused at first, and then astonished, and then the memory of his first wife whom I'd never known was thick in the car with us, and the expression on Fred's face. . . .

Healed. He looked healed, as if an ache he'd learned to live with had disappeared.

We spent the day at the hospital. At some point I gasped out a prayer at the foot of Chris's bed. Just before dusk Fred and I walked across the street and ate fried chicken at a Bojangles' restaurant, or maybe it was a Kentucky Fried Chicken. The floors were so clean, they shone.

We went back to the hospital and sometime after that—it was full dark—we left for home.

We got to sleep around one. The phone rang forty-five minutes later.

"About one-thirty?" Fred asked into the receiver. A few more words, and he hung up the phone.

We lay still beside each other in the dark.

"Chris," I said.

"Yes."

"Was that Alva?"

"Yes."

After a while Fred said, "You have to preach in the morning. You have to get some sleep."

"I know."

Sunday dawned. At seven I phoned two or three of the church leaders to tell them about Chris. I got ready and went to the church where I closed my office door, put on my robe, sat down, and waited for time to pass.

I announced Chris's death at the beginning of the service. Most people already knew, but my saying it out loud, in public, made it differently true.

In one of those odd little twists of grace, Brian, the guest pianist, was there again. He played "It Is Well with My Soul." I sat in my pulpit chair and let the music roll over me. When the time came, I took the pulpit and told the people in front of me, many of whom had tears standing on their cheeks, the story of Lazarus.

Once there was a young man named Lazarus. He had two sisters, Martha and Mary. They were a family who one day along the way met Jesus and fell in love.

They walked with him, cooked for him, learned from him, and believed in him—believed that he was truly the son of God, that he truly had the power of God.

One day Lazarus got sick—very sick—so sick he died.

Jesus wasn't anywhere around. He was off somewhere in a different village. Mary sent for him, because she knew Jesus could heal her brother, but Lazarus died before Jesus arrived.

Mary was furious when Jesus finally came dragging in. She said, "If you had been here, my brother wouldn't have died."

Jesus went to the tomb where Lazarus's body had been laid. The Bible doesn't say that Jesus held his nose, but Lazarus had been dead for three days; you know there was a stench. Jesus asked that the stone in front of the tomb be rolled away, and then he called out, "Lazarus, come forth."

And here's the thing: Lazarus, three days dead, came forth.

Just think what that was like, *I said to the congregation*. Think what it was like for those people to have this formerly dead man walking around, whistling and talking and making jokes and acting like a perfectly normal human being. People must have been beside themselves with wonder and joy. I'll bet they called him a walking miracle.

This week . . . , *I said.*

This week I've been thinking about the second time Lazarus died. Because, you know, he didn't live forever. Scripture doesn't tell us the end, but we know Lazarus was a human being, and that means in the end he did die. Maybe it was a long time after the crucifixion, maybe a short time. But we know that the next time, Jesus wasn't there to return him to physical life. The second time, nobody could do anything.

I wonder what happened to the people who were there when Jesus raised Lazarus from the dead. I wonder what happened to them when Jesus did not perform a second miracle. I'm sure they were grief-stricken and angry and empty, the way people always are when someone they love dies. I wonder if their faith was shaken.

My hope, I said—and I had to pause before I could continue, had to breathe deeply to be sure my voice would remain steady, had to give the congregation a moment to prepare to hear my next words—my hope for them is that in the midst of whatever grief, desolation, and sadness they felt, no matter how far away God seemed, that somehow, deep inside, the people who loved Lazarus were able to remember that once they had watched God perform a miracle.

I remember the day so clearly. I remember how tender the congregation and I were with each other as we shook hands and knuckled our tears away after the service. Fred went with me to Kathy's that afternoon. I spent an hour talking to her, and some time talking to Bertha and Alva. At some point—it must have been around nine o'clock because I think it was dark out—Chris's brother, Jimmy, and I went for a walk in the neighborhood.

The next day I met the family at the funeral home and saw Chris in his casket. I wanted to rub his head, but I felt shy because he looked so formal and dead and all, so instead I patted his hand, which was also dead. That's the thing about bodies: they're always there and then they're not. The item in the coffin is familiar and loved, but it is a vestige.

▲   ▲   ▲

I remember the visitation at the funeral home that night. Somebody from the church criticized me for arriving "late," fifteen minutes before visitation was to begin. I didn't tell them I'd come straight from Kathy's house.

One person, a kind woman who was grieving and in search of a comforting thought, said, "Chris was ready to die."

Lord have mercy on my soul, I lashed out at her. "He was twenty-eight years old. No twenty-eight-year-old is ready to die."

I turned to Fred, who was beside me. "I have to leave now. I'm done"—*done* being our shorthand for "used up," "depleted," "spent." I couldn't bear to be around people any longer. I couldn't bear the thought that somebody might say the death was a miracle because it spared Chris more pain. The death of your child is never a miracle, not even if you're God.

▲   ▲   ▲

The day of the funeral, I went to the mortuary early to give the funeral director a copy of the order of worship. I approached Chris's casket and stood beside him for a while, and then I sat down in the chair I would occupy during the service and mentally walked through the ritual.

Another minister, a man named Cliff who'd been a friend of Alva's and Bertha's since all their children were small, read a nineteenth-century African-American sermon called "Go Down, Death," from James Weldon Johnson's collection *God's Trombones*. Cliff read in a voice so deep, God must be envious. The sermon spoke of Death riding a pale, white horse down from heaven, and then "Death took [Chris] up like a baby, and [he] lay in his icy arms, but [he] didn't feel no chill. And Death began to ride again—up beyond the evening star, out beyond the morning star, into the glittering light of glory, on to the Great White Throne." And it was good.

I read from Isaiah about the lilies of the field, how they neither toil nor spin. I told how three years earlier, we'd gathered when Beth, Chris's sister, died.

Cliff spoke at Beth's funeral about the story where the apostle Paul was in a shipwreck and how Paul clung to a piece of driftwood to survive. Cliff said at times like this, all we can do is grab a piece of driftwood and hang on.

"But what do we do now," *I asked,* "when all of us are too tired to hang on for ourselves?"

Jesus said, "Consider the lilies of the field, how they grow; they neither toil nor spin, yet I tell you, even Solomon in his glory was not clothed like one of these. But if God so clothes the grass of the field, which is alive today and tomorrow is thrown into the oven, will he not much more clothe you?"

Jesus' promise is that when we don't have enough strength to hang on to God, God will hang on to us. God will hang on to us, will clothe us, will sustain us. And for that, and for all that Chris taught us, and all the joy and faith and love he brought to our lives, still today, in the middle of our grief, we can say, "Thanks be to God."

Amen.

I spoke the now-familiar words of committal at the cemetery: "For all that Chris has given us to make us what we are, for that of him which lives and grows in each of us, and for his life that in your love will never end, we give you thanks."

Cliff came to shake my hand before we all departed. "I was at the ordination service this summer. When I saw Chris was there, I knew you were important to him."

I blinked back tears. "We were important to each other."

When we left the cemetery, Fred asked, "Where are we going now?" and I said "To Kathy's."

"Are you sure? Why do you want to go there?"

"Because it's the one place I know where nobody will say anything stupid."

Halfway across town, I remarked, "I'm going out of town, and I'm going to eat everything in sight, drink until I'm shit-faced, and fuck my brains out. You're my first choice to do all those things with, but it doesn't really matter to me one way or the other."

Fred was silent for a moment, and then he said, quietly, kindly, "I wasn't really interested in going along until you got to the last item on the list."

▲   ▲   ▲

My daughter Tara happened to call that night. I told her about the funeral.

She said, "Oh, Mama, Chris was exactly my age."

I said, "Yes. I noticed."

My daughter would grow older. Chris never would. He would be twenty-eight now and forevermore.

For the next two weeks, all I could think about were food, sex, and alcohol. I wanted to get rip-roaring drunk. I wanted to escape to a place, a moment, a space where there was no sadness. I wanted to fuck some-body's/anybody's brains out, preferably while eating a heaping plate of macaroni and cheese. I couldn't because I had to preach. I knew Chris's family would be in their pew, alone, without him. Knowing gave me the courage to speak honestly that next, first Sunday.

I began by offering the congregation a question:

What do we do when God turns out to be something other than what we wanted?

A long time ago I heard Kris Kristofferson sing: "Let the devil take tomorrow. / Lord, tonight I need a friend. / Yesterday is dead and gone, / and tomorrow's out of sight; / and it's sad to be alone. / Help me make it through the night." He added, once that I know of, "I don't want to sleep alone. Help me make it through the night."

I find the song to be an honorable one. It's not the kind of sex I would choose for the youth in this congregation, or the adults for that matter, any more than I would choose for you to use alcohol or drugs to numb the pain of life. But I honor the need to find something to get us through the pain. I honor the sadness that says, "I need something to take the pain away, if only for the next few hours."

I honor it even though I know it doesn't work. There is meaning in getting through the night. It just isn't the meaning we want for each other, or the level of meaning God wants for us. Sex, drugs, alcohol: they're all things we choose to numb the pain. They don't work, of course. They're like standing in the middle of a burning house and saying, "I know what I'll do! I'll pull the ceiling joists down on top of my head."

It doesn't work, but sometimes it seems like the only sensible thing to do. Just get me through the night.

That same sort of thing happened to some of the disciples, the ones who we learn in John 6 turned back and no longer went about with Jesus. They thought they were following God, and then Jesus told them who he was, and he wasn't what they expected or wanted.

Jesus has named who he is, has used the language of food, of bread, to tell them he truly is the son of God. They don't want to hear it. They know Jesus' mother and father. They know he's a real person. And that's not what they want. They don't want God to be incarnate, to be human, to have a body. Bodies aren't sacred, are they? Bodies hurt and break. They feel pain and die. Who needs a god like that?

And so they walk away.

The disciples who departed wanted a god who is not physical, a god free of the body, free of the pain that humans endure, a god who can protect them from the pain of being human, of having a body.

And instead Jesus told them he is the son of God and a human being who feels pain. So some of them went away. And Jesus looked at the ones who stayed and said, "What are you still doing here?"

Helpless, they looked back at him, and they said, "Where else would we go?"

The story is not foreign to us. We all know people who've walked away when God turned out not to be what they thought, when God couldn't fix the pain of being human and loving other people.

I've spent this week looking for meaning. I've been trying to think through what is really important, what really matters. I'm making a list, and I'm surprised at how many things on it have to do with incarnation, with our existence as physical beings—the very thing Jesus named to his followers, the very reason some of them walked away.

Here's my list of what has meaning:

* Getting home from a trip where you've fallen asleep in the car and your dad carrying you upstairs to bed
* The feeling of your mom's arms around you when you're sitting on her lap
* Holding a baby and feeling its heavy sleeping weight on your chest, molding itself into your bones and heart and lungs
* Holding someone's hand
* Rubbing someone's head
* Falling asleep with someone you love
* Sex in the depths of a committed relationship, where the other person's well-being is as sacred to you as your own
* Bumping shoulders with someone—I do this with my brothers and a few other people; it's the only language we have for voicing our affection.

After I worked on my list for a long time, I looked it over and thought, *Isn't that funny? God isn't anywhere on it.* But after I thought about it for a few minutes, I realized that God is everywhere on it, all over it and through it, because who we are, who and how we are with each other, who we are as people with bodies—that was Jesus' message: In these bodies and in the way we touch each other lies the holy.

Jesus says you can't keep the pain away. That's what the disciples who walked away couldn't stand to hear. Jesus turned to the ones who stayed and asked, "Why are you still here?"

And they answered, "Where else would we go? We've lived life the other way—tried dumbing down, tried futility—but nothing else works. Your way may be painful, but at least we're not numb. With you we have life."

That is the great news. Jesus didn't offer us a dream world where everything is just hunky-dory, thank you very much, and we don't have any pain. Jesus offered us life to *live as* we are, in all our humanness, in all our sadness, in our pain, lived in these bodies. That is the life Jesus honored and made sacred and offers us love in the midst of.

And for that we say, "Thanks be to God." Amen.

Death is an absolute condition for the one who dies, but for those left behind, the story of one who has loved deeply and been loved deeply never stops resonating. You have to grow into the loss, its depth, breadth, and heft; the smell, touch, and taste; the tones, notes, and rests of absence. The growth is slow, and painful, and inconsistent, and required.

I'd called Perry Miller, my Clinical Pastoral Education supervisor, the night Chris told me his blood-test results were suspicious, because I knew I needed assistance to steer myself and the congregation through the coming pain. Perry and I met throughout the fall. His upstairs office had one large window that opened into the high branches of a tree. To the background music of a small fountain and a large fan, I watched squirrels wander the branches, and I monitored the passage of time by the falling of leaves from the tree as August trudged into September and September into October. Perry and I talked about Chris, Fred, my parents, the children, the church; and about isolation, insulation, and abandonment.

I kept meeting with Perry because I wanted to learn how to live no matter what happened next. I was hunting for my own center, the space of safety and security and happiness that could sustain me. I didn't know then about pianos, didn't know the task in tuning is to balance the opposing tensions so carefully that they are still and so that from within the stillness, in Anita T. Sullivan's words, "music can spin its way through into our dimension."

At the time I didn't think of myself as a piano and of Perry as a tuner. My controlling metaphors back then had to do with buildings, foundations, keystones, and cracks. I knew if the cracks in my building weren't repaired, a good earthquake or two would knock me down. And I knew earthquakes were coming. People die. People do die. People will die. Parents, siblings, spouse—they will all die. And sometimes the direction of death isn't from above or sideways; sometimes it's downward: children, grandchildren.

I told Perry of an interview in the September/October issue of a magazine called *Alive Now* with a United Methodist clergy couple in Alabama, Kelly and Dale Clem. During the Palm Sunday worship service in 1994, a tornado destroyed the sanctuary of Kelly's church. Twenty people were killed, one of them the Clems' daughter Hannah. She was four years old. Dale said in the interview that "there were people in the city who said immediately that the reason the tornado hit that church was because it had a woman minister."

"Who wants to be part of Christianity if people can use it to say such a thing?" I asked.

"I don't know, but I think the church is too small for you," Perry answered.

"But I got ordained so I could pastor a church."

"Imagine a larger church, where you'd have more room."

"It wouldn't help. A larger church would be the same thing, with more and different faces."

                    ▲   ▲   ▲

Morning after morning I wrote in my journal, in surprise, "I'm still very sad." Sad about Chris. Sad that my children were grown and my husband was now sixty-two and I was forty-eight and chances were he would die before me. Sad about the church's limitations, and about my own. Sad at the futility of my work, because no matter who performed a funeral service, how well or poorly they did it, at the end the person would still be dead and still be buried.

Six weeks after Chris died, I was halfway home after seeing Perry, when it struck me that I was suffering from the human condition. And then: *Sweet Jesus, that's my problem: I'm suffering from the human condition. Human beings love other human beings, all of whom are going to die, and we love life, which we are going to lose.*

Inexplicably, the thought lifted my spirits. Death, pain, sorrow, frustration, disappointment, all those things are the human experience, as much as and as surely a part of who we are as birth, joy, serenity, peace, and pleasure. The maze in which I walked was not of my construction; rather, I was making my way through the bushes and brambles of the human condition. And if the biggest problem I have, and the source of my sadness, is that I am a human being, then there is no solution, nothing to be fixed, nothing to be done . . . although, I reflected, if asked I would tell people not to have children, because as adults we know too much. We know too much about why our parents failed, because it's the same reason we fail as parents and the same reason our children will fail as parents. We fail because there is no chance of success. We are doomed, and we all long for Eden, the place that doom forgot, or for heaven, the place that doom has never known.

In this life, neither Eden nor heaven is an option. There is only now. There is only here. There is nothing but this moment.

Kelly Clem, when asked whether the experience at the Alabama church had changed her as a pastor, replied, "I'm less patient with petty stuff and power struggles that go on in the church, not only in the local church but in the denomination. . . . It's not worth my energy."

That's how I felt: it wasn't worth my energy. I concluded that the most important task of life was to live well in the present, and that the most important element of the present was Fred. I'd given little energy to our relationship in the years of seminary and pastoring. I started wondering what he might like from me. It didn't occur to me to ask him, either because by nature I'm too self-absorbed, or because I knew if he'd wanted something, he'd have already told me. Fred and I know how to tell each other what we want and need and would like. We practiced the skill throughout our marriage, and we reached perfection my first year as a pastor. There was some confusion at first: many models exist for being a clergy wife, but very few people have been clergy husbands. We had to make it all up as we went along: what did I expect from him? what did the congregation expect? what did he expect from me?

We worked out our method one day when I was on my way to a funeral home for visitation.

"Am I supposed to go with you?" he asked. "Do I need to go?"

I was already dressed in my suit, keys in my hand, and had given him a kiss on my way out to the garage. "No, you can stay here. When I need you to go with me, I'll tell you."

I could have asked Fred what he wanted, but it felt important for me to take the time to think the question through on my own. Finally I concluded he'd like me to go to bed at the same time he did every night (rather than staying up late to read or write, falling asleep on the couch, and wandering in to the bedroom at dawn to warm my chilled body against his) and that he'd be happy if I baked peanut-butter cookies or a coconut cake once in a while. So simple. So little.

We are so very different, Fred and I. He was born on February 1,

1935. He is five feet ten inches tall and weighs 180 pounds. He has straight, fine blond hair and blue eyes of the shade that make you trust every word he utters. The collars on his dress shirts are sixteen inches. The sleeves are thirty-three inches. He looks wonderful in black, white, khaki, and sky blue. Fred's favorite hymn is "I Would Be True" because when he was a child his mother led evening devotions that concluded with the whole group—her, her children, her children's friends from the neighborhood—singing that hymn. One of the statements Fred makes with annoying regularity is "There's a reason for that."

I was born on September 2, 1949. I'm five feet seven inches tall and admit to weighing the universal driver's license weight for women over forty, which is 135 pounds. I have naturally curly brown hair and green eyes. I look fabulous in black, white, and turquoise. My favorite hymn is "Lord of the Dance" because it's the only song I know that's strong enough to sing into the face of death. One of the statements I make with annoying regularity is "I'm thinking. As soon as I figure it out, I'll let you know."

The two parts of Fred's body that I love best, not counting his penis, are his wrist bones and the hollow just above his right collarbone. I fell in love with the hollow above his collarbone so slowly that I didn't even recognize it as love for the first ten or fifteen years. Fred and I are just the right heights so that when I step close into his body and his arms encircle me, my nose fits naturally against that hollow and I can breathe in his elemental nature: pulse, skin, heat, bone. I love breathing him in.

I reached one firm conclusion: I wanted more time with Fred.

chapter fifteen

HOLY COMMUNION OPERATES IN SACRAMENTAL TIME and space, which is different from regular time and space. Any time you take communion, you're taking it with everybody, everywhere, any time, any place across the centuries, living or dead, who has ever taken communion.

If that sounds ghoulish to you, it's because you aren't God. One of the joys in being God is that you get to do a few things exactly the way you want to do them, and the hell with physics. The way God chooses to operate sacramental time doesn't require a clock because there is no beginning and no end.

As I selected the texts for the first Sunday in October, the tenet that I would be taking communion along with Jesus, John Wesley, Elizabeth Cady Stanton, Martin Luther King, Jr., and Terry's parents didn't seem like such a good thing, because Chris Flynn was dead, and yet he would be partaking of communion with us. At our last communion service, we'd watched Chris rocking on his feet a bit, the plate trembling in his hand, as he offered the body of Christ. Back then everything was still possible. He was getting stronger, working, heading for the golf course. How were we going to contend with the changed reality?

I tried to convince myself I'd be fine, that I'm a professional, that I could carry on as though nothing were missing and carry the congregation with me. But here's the thing: I didn't want to carry on as though nothing were missing. I wanted to honor the memory of who Chris was with us and who we were with him—but to do so meant touching wounds that had not yet scabbed over, let alone healed.

I did the only thing I could think of to do. I called Alva, Chris's father.

"Alva, we're having communion on Sunday, and I need you to serve the bread."

I listened to the silence of Alva remembering.

Then he whispered thickly, "I don't think I can do that."

I wanted to release him from the obligation, but I was choking on tears. "I don't think I can get through it without you," I whispered back.

More silence.

"I'll do it then. Somehow."

▲   ▲   ▲

Somehow, together, we did.

When I nodded to Alva at the beginning of the ritual and waited for him to join me behind the altar, I was peripherally aware of the congregation's response: a gasp, and then recognition flowing in, and then an exhalation. I have no other memory of the service except that at its conclusion Alva went to the altar rail and knelt in prayer. I observed his bowed head for a few measures of the closing hymn, and then I followed, knelt beside him, and linked my arm through his. Neither of us spoke. I believe we were both trembling.

When he rose, Alva whispered to me, "Thank you."

▲   ▲   ▲

By mid-October I was reconciled to the knowledge that there was nothing I could do about the future, that my task was to live well within the present. My thoughts had been churning like a river during a torrential storm. Now some days they felt more like a quiet river spotted with shade, the waters sparkling over rocks.

In the quiet I did the math. If I retired from pastoring at age sixty-five, Fred would be seventy-eight. Would he still be well enough for us to go places and do things? Would he still even be alive? Did I really want to spend what we had left of life together focused on sermons, committee meetings, and death, a bystander to our life? Was that what I wanted? I'd stood in the hospital room as Chris lay dying, the oxygen turned up full blast, Kathy nestled against him on the bed, the rest of us changing positions as though we were dancers in a perfectly choreographed sacred dance. Some day, if the actuarial tables held, I would be engaged in that dance once again, but Fred would be in the hospital bed instead of Chris, and I would be playing the role not of pastor but of wife.

When that day came, I wanted to know I had savored every moment of life with Fred.

But how? How do you savor life, how savor another human being, especially when one person is Fred and the other me, two people who had always balanced deep intimacy with distance?

Months earlier I'd registered for a conference in San Francisco. I was supposed to fly out alone, but now I decided Fred and I should take a road trip together. We could visit my sister, Amy, in Arizona and go from there to Los Angeles, where Fred could visit relatives while I caught a plane to San Francisco for my conference.

The church and I were in a state of mutual fragility. We'd been through so much with Chris, loved so much, lost so much, that even though we were just as busy—in fact, we'd begun a campaign to raise $50,000, a thousand dollars for each year of existence, by the church's fiftieth anniversary in August—the rough edges had all disappeared. And so, when I told the personnel committee my plans, I simply explained that we'd have to be gone two full weeks because on retirement Fred had vowed he'd never board another plane. "The real reason we're driving, though, is that I haven't talked to my husband in five years."

The three committee members in attendance laughed and applauded. "Go. You and Fred go. Relax. Enjoy yourselves."

Fred wasn't enamored with the idea, but he couldn't come up with any good reasons for refusing, so in November I loaded the backseat of the car with six months' worth of back issues of *The New Yorker* and *The Christian Century,* an annotated Bible and three scholarly commentaries in case I wanted to work on Advent sermons, legal pads, pencils, pens, and three mystery novels, variety enough to keep me engaged when I wasn't driving.

I didn't read a word. For the first two days, as we drove through Georgia, Alabama, Tennessee, and Arkansas, I talked nonstop, rambling on about the church and new projects and what I might do for the Christmas-Day worship service. On the third day, somewhere in the middle of Oklahoma, I finally stopped talking. I stopped thinking, too. I simply looked out the car window.

Oklahoma is not known for its scenic vistas. The terrain matches my favorite foods: coffee, cocoa, chocolate, almonds, and oatmeal, highlighted with dashes of tapioca pudding. Looking out across the emptiness, I felt as though the past were behind us, the future ahead of us, and the present somewhere far beyond the confines of our car. Sick to death of living in the present, I was glad it was outside the car, where it couldn't touch us. I wanted us to drive through Oklahoma forever.

We couldn't stop time, of course. We reached the western border of Oklahoma and pushed across the Texas panhandle, pausing in Amarillo, Texas, for repairs on the car. There was snow on the ground in Gallup, New Mexico, and heavy rain blocked our view when we detoured to see the Painted Desert in Arizona. I lavished songs of geography on Fred: "Old Man River," "Oklahoma," "The Old Chisholm Trail," "Abilene," "Luckenbach, Texas."

We reached Amy's house outside Kingman, Arizona, late Friday afternoon and kicked back. We made two sightseeing trips, one to the Route 66 Museum, the other to Wal-Mart; we helped her put out Christmas decorations; we visited some antique shops. In the evenings Amy kept a close watch on the time and sent us outside at the right moment so Fred and I could watch the big-sky sunsets, 360 degrees of light and color.

After a few days we drove on to Los Angeles ("California, Here I Come," "I Left My Heart in San Francisco"). There we went to an Italian restaurant and sat across from the actor who played Mr. Roper in the television series *Three's Company* and three booths away from the comedian Andrew Dice Clay, who was jotting notes for a new routine on a napkin and then calling over the waiter to try out the lines on him.

Saturday, I flew alone to San Francisco. I'd been seduced into attending the conference by the colors on the brochure—black, cobalt blue, and hot pink—and by the title: *Holy Boldness*. When I'd registered, Chris was regaining strength after his bone-marrow transplant, and I believed boldness was a good thing. My conviction sagged when Chris died. I hoped the conference would invigorate me.

I dropped my luggage in my room at the Marriott, rode an elevator down to the lobby and an escalator down another level, went to the conference registration desk, picked up my packet, and then stepped out of the flow of traffic to take a good look around the room. Around me surged a sea of somber suits and earnest expressions. There were no signs of hot pink or cobalt blue, of joy or power.

The conviction shuddered through me that I was wasting my time—an entire weekend of my precious life—at a conference where nobody was likely to say anything I didn't already know, and where people would speak with passion and urgency about the need for strong ministers and strong ministries. I no longer believed a word of it. From what I had seen, the task the Church prefers, and is best at, is burying the dead. It's an honorable task, but I had already done my fair share of burials.

My life had lost its meaning. I could no longer tell the difference between the trivial and the holy. I didn't know which was more important, the water that ran through my fingers when I performed a baptism or the pair of black oxfords now cramping my toes. I couldn't attest any longer that serving communion was any more urgent or necessary or productive a task than staring out a car window at the Oklahoma plains. The core beliefs that made pastoring an honorable endeavor had slipped away.

And here's the oddest thing: It felt like a redemption.

Fred and I drove the southern route home: Phoenix, Tucson, El Paso. At two in the afternoon on Thanksgiving Day, we drove through Fort Worth and Dallas, an unsettling experience because the interstate was as empty as a mall parking lot at midnight.

"Do you think one of those bombs exploded that kills everybody but leaves the buildings standing?" I asked.

"It's possible, but more likely everybody's either eating turkey or watching a football game."

We ate that evening in a Cracker Barrel restaurant. Fred went with tradition: turkey, dressing, cranberries. I ordered scrambled eggs and hash browns. It was the first time in thirty years I hadn't prepared Thanksgiving dinner, and I'd decided if I were going to break with tradition I'd do it wholeheartedly.

We'd started on dessert when Fred said, "I've found out one really good thing on this trip."

"What's that?"

"I found out that I still really like you."

My eyes were sparkling back into his when I said, "That's good. I still really like you, too."

What better benediction can there be to a vacation?

▲   ▲   ▲

Our children were disgruntled on our return home.

"It was all well and good that the two of you took a vacation," said one. "But from now on, don't do it in November."

"Thanksgiving was fine," said another mournfully. "Some friends knew I was a Thanksgiving orphan, so they invited me to their house to eat."

"Oh, don't worry about it," said a third. "You can be gone over Thanksgiving whenever you want to as long as you buy all the food and put it in the refrigerator and leave the door unlocked. That way we can still all meet at your house, and we won't have to go to the grocery store, and we won't have to wash dishes alone."

Some members of the church were unhappy as well. I'd missed the annual community Thanksgiving worship service, as well as two Sundays in the pulpit. How much vacation time did I get? Isn't a preacher supposed to be in the pulpit rather than gallivanting off to California? Why wasn't I there doing my job?

I had little energy (and less interest) to give to their questions. Lightning had struck near the parsonage two days after Fred and I left for California. One result was a pinhole leak in the water pipe leading into the washing machine. When we unlocked the kitchen door of the parsonage we found three inches of standing water on the now-warped kitchen floor; saturated carpet in the den, living room, and hallway; and the stink of mold.

The repair people told us the house would be uninhabitable for at least six to eight weeks. It was December. Christmas was coming. We had five children, none of whom lived in town and three of whom had spouses. We had four grandchildren. All of them would be home for the holidays.

We spent days loading the trunks and backseats of our cars with clothes, shoes, books, pots and pans, the microwave, the computer, and other important items to haul home.

We never moved back into the parsonage.

▲   ▲   ▲

Throughout Advent I sorted out my future. What now? Where was I to go from here?

I was clear on one thing: I was not going to request a leave of absence. Not again. This time I'd find an option that didn't require I explain myself to a disapproving committee.

While I was sorting out my future, the sermons I was preaching were sorting out my spiritual life in the present. One Sunday, my sermon illustration was Berkeley Breathed's book *A Wish for Wings that Work.* Breathed is the cartoonist who created Opus the penguin, Bill the cat, and a number of other characters who wrestle with theological questions as often as not.

Opus can't fly. He's a penguin, and he's not structured for flight. But he has two wings, and he'd really like to fly, so he writes a letter to Santa and asks for wings that work. On Christmas Eve, Santa's sleigh breaks down and plunges into a lake. Snow ducks who live in the neighborhood rouse Opus from his bed. Opus jumps in the lake and swims, "strong and fast, through the icy water, a wonderful, roaring, graceful torpedo" to rescue Santa and the sleigh. The next morning Opus wakes to find his lawn full of snow ducks. The final illustration is of Opus borne aloft by the snow ducks. He is laughing. He is flying.

The Opus story is like the Christmas story: The gift of the baby Jesus wasn't the gift people thought they wanted. People then, as now, want more impressive gifts: CD players, blue bicycles with chrome, wealth, power.

God doesn't always give us the gift we want. One person might want to be a poet and realize with time that their real gift is to be a pastor. Another person might want to be a pastor and realize with time that their real gift is as a poet. To live into the gift of Jesus means living into the gifts God gave us.

I read the book to Molly, my friend and comrade in ministry, over the telephone that afternoon. Halfway through, she stopped me.

"No."

"What?"

"No. I don't want Opus to have some other gift. I want him to get wings that work for Christmas." I think she was crying.

"Oh, Molly, so do I. But that's not how the story goes."

Molly and I were luckier than Opus. Our wings worked; we had the gift of flight; we wanted to keep flying, to continue in the excitement of seeing our churches stabilize and grow, in the wonder of sitting with sad or frightened people and by our natures telling them something rare about the nature of God; in the amazement of seeing faces transformed by the goodness and mercy of the God we worship. For all the idiocies, we loved our work, but within a month Molly would leave her pastorate and five months later I would leave mine, too. So tell me this: which is worse, to have wings that don't work or to have working wings but no sky in which to fly?

The next day, Monday, December 22, we got a phone call saying Fred's best friend, Leonard, was dead. Leonard and Fred had played golf together two, sometimes three, times a week for eight years. Fred frequently came home from the country club with new Leonard stories, mostly about how he'd bought another new golf club and sworn his golf mates to secrecy. "He said his wife will kill him if she finds out," Fred would tell me.

I knew Leonard's wife. I didn't much believe he had any secrets she hadn't already figured out.

Leonard's funeral was on Tuesday. Wednesday night, Christmas Eve, I woke up in the middle of the night with the flu. Still awake at daybreak, I called the church lay leader to ask him to lead the Christmas Day worship service. I spent Christmas huddled under blankets on the couch while around me the children and grandchildren opened presents and played. Four days later my grandmother, the one in England with whom I'd corresponded from the month I learned to write in cursive until the month she forgot how to write in cursive, died. That night I went to visitation at a funeral home—the elderly mother of a member of the congregation had died—and, for once, instead of standing in line, I went straight to the family to offer my condolences so that I could hurry home to where my own sorrow awaited me.

On January 10, my daughters' paternal grandmother, my ex-husband's mother, the first person I ever met who dipped snuff, died, and my sad daughters came to my house.

It was deep midwinter, and grief was falling, grief on grief without end, amen, and Chris Flynn was still dead, and so was my grandmother, and yet the world went on. I tired to prod myself out of the doldrums by signing up for a course on creativity and the arts at a local university. The class combined hands-on art projects with both a theoretical and a practical examination of creativity. One week, the assignment was to answer the question, "If you could do anything on earth, what would it be?"

My answers spilled out: I'd compete in the Olympics in the luge so I could smell the ice, feel the wind, and whoosh around the track. I'd own a horse farm in Oklahoma, where I'd complain about the weather, breathe deeply, and look out across the fields. I'd be a nuclear physicist and explain the mysteries of time to theologians, or a lumberjack so I could scamper up trees, figure out exactly where they should fall, hack away while the chips fell, and then watch the tree fall—*whack! kaboom!*—exactly where I'd said it would.

I could almost feel my synapses sparking. To think, to imagine, to dream: I'd nearly forgotten how. This isn't to say there was no intellectual or imaginative challenge in sermon preparation, but the challenges arose within tight boundaries: the biblical texts determined themes, and both Church tradition and cultural norms determined my conclusions. It was like being a Maserati in a rose garden, afraid to shift out of Park because I would disturb the American Beauties. Until now, I hadn't recognized my own intellectual stultification, nor had I acknowledged the curtailment of intellectual freedom implicit within the demands of pastoring. In writing a weekly sermon, I'd learned to ignore any questions I came up with that were too complex to be addressed in four double-spaced pages. I had the same problem newscasters face: some issues, some events, some ideas can't be reduced to a sound-bite, not even a twenty-minute sound-bite. After a while, I lost the habit of raising questions, even to myself, that didn't fit the exigencies of the job.

You hear a lot about sacrificial giving from religious people. Some of the talk is authentic, but some is manipulative, intended to keep people in their place ("You don't like your job? Don't you know the ordained ministry requires sacrificial giving?"). I'd questioned my own motivations, wondered if my desire to move into another form of ordained ministry indicated a failure—of goodness, of commitment, of responsibility. Studying learning theorists, experimenting with art and my own creativity, I resolved any twitches of guilt. Whatever God wanted for me, it wasn't a self-lobotomization—nor was it an emotional shutdown, which I'd also achieved.

I knew I'd lost my emotional connection in January when I buried the third young person in three years. This young man was older than the other two—he was forty—but he had a wife and a child in first grade. His dying was different as well—not a lingering illness but a sudden massive heart attack while he was at work. I didn't know him as well as I knew the others, but I knew his son very well; a hearty and affectionate child, the boy had once proclaimed to me, "I'm going to be here every Sunday FOR THE REST OF MY LIFE." So things were both different and the same about this death, but what was most different was me.

I don't know that anybody but Fred recognized the change. "Are you all right?" he asked me several times that week. "Are you sure you're all right?"

I was, and I wasn't. I was my usual careful, connected self, spending time with the family and especially the child, giving my usual painstaking attention to the funeral meditation, regretting just as deeply the truncation of a life. What didn't show, except to Fred, was my absence of tenderness. I'd locked it into a closet hidden at the back of my emotional staircase. My friends who'd urged me early on to separate my emotions from the job would have been pleased if I'd told them. It may have been the greatest achievement of my pastoral career. The only problem was that I counted it as loss, because I didn't want to live this way. I had become less of myself, not more, a certain contradiction of the gospel. Worst of all, I no longer knew what was trivial and what, if anything, was redemptive.

By February I was intent on putting my life in order. I plunged into emptying the reams of paper in the file cabinet, arranging the photo albums on the bottom shelf of the living-room bookcases, calling Joe Turner to come tune the piano, and wondering what to do with the damn piano once it was tuned. As it happened, Joe tuned the piano the same week I told the congregation I'd be leaving in June. Rumors were spreading; I didn't want the information restricted to those few people who had wheedled the information out of the personnel committee members.

That Sunday morning I took to the church the only item Fred received when his mother broke up housekeeping prior to moving to a rest home: a bun warmer consisting of a wicker basket and a yellow quilted-cotton hen with a red beak that fit over the basket. Into the bun warmer I put a purple plastic egg in which I'd place twenty fuzzball chicks—a dime each from a cake-decorating store. Come time for the sermon, I lifted the bun warmer high and said, in the same phrasing used for flowers on the altar, "The chicken on the altar this morning is to the glory of God." I extricated the purple egg and took it to the pulpit.

The day's lectionary text was from the thirteenth chapter of Luke. A group of solicitous religious leaders, Pharisees, came to warn Jesus that

Herod wanted him dead. Jesus was not frightened. Instead, he said, "Go and tell that fox for me, 'Listen, I am casting out demons and performing cures. . . . Yet, today, tomorrow, and the next day I must be on my way, because it is impossible for a prophet to be killed outside Jerusalem.'" Breaking off, he mourned, "Jerusalem, Jerusalem, the city that kills the prophets and stones those who are sent to it! How often have I desired to gather your children together as a hen gathers her brood under her wings, and you were not willing."

The scene is being set for Jesus' crucifixion, *I said to the congregation.* The three major players are on stage. The first is Herod, the fox, a predator both sly and destructive. The second player is Jesus, the life giver, the one who cast out demons and cured people's illnesses and claimed the kingdom of God as here and now and yet to come. The third player isn't a person; it's a city, the city of Jerusalem, the place where prophets are killed, the setting for the crucifixion.

Herod's goal is to keep Jesus from doing the work he's called to do. Herod thinks he's in control, but he isn't. He can't stop Jesus, because Jesus isn't controlled by Herod. Jesus is controlled by his faithfulness to God.

And then we find that amazing, life-giving statement where Jesus compares himself and God to a chicken. It isn't the only time in the Bible that God is compared to a bird. Deuteronomy speaks of God as an eagle stirring up its nest and hovering over its young. Psalm 91 says that under God's wings we will find refuge. Isaiah says that, like the birds hovering overhead, so will God protect Jerusalem. That's God: hovering over us, offering refuge, protecting. Jerusalem is in a time of great danger, and Jesus is saying that one of God's deep desires is to protect the community.

The image of God as a chicken, specifically a mother hen, gives us a glimpse of who God is and how God sees us.

How many of you have ever raised chickens? *I asked. A few hands went up.*

Well, then, you'll understand what I'm getting ready to say. When people hear about Jesus sheltering Jerusalem like a hen shelters its chicks, most people probably picture sweet, fluffy, well-behaved baby chicks, don't you think? But people who've been around chickens know better, don't we? *By this time, the people who'd raised chickens were snickering.*

We're an exclusive society, chicken farmers past and present. I'm a chicken farmer past. When I was growing up, my family raised Leghorns, white chickens that produce white-shelled eggs. My father built cages for them and installed a watering system, but in the winter the system often froze out. I'd carry buckets of water, and the water would slosh over the side and down into my red boots. To this day I believe that the only good chicken is a fried chicken, but that doesn't change the fact that I loved the days that fifty peeping chicks arrived for us at the local post office in a waxed box studded with airholes.

Baby chicks are delicate souls committed to freezing to death if possible, an outcome that seemed likely the year the electricity cable from the mainland to the island was cut by shifting ice on the lake. It happened that a box of chicks had arrived the day before.

My father carried half of a small wooden rowboat—the front half, if I remember correctly—into the kitchen. I don't know why we had half a rowboat in the backyard, but it certainly came in handy. My mother blocked off the open end, covered the top with a large piece of cardboard, and anchored it in place with something heavy, probably a box of laundry detergent.

That method for keeping the chicks safe and warm worked well right up until the chicks developed pin feathers. Until then, they stayed in the boat, either running around tripping over each other and peeping their heads off, or sleeping in one big fuzzy heap in which the weakest always suffocated. The day their pin feathers arrived, though, everything changed. Now they could fly.

When my mother slid the cardboard cover back to feed and water the chicks, they erupted over the sides of the rowboat and flowed in every direction: under the stove, behind the washing machine, into the dining room. Our cat George, who was napping in his favorite spot on a chair pushed under the dining-room table, stuck his head out from under the tablecloth to see what was happening. In the same moment the front door opened, and my father walked in with Nick, our dog, who was clearly thrilled to have arrived home at such an interesting time.

This is what the chickens looked like.

I reached into the purple plastic egg, picked up a yellow fuzzball, and lofted it toward a woman sitting in a front pew. I picked up another fuzzball, and another, and another. I flung chicks to the left of me, chicks to the right of me, chicks behind me into the choir loft, and chicks straight ahead toward the acolytes' feet. I pitched chicks as though they were popcorn kernels and I was hot grease in a lidless pot.

Jesus knew about poultry, *I said when I ran out of chicks.* So when he said he wanted to shelter Jerusalem like a hen shelters its chicks, he was talking about the way both chicks, and people, panic and run like mad.

Do you see now that God sees us in that same way, sees us racing around down here with no idea where we're going, with cats and dogs and foxes all ready to take advantage of our frenzy?

Today's text promises us that the God we worship is not only a re-deeming God; the God we worship is a protecting God as well.

I paused to breathe, to center myself, and to create a stillness that would focus the congregation on my next words.

I'm using this text and these chickens this morning because I have something important to tell you. I'll be leaving in June, and you'll be get-ting a new pastor. I've applied to graduate schools to get another degree, and I'm waiting to hear if the bishop is going to approve an appointment for me to attend school.

I spoke of the time of transition ahead and of the emotions congre-gations experience when a pastor departs: sadness, relief, anger, guilt, and fear. I said we'd be doing a funny little dance together over the com-ing months, a dance of love and separation, that I wasn't all that good a dancer but I wanted us to do it well enough together that at the end they'd be free to invent a new dance with their new pastor.

I spoke of the choices facing us and told about a friend who was now pregnant after a series of miscarriages. She didn't know whether to celebrate or not, because if she celebrated and then miscarried, she'd cry. I wrote her a note a few days later telling her that I'd decided to cele-brate because, while I was willing to take the risk of crying, I wasn't willing to miss the celebration.

So here's the first thing I want you to know: Here and now is a time to celebrate. The second thing I want you to know is that God's grace is suffi-cient for this transition. For fifty years God has protected this church like a mother hen gathering chicks under its wings. God's wings have sheltered church members whether they're here or off in college or in the service in Okinawa, in life and in death. It is the truth Jesus proclaimed in his life, in Galilee and in Jerusalem, in his death on the cross, and in the resurrection promise of life everlasting.

God has kept us safe this far, and God will lead us home. Amen.

The cynical view of sermons is that one person stands up in the pulpit and casts pearls he or she has gathered toward the assembled mass, who may or may not want them. That's not how it works, really. Sermons are conversations. Granted, the preacher gets to do all the talking, but the congregation participates as clearly as if they were speaking. They converse by gazing at the preacher or at the floor, by lounging in the pews or leaning forward, by their rustles and their stillness. The pattern of their breath is a part of the conversation, as is the pattern of their facial muscles: tension, relaxation, wonder, sorrow, peace. There's a third party to the conversation, too: that would be God. At least, God will be there if the tensions are balanced well enough to make room for God. If not, everybody would be better off getting drunk Saturday night and sleeping in Sunday morning. But when there's room, when the preacher is listening both for God and to the congregation, and when the congregation is listening both for God and to the preacher—well, on those days you have a sermon.

I had half a sermon the day I announced my departure. The second half got lost because, although the congregation seemed willing to listen, they kept retreating into themselves. They looked to be puzzling out a question, and an answer, they couldn't quite articulate. Nobody said much as they left.

"We knew this time would come," said one person.

"I'll miss you," said another.

Some said merely, "Well," with the distinctive drawn-out southern intonation that means "I wasn't expecting this, and I don't know quite what to make of it."

▲   ▲   ▲

Fred had already changed from his suit into blue jeans and a golf shirt when I got home. "You did it," he said.

"I did."

"It was a good sermon. I just wish you hadn't had to preach it."

"Me too. Do you know what's awful? I can't wait for Moving Day to get here, but now that it's official, I can hardly bear the thought of leaving."

Molly called that afternoon. When she left her pastorate, we'd decided to throw a joint party when I left mine. "Can we set the date now?" she wanted to know.

"Not yet. I'm too sad."

Molly's silence carries more kindness than most people's speeches. After a minute she said, "I know. I remember. The same thing happened to me."

Ambivalence is a stern partner, requiring honesty from you whether you want to give it or not, pressing you to understand your own emotions. What my ambivalence taught me is that while I'd have chewed my right leg off to get away from the local church, I'd have given my left leg to have been able to stay.

chapter sixteen

———

A GOSPEL TRIO WAS PERFORMING AT THE CHURCH, AND Brian Mallory had been invited to play during intermission. As he approached the piano, I noticed he walked with the sureness of foot children have, as though they're growing out of the earth's core. It's a walk most of us lose long before adulthood. After the concert we gathered in the basement social hall for refreshments. I looked across the buffet table laden with ham biscuits, pimiento cheese sandwiches, three kinds of potato salad, pea salad, deviled eggs, pistachio salad, pound cake, chocolate cake, pecan pie, banana pudding, and at least five varieties of cookies and saw Brian on the other side.

"Good job tonight."

"Thanks. What's that?" Brian asked, nodding toward the sandwich I was lifting onto my plate.

"An asparagus sandwich. You'd better get one before they're gone. They're really good."

"What's in them?"

"Asparagus spears, with mayonnaise on both sides of the bread."

He shook his head. "I think I'll pass. Thanks anyhow."

We found chairs together at a table covered with a pink plastic tablecloth with a milk-glass vase of silk pansies as its centerpiece. While we were eating, I asked if he gave piano lessons.

"Do I give lessons? Yes. Why do you ask?"

"Because I need to learn to play the piano."

"Why do you need to learn to play?"

"Because I just found out the piano in my living room is worth ten thousand dollars."

"What?"

"I had the Yamaha at my house tuned a few weeks ago, and the tuner said it's worth ten thousand dollars."

"Is that the only reason you want to learn to play?"

"I think so." There were more reasons, but how much do you want to confide to a stranger?

"Have you taken piano lessons before?"

I was chasing a bit of banana around my bowl of banana pudding with my spoon and retrieved it before I answered him. "No. Is that a problem?"

"No. What kind of music do you want to play?"

"I don't know enough about music to answer that question."

"Not a problem."

"Oh. So will you teach me?"

"Sure. When do you want to start?"

▴   ▴   ▴

My first lesson was on Thursday, March 19, 1998, at 9:30. At about eight-fifteen that morning, Fred looked up from the crossword puzzle he was working in the newspaper.

"What are you doing?" he asked.

"Fixing a cup of coffee."

"Was the one over here not any good?"

On the table beside his elbow was a mug of coffee, with milk. Fred drinks his black with half a spoon of sugar.

"Is that mine?" I asked.

"Yes."

"Is it warm?"

"It should be. You set it down here a minute ago, just before you put that cup of water in the microwave to heat."

"Oh."

I turned the microwave off and joined Fred at the table. He wrote another word into the puzzle before he glanced up at me. "You're a little distracted this morning. You're not nervous about the piano lesson, are you?"

"I must be."

The truth is I was afraid of the piano. I wasn't a musical person. I'd taken guitar lessons when my daughters were young, but all I learned were the names of the notes in the treble clef and that I had no ear for music. Then, too, the guitar had six strings. If I couldn't manipulate six strings, how could my fingers manage eighty-eight keys?

The world of music felt off-limits, like farmland posted with a sign saying, NO TRESPASSING. VIOLATORS WILL BE SHOT. I thought musical performance was reserved for people anointed in utero as musicians. I was not one of them. To take lessons I'd have to push my way, without invitation, onto their property.

My resolve to put the piano to use might have evaporated like a New Year's resolution if it hadn't been for Howard Gardner, one of the theorists I studied in a learning-theories class. Gardner's a professor of education at Harvard University and an adjunct professor of neurology at the Boston University School of Medicine. For twenty-five years, as Gardner says in the preface to his book *Creating Minds,* his research area has been the way "artistic capabilities develop or atrophy within our own and others' cultures." Gardner has studied normal children, gifted children, and people with brain damage. He's crossed cultures and even species in his attempt to document how human brains take in and respond to information. He's used both classroom settings and laboratories (where he utilized brain scans and other measuring instruments) in his research.

Gardner holds that intelligence isn't one solid block like a bar of gold bullion. Rather, it's like a bag of gold dust—or, as he puts it, "an ensemble of relatively autonomous faculties." He calls these autonomous faculties "multiple intelligences." He's documented eight of them through cross-cultural and cross-species research. The first three intelligences are familiar: linguistic (language and communication skills), logical-mathematical (sequential, algebraic skills), and spatial (the sorts of things people learn, or don't, in geometry class). These skills are the ones IQ tests and S.A.T. exams purport to measure and are often regarded as the totality of intelligence.

Gardner says that view of intelligence is too limited. He says we have at least five more intelligences: bodily kinesthetic, which is the ability to use your body to solve problems; interpersonal, which has to do with understanding other people; intrapersonal, which has to do with understanding yourself; naturalist, which is a sensitivity to plants, the weather, rocks, the entirety of creation outside the limitations of the human body; and musical intelligence, the capacity to hear and remember patterns in music.

Gardner believes all eight intelligences will increase if they're nurtured. People don't have to be stuck in one place. We can actually learn.

Now, I know people can learn. I myself that same month had watched five second-graders learn to light the candles on the altar without setting my hair on fire. Somehow, though, when it came to music, I thought different rules applied.

But I was ready to learn something new. The intelligences I'd spent my life developing were the touchy-feely ones: linguistic, interpersonal, and intrapersonal. I was sick to death of using those intelligences. I wanted to give the analytical side of my brain a chance to come out of hiding and explore. I wanted to do something mechanical. I mulled over the question of which of my less-developed intelligences to nurture. I knew my spatial intelligence needed some prodding because of the C I got in high-school geometry and because of my predilection for trying to stuff two quarts of leftover spaghetti into a one-quart plastic bowl. But my musical intelligence was even less developed. I couldn't hear patterns in music, let alone remember them. After Fred declined the idea of piano lessons, though, I was forced to wonder if I could raise my musical intelligence. Seeing Brian had pushed me over the edge. Now that it was actually happening, I wasn't sure I wanted to proceed.

▴   ▴   ▴

Brian arrived wearing khaki pants, a green plaid shirt, and a three-day beard. He carried two music books: a thin volume titled *Michael Aaron Adult Piano Course, Book One,* and a thicker, spiral-bound book called *Adult All-in-One Course, Level 1.*

We walked into the living room, and I waited for him to sit down on the piano bench, vaguely assuming that for the first few lessons he would play while I hovered at his elbow, watching and listening like a starstruck groupie while he expounded about notes and clefs and where pianists put their feet.

I was wrong. Brian gestured me to the piano bench and politely inquired whether it was all right if he sat on the arm of the overstuffed couch, the only piece of furniture near the piano. I said it was fine. We seated ourselves, and he began to ask questions.

Yes, I told him, I knew the names of the lines and spaces in the treble clef. I'd learned them when I took guitar lessons for four months twenty years earlier. Why did I stop studying the guitar? Because I could never tell if it was in tune or not. Yes, I knew where middle C was on the piano. Somebody showed me when I was in high school. No, I didn't know where the other Cs were on the keyboard. I didn't know the keyboard *had* other Cs.

"There's a pattern," Brian told me. He leaned forward to touch a series of keys. "Do you see the two black keys together here, and then the three black keys together here, and then two more black ones here, and how that pattern repeats itself all the way up and down the keyboard?"

I nodded.

"The white key to the left of the two black keys is always a C."

"Always?"

"Always."

Imagine that: repeating patterns. Not an evolving mystery of keys, but patterns.

Brian placed the Aaron book on the piano.

"Can you play this?" he asked.

"This" was Beethoven's "Ode to Joy."

I recognized the song from church hymnals where it appears under the title "Joyful, Joyful, We Adore Thee," and from my daughter Tara's wedding. The arrangement in front of me had a total of five notes, arranged and rearranged across sixteen measures. Slowly, searchingly, one note at a time, I picked out the tune. Music came out, a simplified rendition of the hymn, but still recognizable as Beethoven's composition.

I once read that the late pianist and composer Leonard Bernstein loved to tell the story of the first time he put his fingers on the keys of a piano. He was ten years old.

"I touched God," he'd say.

I didn't know about that, but I did know I was in love, boom, instantly. It was shocking, because I had no prior affection for the piano, knew nothing of its character, of what loving it would be like for the long haul, of whether its tones and range would satisfy me. I didn't care. The great cave of music, the universe from which I'd felt barred my whole life—in a moment, in a twinkling of my fingers, the rock rolled away, and I entered, mind and body and soul. From that moment, and for months after, nothing much mattered except there was a piano in the house and when I touched its keys in a particular order, music came out.

"Why are you laughing?" Brian asked.

"Because this is so cool."

We switched books, and he watched me pick out the notes to "Aunt

Rhody," "Mexican Hat Dance," and "Lightly Row." The first half of each song was played with the right hand, the second half with the left. Between the songs, Brian talked about position: knees under the outside edge of the keyboard, elbows tucked in against my body, fingers rounded.

"My fingers don't do round," I said.

"Mine didn't do round, either, when I started. My piano teacher made me play holding a golf ball at first, and then a racquetball, and then an orange."

I wiggled my fingers, trying to imagine a golf ball in my palm. "How old were you when you started taking lessons?"

"Two."

"Two? Two years old? You started piano lessons when you were two years old? Oh, my God. I'm forty-six years behind."

Brian showed me an octave, spreading his hand across the keys so his thumb rested on one C key and his little finger on the next C key up, a total of eight keys. "Can you reach that far?' he asked.

I tried. Yes, I could reach.

"Can you push any keys down?"

I couldn't. My fingers were stretched so wide not a single finger could move.

"How about an octave plus one key? Can you reach that?" Brian asked.

No matter how I stretched, my fingers couldn't reach. Brian, on the other hand, could reach an octave plus two, a total of ten keys, and he could push down each key, and he didn't wince when he did so.

Curious, I held my right hand toward him, palm flat and facing him. "Let me see your hand."

He placed his palm flat against mine, his fingers stretched wide. Our hands were nearly identical in size. His palm was the same width as mine, and his fingers were only a bit longer. His fifth and fourth fingers, though, were both exposed on the other side of mine. How could they be visible when our hands were the same size? I twisted our wrists sideways for a different view. Ah: the spaces between his fingers were double or triple the area of the spaces between my fingers.

"Don't worry about your hands. The more you play, the more you'll be able to stretch. And it will help if you do this." He put the fingertips of his hands together and pushed so hard his fingertips turned white.

"My piano teacher had me do this exercise to strengthen the muscles in my fingers."

I practiced the pushing exercise while Brian searched through the orange book.

"Here you go. This is the C scale. You need to practice it this week, along with the songs we've worked on." Then he asked again what kind of music I wanted to learn. Again I told him I didn't know.

"In that case, you might as well learn to play classical music. If you can play classical music, you can play anything."

Oh, Lord, spare me: classical music. The little I knew of it came from television commercials. A pizza company once used the *William Tell* overture as background music for a ditty that began, "Have a piz-, have a piz-, have a pizza roll"; and the Rice Krispies cereal people once ran a commercial where an opera singer sang, with great drama, "No more Rice Krispies / We've run out of Rice Krispies / I shall not stop, till I hear snap, crackle, and pop."

It hardly seemed enough exposure to work from.

To Brian I merely said, "Classical music? Okay, fine."

After Brian left, I played "Ode to Joy" five or six times, and "Aunt Rhody" nine or ten times (I've loved the song ever since I was a child and found out that singing it drove my sister, Amy, crazy). I practiced another two or three hours after supper. I worked first on the assigned songs and scales. Invariably I'd hit two or three notes incorrectly, but the songs still sounded right. I paged through the books to see what else looked interesting and took a shot at playing every song I recognized. I could do three of them without much effort, as long as I moved my fingers very slowly: "Au Claire de la Lune," "Tisket, A Tasket," and "Good King Wenceslas."

Further on in the book I found "Michael, Row the Boat Ashore." I wanted to play it, and also "Jingle Bells" and "Mary Ann" (the woman who's been sifting sands all day and all night since the 1950s), but each song required I play with both of my hands at the same time. I couldn't do it. Near the back of the book I found "Scarborough Fair" and "Greensleeves," both of which I'd loved in the sixties, but the former had too many notes, and the latter had the small tic-tac-toe boards indicating sharp notes. The songs were far beyond my capabilities.

All in good time, I thought. *All in good time.*

It was a slow, steady, Zen kind of thought, but I'm not a very Zen sort of person. Consequently, when I found "Drink to Me Only with Thine Eyes" in the middle of the Aaron book, I searched out Fred, who was in the laundry room putting clothes in the dryer.

"Will you show me how to play a chord?" I asked.

"A chord? What are you practicing that has chords?"

"Come see."

"That song's pretty advanced for someone who's only had one lesson," he said.

"I know. But I've always liked it, and I want to play it. Will you show me how to do the chords?"

"Chords are simple. You just figure out the notes and press all of them down at the same time."

He demonstrated, and as he stepped away from the piano, I forgot he was in the room, absorbed as I was in the music.

▲   ▲   ▲

I began sorting files at the church, selecting which papers stayed with them, which belonged in my personal file cabinet at home, and which could go in the recycle bin.

Back home, I decided to tackle my front yard. Virtually untouched by human hands since we'd bought the house eight years earlier, it was a disgrace to the neighborhood. On Wednesday I raked two or three billion leaves to the curb and scattered hollyhock and black-eyed Susan seeds and a wildflower mix guaranteed to bloom in the shade. Thursday afternoon I planted yellow day lilies. As I sweated and breathed in the smell of earth, I came to the conclusion that a major reason I was leaving the pastorate—a reason as important as wanting more energy for Fred and wanting more intellectual stimulation and thinking God wanted me doing something else—was that I was tired of loving.

Back when I started divinity school, the dean lectured all the students about how each of us was called to give our lives to serving others. In ensuing semesters various professors talked about how the best service that ministers can provide is to love as Christ loved, which means loving everybody.

Loving everybody, I've noticed, is an awful lot of work. Some days I can hardly bring myself to love Fred. If I can't do that, how am I to care for the other six billion people who inhabit the planet?

The concept is suspect, but the reality of life in the church gave me insight into the dean's meaning. As a pastor I kept running into people who were goofy and conflicted and alive, just as I am. When they got sick or wounded—in other words, when life happened to them—my job gave me permission to be there. I was glad to be there. Why? Not for any profound theological reason, but simply because I'd come to care about them. To (damn it) love them.

And yet the loving was hard. One night Fred and I went out to a restaurant with a buffet. Preoccupied after an afternoon spent visiting people in the hospital—I think that time it was a young man with a broken neck and an older man with heart problems, or maybe the six-year-old who'd had a tonsillectomy—I filled two dinner plates. When I reached our table and set the plates down, Fred studied them and observed, "You must be hungry."

I looked at what I'd gathered: macaroni and cheese, mashed pota-toes, gravy, corn, red Jello, chicken, vanilla pudding. Comfort foods, double portions of each.

"I could take a spoon and start eating at one end of the buffet and keep going down the line until I emptied it," I said. "I'm famished."

"It's okay," he said. "Eat until you're full."

It's hard to get full when you lead a congregation, harder still to stay full. Episcopal priest Barbara Brown Taylor wrote an essay pub-lished in the November 4, 1998, issue of *The Christian Century* about the difficulty she had as a pastor when people complained to her because the coffee was cold or the bathroom was out of toilet paper. It was difficult, she said, because her primary job had nothing to do with fixing those things. "The main reason I was there was to get them out alive if the plane went down."

Here's the main thing you learn as a pastor: planes go down. All of us, every last one of us, is always and only one aneurysm, one slick tire on a rainy night, or one blood test away from crashing and burning.

Here's the main thing you learn in your first piano lesson: you have to concentrate. Life, death, eternity, redemption, salvation, where you're going, what you're going to do when you get there, how you make the trip, why you're going: You can't concern yourself with such things when your hands are on the keys. Like pastoring, learning to play the piano demands a quality of absorption, the ability and will to forget yourself and give your total attention to the music and the keys. Devo-tion: they both demand devotion.

▲   ▲   ▲

In my creativity class after my first piano lesson, the instructor taught us how to do mandalas. First she had us spread a number of colored pens and markers on the table. Without thinking, we were to pick up the first color that appealed to us and use it to draw a circle on a white sheet of paper. Then we were to sit still and breathe for a few minutes.

"Take some time to be quiet," she said, "and then pick up the color that attracts you and begin filling in the circle however you want. When you feel as though you've done enough with that color, choose another. Keep going until your picture feels complete."

While I worked, I stole glances at the other students' mandalas. Theirs were prettier than mine, harmonious, with careful lines and tidy colorings. My mandala contained wild lumps of color: grass green, blood red, royal purple, a touch of cobalt. I drew from my shoulders, from my chest. I could see my heartbeat in the colors and hear it as my hand moved across the page.

Near the end of the class, the instructor told us the underlying impulses the colors supposedly revealed. Green stood for cyclical renewal and natural healthy growth. Red indicated life, lust, libido, raw energy, fire. Purple was the color of self-absorption, vivid imagination, and the ability to generate excitement. Blue meant serenity, relaxation, devotion, and the awakening of intuition and wisdom.

I am as leery of mandalas as I am of other spiritual games (horoscopes, Tarot cards, reading the entrails of birds, casting runes, apocalyptic visions, Ouija boards), but that didn't stop me from going on a mandala rampage. The first was *Dueling Tornadoes,* eight squiggly towers in varied shades of blue amid vast patches of white. According to my class notes, the picture indicated clarity, readiness for change, a loss of energy, and the reluctance to embrace life in the body. I drew two more mandalas. *No Red* was curves of purple on a white background. *Connect the Blocks* was a series of purple and black squares connected by straight purple lines. I drew a mandala with green, yellow, and white stripes, which a handout told me indicated autonomy, hope, and the readiness to pursue something new.

For two solid days, I created mandalas and read texts and discovered I was full of growth, lust, self-absorption, and hope; that I was trying to connect the dots of my life in a new pattern; and that on different days different impulses predominated. At the end of the two days I was done

with mandalas. I put down my sketchbook, went to the piano, and practiced for three hours, working first through the assigned pieces a dozen
times each, and then practicing "Drink to Me Only with Thine Eyes" for
an hour or so. Somewhere within its notes I thought, *The piano is my
mandala,* because in playing the piano, I was myself freely flowing, moving, growing, springing, knowing, graceful, cherished, beautiful, beautiful heart, beautiful hands, beautiful fingers, beautiful scars, too, the
scars of love, all beautiful and graceful, moving, flowing, flowing on,
flowing on, flowing on and on and on.

▲   ▲   ▲

Brian's hair was unleashed when he arrived to give me my second lesson.
It floated around his shoulders, a frizzy halo.

"How's it going?" he asked.

I said, "Your hair's even curlier than mine. I've been waiting for you
to get here so that you can show me how to move my hands."

Untroubled by the non sequitur, he asked, "What do you mean,
'move your hands'?"

"I have to move my hands from one place to another in 'Drink to
Me Only with Thine Eyes,' and I don't know how."

He cocked his head and squinted at me. "Did I assign that piece?"

"Nope. I found it in one of the books."

He followed me through the kitchen and down the hall to the living room.

"You're wearing jeans," he observed.

"Why, yes, I am." Along with my Levi's blue jeans I had on a white
turtleneck and the navy sneakers with four-inch-thick soles Fred had
bought in California to give me for Christmas.

"I don't believe I've ever seen a preacher wear blue jeans before,"
Brian said.

"Really? I wear them all the time."

I played the first four lines of "Drink to Me Only with Thine Eyes."

"There. Right there is where I don't know what to do next. My
third finger is on the E, and now it's supposed to be on the G. How do I
get it from the E to the G?"

"Just pick up your hands and move them." Brian snorted, lightly.
"You're taking this much too seriously. Get over it."

Oh, well, damn, of course I was taking it too seriously; I take most things too seriously. I'd thought maybe I was supposed to slide my hands across the keys, or . . . well, I don't know exactly what I thought the *or* might be, but it was critically important to me that I do everything on the piano exactly right.

I picked up my hand and moved it. It worked out well, except I then played an F instead of the G, resulting in a somewhat peculiar sound. Brian applauded my effort and told me to keep practicing the piece.

Next I played "Aunt Rhody." Rhody and the dead gray goose and I got along fine, except when I played the wrong notes.

"The alternate notes you're playing sound good. You could probably play really well by ear."

I could play by ear? Me, the one who couldn't tell if a guitar was in tune or not? I was secretly pleased by Brian's comment. What I told him, though, was "I don't want to play by ear. I want to play by the rules."

Brian shook his head so hard, his curls danced. "One of the rules is that you have to interpret the music you're playing. Sometimes that means changing the notes."

"You can't expect me to interpret the music. This is only my second lesson."

"It's not something you add in later. Any time you play, you're interpreting."

"Oh, it's like preaching. Any time anybody preaches, they're interpreting."

"I don't know about that. Maybe."

"You're not Methodist, are you?"

"No, I'm a Southern Baptist."

"Mmm. That explains it. Some Baptists try to pretend they aren't interpreting. But never mind. Show me something else on the piano."

Brian walked me through "Song of the Cello," "Alpine Melody," "Intermezzo," and "How Can I Leave Thee?" The latter three required the use of both my left and right hands.

"Do I need to practice these before my next lesson?"

"Nah. You already play them well enough. Are you sure you've never taken piano lessons before?"

"I think I'd remember if I had. Why would you ask me that?"

"Because you're playing so well so quickly."

I flushed. Me? "Am I really?"

"Yes. Now try this piece."

"Lullaby" had tied notes and quarter rests in it. So did "Soft, Soft, Music Is Stealing," a selection a few pages further on, and it had something else new.

"See the little *p*s and *f*s?"

I nodded.

"They tell you how loudly or softly to play. You're to play the first half softly, and the second half loudly. Practice doing that, and keep working on 'Drink to Me Only with Thine Eyes' and the C scale."

We moved on to the spiral-bound book, in which Brian assigned "Jingle Bells" (I was to pay attention to the places where the chords changed), "Merrily We Roll Along," and "Largo."

"See the curved line between this note and the next one? That's called a tie. When two notes are the same and joined by a tie, you don't play the second note. You just hold the key down."

"I can do that. What else?"

"You want more?"

"Yes."

Brian studied my face. "What would you think about taking two lessons a week?"

"Two lessons a week? Is that possible? Can I really do that? I'd love to."

"Of course we can do that. We can do lessons on both Thursdays and Mondays. But you're going to need more books. Will you be here a few minutes? If so, I'll run up to Case Brothers and see what they've got."

Case Brothers, the music store where Fred originally bought the piano, is only half a mile from our house. Brian was back in fifteen minutes.

We stood at the butcher block in the kitchen and went through the new books. Two were written for children and illustrated with dragons and birds. "These are finger exercises to get your fingers moving better and let you practice some techniques. Work on this one for the staccato." He put a check mark on the upper right corner of the fourth page.

The third new book was *John Thompson's Modern Course for the Piano, The First Grade Book* (*Something New Every Lesson* a subtitle promised). Brian put an X beside "Swans on the Lake."

"If you run out of things to play, work on this one. It'll help your tonal shading. Instead of just piano and forte, it has gradations in volume between the two: mezzo-forte, mezzo-piano, and pianissimo."

"Do what?"

"There's more variation to volume than just loud and soft. You need to practice the shadings in-between." The final book was *Favorite Melodies the World Over,* arranged by Jane Smisor Bastien. "I got Level Two because they were out of the Level One book. I think you can handle some of the music."

I flipped through the pages. Piano Concerto No. 1 by Tchaikovsky, "Christ the Lord Is Risen Today" by Charles Wesley, "She'll Be Coming 'Round the Mountain," composer unknown. Each song looked to contain hundreds of notes.

"If you need one more thing to practice, do 'Sweet Betsy from Pike.' It'll let you work on moving from one chord to another."

I studied the page. Yes, I could see all the chord changes.

"Okay, then? Do you think you're set until Monday?"

"I think so. If not, can I call you?"

Brian laughed. "You're amazing. I've never had a piano student like you before. It's hard to believe I almost said no when you asked me to give you lessons."

"Why would you have said no?"

"I was intimidated."

"Intimidated? Why were you intimidated?"

"Because you're a preacher."

I forget that my ordination has this effect on some people. They regard me as paranormal, like an alien who's fallen to earth, and not necessarily an alien who's come in peace. I thought back to my impression of ministers before I joined the ranks. Oh, yes, I remembered: I thought them strange, different. It's not that I thought clergy were unhuman, exactly, or inhuman. Para-human, maybe. They didn't seem to inhabit the same universe I did.

I understood a little of what Brian was naming. I was just surprised to find the stereotypes applied to me, especially because I felt as intimidated with Brian as he was with me. I knew when he played he was accessing a power greater than himself. Somehow, the power of God looked different when I saw it moving through Brian.

chapter seventeen

I COULDN'T PLAY "SWEET BETSY FROM PIKE." THE PIECE had five different chord changes; it was too hard. To make up for my inadequacy, I played my other assignments seven or eight times each after Brian left, and then I looked all the way through the Bastien book.

It felt like the first day of school all over again, back when I was in grade school and investigated my readers to see how big the type was and whether the illustrations looked interesting. Learning to play the piano is a whole lot like learning to read. The musical notes were as obscure as the words in my Dick and Jane book when I entered first grade and words were nothing but mysterious blobs of ink crowded together. I remember the halting unknowing when every new combination of letters was a task to be labored through. I remember, too, when I was able to read and could effortlessly and freely sound out the word and keep sailing. But never, no matter how hard I tried, could I recall the precise moment I learned to read.

I found myself hoping that this time, in the new alphabet of notes and dots and lines, I'd be able to notice the exact instant. I wanted to be able to say, *Yes, that was it, the very moment the world changed.*

I should have known better. Epiphany—the idea that in one bright, shining instant everything becomes clear and life is transformed from that day forward—is an overrated theological concept. My experience in the Chevette aside, life's most important events—birth, death, learning to read, being ordained—don't happen in an instant. Even if there's a clock in the room and somebody documents the time, it's still an invention, a pretense. Who can define the singular moment when love is born? Is it the day a couple meets? The day they say "I love you" for the first time? The day they make a commitment?

I document my love for the piano from the moment I played "Ode to Joy," but that begins the story in the middle. My infatuation grew out of, blew up out of the nights of music on the island, the ones in the winter and the ones in the summer; and of my sense of inadequacy because I couldn't tell if a guitar was in tune, and of my longing for a sense of the holy even after I stopped believing in it.

I found "Stars and Stripes Forever," a march by John Philip Sousa, in the Bastien book. I'd loved Sousa's music ever since I watched a black-and-white movie about him on television when I was growing up. I tried to play the march. After I played the first two lines four times, I noticed the chords were made up of three notes, rather than the two I was playing (two notes, I learned later, don't constitute a chord; they're an interval). I plugged along but stopped after half an hour, frustrated. Then I chastised myself for my frustration.

I'd just read a book called *When Work Doesn't Work Anymore* by Elizabeth Perle McKenna. McKenna surveyed a number of women who left corporate positions at the height of their executive careers; she wanted to learn why the women opted out. One of her conclusions was that often women leave their jobs because, even though they were given consistently superior marks on performance reviews, the women themselves were unhappy with what they were able to achieve. The women, according to McKenna, were measuring themselves against their personal standards of what they wanted to achieve, rather than against the standard of what actually could be achieved.

I saw myself reflected in McKenna's research After two weeks of piano lessons, I wanted to play every assigned selection perfectly, every time. I was making steady progress—rapid progress if I were to accept Brian's evaluation—and yet I wasn't satisfied. I expected more from myself than could actually be achieved. When I thought over my work at the church, I saw the same dynamic, especially at the beginning. No wonder I was often frustrated; the standards I set for myself were unattainable.

▲   ▲   ▲

The next day I drove to North Carolina for a meeting. On the way I listened to a tape of Mozart's music my sister had sent me. Previously, instrumental music had been white noise to me, as meaningless as the sound of other vehicles' tires on the highway. In the car that afternoon, though, I was able to listen for as long as three or four minutes at a time, because when I heard the notes I was able to visualize hands moving up and down the keyboard. It was as though until now I'd only been aware of instrumental music as a distant forest. Now I could glimpse the particulars of some notes: a maple leaf here, a laurel tree there, a frond of honeysuckle.

Driving home, again listening to Mozart, I had a wild idea, an idea so good that as soon as it occurred to me, I wished it hadn't. I wanted Brian to do a sermon with me, him on the piano, me preaching. Immediately I knew the Sunday: Pentecost, my favorite day of the year, the day that celebrates the coming of the Holy Spirit to the Church, the perfect day for God to draw us out. My excitement grew as I thought about the intersecting powers of the biblical texts, Brian's playing, and my preaching. I pondered mechanics as I wove through the traffic on Interstate 85. Would Brian be willing to play? If so, would I write the sermon first and give him my text? Would the piano stay in the background all the way through, or should it dominate at times? How complicated would it be to pull such an event together? And did I really want to spend the amount of time it would take, thirty to forty hours, to plan and prepare?

No. No, I didn't. Pentecost was May 31, my next-to-the-last Sunday at the church. At this late date, I wasn't going to commit to a project as time-consuming and risky as this one. I had enough other things to do.

▲   ▲   ▲

Friday morning I worked in the front yard and meditated. I'd been thinking about Sunday's sermon off and on since Monday, when I'd read the text and scanned the scholarly commentaries. The gospel text for the week told about Mary pouring expensive oil (*pistikos nard*) on Jesus the night he was betrayed. Judas Iscariot got angry with Mary because he'd planned to steal the money she'd spent on the oil. While I raked leaves out of the ivy, I got tangled up in questions about love: Mary's love for Jesus, Jesus' love for Mary, Jesus' love for Judas. It was a week when two young boys in Arkansas had shot a number of their schoolmates. The shootings, coupled with the biblical text, spiraled me into thoughts about families, about the parents of the people who did the killing, about the parents of the people killed.

How do people ever figure out what they're doing in relationships, as parents, as partners, or even as friends? How do we know the best expression of love, and whether it's love at all, or if instead it's need, or power? Loving is complicated.

I was still thinking through the ideas—which warranted more than six days of thought—when I preached on Sunday.

Have you ever noticed how very complicated love is? *I asked.* It's hard to know what love is, really. Some things look like love, and it turns out they're the opposite, and some things look like foolishness, and it turns out they're love at the deepest level.

Look at Judas Iscariot in this passage. He says, "Why was this perfume not sold for three hundred denarii and the money given to the poor?"

His words sound like a reflection of Jesus' words, "Sell all you have and give the money to the poor." Judas seems to be criticizing Mary because she's not following Jesus' teaching.

Except love of the poor wasn't the reason Judas made the comment. He made the comment because he was a thief. He wanted the three hundred denarii to go inside the common purse so that he could steal it. What looked like love was really greed.

On the other side is Mary, who anointed Jesus' feet with expensive perfume. *Pistikos nard* is the phrase in Greek. *Pistikos nard:* the oil of a fragrant plant imported from India, the fragrance so sweet it filled the entire room as Mary rubbed the oil on Jesus' feet and wiped it off with her hair. Three hundred denarii, says the text: almost a full year's wages for a laborer. So much work, so much money, and Mary poured it out on Jesus' feet, poured it all out in love for him, in the same way that in six days Jesus would pour out his life in love for the world.

I wonder how complicated the decision was for her, if it was difficult for her to decide or if she'd listened to what Jesus was saying about his coming suffering and death and chose to honor him this way. She wasn't like Judas, wondering what would be in it for her. She brought a different question: how can I respond in love to Jesus' love for me?

It's a complicated question. Sometimes we don't know the answer, and sometimes we're certain we know the answer but later realize we got it wrong, and sometimes we know the answer, but it's just too hard for us to do.

There was a trial in Florida earlier this year, the trial of a seventeen-year-old boy who set fire to a United Methodist Church and caused $750 worth of damage. The young man spilled gasoline all over himself in starting the fire, and he was badly burned. The prosecutor wanted the boy sent to prison as an adult and asked for a sentence of up to fifty years. The pastor of the church that burned asked the court to be lenient, that instead of prison the boy be sentenced to counseling, drug rehabilitation, and a group home. The judge agreed.

Later, somebody asked the pastor if he'd have been as supportive if the church had been destroyed in the fire. The pastor said, "I would have been really angry, and I would have had to sort through my anger, but I still would have made the same request."

It's complicated—love, persistent love, some would say foolish love. I don't know if this church were destroyed by arson if I could do what the other pastor did: sort through my anger and choose to love. I don't know how many of you would want me to do that. How do we sort it all out when what we want to do is to place blame and make sure somebody is punished?

The shootings in Arkansas this week are another example. People seem to be either furiously angry or quietly heartsick. What I've read suggests it's one of those weird kid-brain things: they planned to shoot, and they meant to hit people, but I don't think they grasped that people would end up really dead. It's hard to understand what death really is when you're an adult, let alone a child.

Children are dead, and the country is walking around dazed, and some people want the children who did the killing to be killed. It's as though if we can blame the right people and punish them sufficiently, then everything will be all right.

I don't have an answer. There are too many questions to have one answer, questions like How do we live as a society? How do we create limitations so a dumb game played by children doesn't destroy lives? How do we live together with the children we know so that through us they learn how to set boundaries and how to protect themselves and their souls so that they can honor their own lives and the lives of others? And how do we balance the limitations we place on them with the freedom we must allow them if they're ever going to mature?

The questions are so complicated that the one thing I know for sure is that if the response we offer is, "Oh, that's easy, all you have to do is (fill in the blank)," then we can pretty much count on being wrong. Because love isn't simple, and the answers aren't easy.

Judas had the easy answer: Mary should give the money to the poor rather than wasting it on Jesus.

Jesus had a different answer: "Leave her alone. She bought the oil so that she might keep it for the day of my burial."

Except Mary didn't keep the oil. Six days before Passover she poured out the oil she'd bought to prepare Jesus for burial. She poured it on his feet, and then she rubbed it in, and then she dried his feet with her hair. And Jesus said, "Leave her alone, because this is love, this is devotion, this is the act of a disciple."

We are called to be disciples, too, to follow Jesus down a tortured, complicated path. We're called to follow him into a rose garden at midnight on a moonless night, blindfolded. We stagger along in territory we don't really want to be in, our hands and arms ripped by thorns, having to make decisions about which way to turn, not knowing for sure if they're right or wrong, not knowing if we're taking the most holy action of our life or the most stupid.

Love. Love. Complicated love. That is the cost of discipleship.

Amen.

In his book *Piano Pieces,* classical pianist Russell Sherman posits that the piano is "the ideal therapist for human ails, breaches, and distresses." Was it so for me? Certainly there was a breach, and certainly the piano was a bridge: in my adventures with it I was figuring out death, disillusion and despair, sexuality and life and happiness. When I'd ask Fred, "Is this driving you crazy?" he'd smile and say, "No, I love hearing you play." He liked it because the house was filled with a rare sort of beauty: not the beauty of perfection, of notes played accurately, correctly, smoothly, and in perfect time. There is no perfect time, or perfect place, or perfect way to live or move or have your being. There is only the possibility of beauty, here and there and now and then, as the ultimate repayment for devotion.

That afternoon when I practiced the C scale, first with my right hand, then with my left, then with both hands, my fingers were stricken with transient paralysis and refused to depress any key. Brian assured me it wasn't a grievous problem.

"You're doing better than any other student I've ever had. The trouble is your fingers have never had to do any work before, so they don't know how. Your thumb and the first two fingers on your right hand are used to taking instructions, but the rest of your fingers aren't."

"What do I do about it?"

"The same thing you do with every other problem on the piano. Keep practicing." He said books were available with exercises to help strengthen fingers; he was trying to locate one for me by someone named Hanon.

He was not nearly impressed enough to suit me when I played "Drink to Me Only with Thine Eyes" and "Stars and Stripes Forever." He said, "You'll be working on these two a long time. They're both very complicated. Look, you've got staccatos in 'Stars and Stripes Forever,' not to mention chords, which you didn't even know how to play last week." He demonstrated staccato. It's not the sharp drumming on keys I'd imagined but a inward brush of the fingertips across the keys toward the body. He showed me some selections in the technique books that would improve my staccatos.

"Keep practicing what you've already got, and work on the staccato pieces. Will that be enough?"

"I don't know. Maybe you should give me some more."

Brian laughed. "You really love this, don't you?"

"Yes, I really do."

He offered three spare pieces, "Contrary Motion," "Hunting Song," and "Old English Dance." "If you get to them, fine; if you don't, fine."

▲   ▲   ▲

Practicing that night, I could only do one thing at a time. If I paid attention to the notes, I could play them correctly, but I couldn't bring any shadings into the piece. If I focused on the shadings—the piano and forte and layers of volume in between—I hit every third note wrong. And whatever I was doing, my fingers were flopping around like head-less chickens. I shifted to practicing the C scale and concentrated on each finger as my hands moved up and down the keyboard. Now here was a peculiarity: I couldn't feel my fingertips. If I wasn't looking at my hands I didn't know what finger was pressing a key. I could only suppose I lacked the brain circuitry necessary to differentiate between my second and fourth fingertips or my third and fifth.

It's strange learning that parts of your body aren't fully connected to the rest of it. My hands looked normal—the muscles, tendons, and bones were where they belonged—and yet here was an aspect of my physical reality I'd assumed functioned correctly which, in fact, didn't.

The information gave a new edge to the learning theories I'd studied earlier that winter. It wasn't only my brain that was being rewired by the piano lessons; it was my body, too. And, no doubt, my soul as well.

▲   ▲   ▲

Fred and I made a day trip to deliver tax information to our accountant. While Fred drove, I read the book *Tone Deaf and All Thumbs?* by Frank R. Wilson. Wilson, a neurologist, started taking piano lessons when he was forty-two. Lo and behold, he felt incompetent before he started his lessons, just as I had. Wilson said most of the world feels the same way, but, he insisted, you don't have to be a prodigy to make music. And why should people beat themselves up for not knowing how to play when they've never been taught how?

Beating yourself up when you've never been taught . . . What a concept. Music not as a genetic inheritance but as a skill that can be taught, and learned. I was relieved. I'd fallen so deeply in love with the piano that I couldn't bear the idea that I might never play well enough to satisfy my own desires.

After we saw the accountant, we stopped to see Fred's sister. She'd inherited their mother's piano, the one on which all the Hayes children took lessons. I picked out the first two measures of "Stars and Stripes Forever," which was all I could remember of it.

"Did you look at the music in the piano bench? I don't even remember what all is in there."

We dug through it.

"Look!" she said, holding up some sheet music. "Did you know Fred played this piece in a recital when he was a teenager?"

It was his copy of "Rhapsody in Blue."

"You can take any of these home that you want to."

We ended up with "Rhapsody in Blue" and a book of finger exercises by C. L. Hanon, the same book Brian had recommended. The title page reads, in part,

The Virtuoso Pianist in Sixty Exercises
For the Piano
For the Acquirement of Agility, Independence, Strength, and Perfect Evenness in the Fingers, as well as Suppleness of the Wrist.

It was translated from the French by Dr. Theodore Baker, copyright 1900 by G. Schirmer, Inc.

I read sections of the preface aloud to Fred on the way home. My favorite was *"If all five fingers of the hand were absolutely equally well trained, they would be ready to execute anything written for the instrument"* (italics Hanon's). I took the statement to mean mechanics are the critical factor in piano playing. Good: the mechanics were something I could control.

Brian and I would argue later over my conclusion. He said, "Anybody who spends enough time practicing can get the mechanics right. That doesn't mean they're good pianists. It's not the keys you strike. It's how you strike them: the shadings, the speed, the power, the interpretive skills."

"That's silly. If I can't get my fingers to press the keys I want them to press, I'll never be able to play diddly."

I was wrong, of course. Many of the world's greatest pianists weren't bothered by technical niceties, according to Harold C. Schonberg in his book *The Great Pianists.* Beethoven "broke more pianos than anybody in Vienna" and was probably never an accurate pianist. Liszt would have made a great rock star. When he performed, "ladies flung their jewels on the stage instead of bouquets. They shrieked in ecstasy and sometimes fainted." Liszt, who could play anything on sight and never forgot any of it, wasn't concerned with getting every note right. And then there's my old friend Anton Rubinstein, the pianist George Bagby wrote about. Schonberg says when Anton got carried away, he "did not care how many false notes fell under the piano and wiggled on the ground."

I was touchy on the subject of notes, false and otherwise, because my fingers were still locking up. Not every time, but often. The times a finger *would* deign to depress a key, either the rest of my fingers flew up in the air or several of them joined in solidarity with the playing finger and pressed other keys. My thumb, meanwhile, acted like a six-year-old in his first game of T-ball, wandering here, wandering there, oblivious to the concept of position.

▲   ▲   ▲

I did have one moment of glory, late on a Wednesday night. I was tinkering with "Christ the Lord Is Risen Today" when everything came together. After four measures my fingers knew the pattern. They knew exactly where to go, and they went to exactly the right places throughout the song, showing up where they needed to be the instant they needed to be there. I played smoothly, effortlessly, without thinking, eyes and fingers coordinated.

I tried the song again immediately, but I'd lost the pattern. The moment was over, the skill gone. For a few minutes there, though, I wasn't hunting and pecking, nor searching and straining; I was simply playing the piano. It was like in the middle of February when you walk outside and, if only for a moment, smell spring, or like preaching after the pettiness has lost its sting and you and the congregation are able to look into each other's eyes and name the grace and goodness you've shared.

▲   ▲   ▲

Brian was pleased about Hanon.

"These exercises will strengthen your fingers. That's the problem you're having. Your fingers are weak, especially the fourth and fifth ones."

"You're sure this will help?" I asked, looking at the multiplicity of notes crammed onto the page. "It looks hard."

"I'm sure it'll help. And it's not hard."

My new assignments that day were "What Can I Share?" to get some more work with shading, and "Thoughts at Twilight," which included both sharps and flats, meaning instead of just playing white keys I would now be using some black ones. I was disappointed when I played "Drink to Me Only with Thine Eyes." I'd practiced it dozens of times. Nevertheless, in the fifth measure I hit four consecutive wrong notes.

"Goddamn it," I muttered.

Brian stiffened. "What did you say?"

"Excuse me," I said (I was so accustomed to practicing alone, muttering all the while, that I'd forgotten he could hear me). "I didn't mean to offend you."

"I'm not offended. I just didn't know preachers knew words like that."

"Brian, honey, you don't know the half of it."

"Maybe you need to take a break," he offered.

"Maybe I do. Let's go out on the back porch."

On the way outside I grabbed a pack of cigarettes. Brian's eyes widened.

"Oh, my God. Don't tell me you smoke, too?"

I patted him on the arm. "Brian, I know this is taking you some time to absorb, but I'm a human being. I do all kinds of things."

"Oh. Okay. In that case, do you mind if I get my cigarettes out of the car?"

"Go right ahead."

We had a cigarette, and then another. I asked Brian what he did in the spare moments of his life when he wasn't giving me lessons. He said he was in college and that he worked in a veterinarian's office and also tended a doctor's horse stables. He was twenty-one and had gone to college in Charleston for two years but had moved back home around Christmas. He was the youngest of three children.

"Well, that explains it," I said.

"Explains what?"

"Why our lessons are working so well. Why I'm so comfortable with you that I laugh during the lessons. I'm a third child, too."

"And does that mean something?"

"Sure it does." And then I told him my Lindsay story.

Lindsay is my brother Douglas's daughter. Lindsay has twin brothers, Jeff and Jon. When Lindsay was three or four and the twins seven or eight, the boys got sick. My sister-in-law Gayle took them to the doctor. She couldn't find a baby-sitter, so she took Lindsay along.

After the doctor diagnosed matching ear infections for the boys, he volunteered to check Lindsay's ears, too, since she was there. A few minutes later he gave his diagnosis. Lindsay had walking pneumonia.

"You're kidding," said Gayle. "How could my child have pneumonia and me not know?"

"That's easy," said the doctor. "She's a third child. Third children are so afraid that they're going to be left behind that they don't pay any attention to their bodies. They just keep moving."

"That explains a lot," said Brian. "I don't seem to operate like other people. And my being a third child explains some of it."

"Yep. The doctor didn't bother telling Gayle that third children are sweet. First children are in charge, and second children fight for a place in their parents' affection. Third children are so grateful that the rest of the family lets them live that they're nice to everybody."

Somewhere in the ensuing conversation, which ranged from the question of whether God does, in fact, love third children best to a discussion of what kind of flowers I might plant in the backyard, Brian and I talked about the day Chris Flynn died.

"I'd rehearsed 'It Is Well With My Soul,'" Brian told me. "When I got to the church and found out about Chris, I thought it was the worst possible thing to play. But my friend in the choir said no, it was the perfect song."

"She was right. The grace—" I stumbled, started again. "Your playing kept me steady. The grace I was offering in my sermon . . . you offered it to me first." That's where our surprising friendship originated: in the shared grace of those two Sundays with Chris.

I gave Brian an hour-by-hour account of the day of Chris's funeral, even telling him my comments afterward to Fred on the way to Kathy's.

Brian said, "I know that feeling, the one where you want to be where nobody's going to say anything stupid."

"You do?"

"Yes." Brian also understood how disconcerting it can be when you're concentrating on something important—the concept of grace or how to finger a run on the piano—when someone interrupts you to say, "I hear it's going to be a scorcher tomorrow," and you look at them like you've never seen a human being before, and they look at you as though you've insulted them.

Until that afternoon Brian had made assumptions about me—a minister, a wife, a grandmother—and I'd made assumptions about him—a kid, living with his parents, in college. Now, though, as he spoke of concentration and focus, I could have been speaking the words myself. Something sparked in me—nothing so dramatic as the pyrotechnics when I played "Ode to Joy" for the first time, and yet a spark.

Fred joined us on the back porch for a cigarette. He raised an eyebrow sardonically when I told him Brian was a third child. "Not another one."

"Yes. And look: his eyes are green. Brian and I would almost be twins, if I were thirty years younger and male and could play the piano."

"My eyes are blue," said Brian.

"And he's got naturally curly hair like yours," Fred observed.

"Your eyes are green, Brian," I said.

"Only because I'm wearing a green shirt. And yes, my hair is naturally curly, and I'm having trouble keeping it out of my face because of the breeze."

▲   ▲   ▲

"Why doesn't he get a haircut?" Fred asked me that night. "Do you think he keeps it long like that just to annoy his parents?"

"I don't know. I think maybe he likes the way it looks."

Fred rolled the idea around for a minute. Then he said, "He sure can play the piano."

"I know. He plays the piano the way I preach."

"All out? Holding nothing back? Like it's the most important thing in the world?"

"Is that what it is? Is that what I do?"

"That's what you do. It doesn't matter if you're preaching or raking leaves or learning how to play the piano. That's how you live."

▲   ▲   ▲

Lent lasted a long time that year. Come April, I was still in limbo, waiting to hear from graduate schools, waiting for June and Moving Day. Clark didn't think the bishop and cabinet were going to agree to my appointment to school. I might end up being put on involuntary leave of absence.

"Involuntary absence!" I ranted to Fred. "That's where they appoint people who screw the choir director or steal money out of the collection plate. What the hell is the problem?"

"Do you really not know, Mary Jo? Don't you know what's happening at their meetings?"

"No. What?"

"They're shaking their heads and saying to each other, 'That bitch won't do what she's told.'"

Startled, I laughed out loud. Finally I was annoying them as much as they annoyed me. Life was improving. Still, I couldn't stop thinking about the new pastor who'd be coming, how he or she would not know the other loves and sorrows that united the congregation. Even after all I'd been through, I didn't want to leave the congregation to someone else. It was as though a piece of Chris would disappear when I left. He'd been dead eight months by then, but his death was still evolving. Bit by bit, the pieces of his life were being scattered as the people who were bound together by love, hope, and loss moved on and away from each other.

Grief is one aspect of the human condition. Movement is another. Movement is important, but it doesn't erase the pain.

▲   ▲   ▲

Brian had lied to me. Hanon was hard. Each measure contains eight notes. You play those eight notes, and you shift your hands one white key to the right and play the identical pattern on the new keys. You repeat the pattern twelve times. If my hands had been well-behaved, it might have been a simple exercise. Given my hyperactive fingers, it wasn't.

People tell me when they took piano lessons as children, they hated playing scales and finger exercises. It was boring, they say. Not for me. I loved the regularity of Hanon. I loved how the music looked complicated on the page, and yet once you knew the pattern, you could play on and on. I loved not having to think about shading or slurs or accidentals. I loved the feel of my hands moving up and down the keyboard, loved the sound of the notes, loved the sound of the edges of the keys rubbing against each other as I played. After half an hour with Hanon, I was as relaxed as a baby falling asleep in a high chair. I warned Fred he might come into the living room one day to find me with my face in the keys, asleep and drooling.

I'd argued with Brian over mechanics versus interpretation because I was sick unto death of interpretation, of the search for meaning and the means to communicate meaning. I loved the piano because it let me concentrate on the physical, to forget for a little while that the physical, spiritual, and mental are an indivisible and holy trinity, to forget that young people die, to forget that people like me are a problem for the Church.

chapter eighteen

HOLY WEEK SUCKS IF YOU'RE ORDAINED.

It's the one week in the liturgical year when you can't pretend that God is all-powerful, or that suffering is somehow incidental to life, or a tragic accident, or God's will. Holy Week insists that death is as much a part of life as birthing and breathing. On Palm Sunday, worship services begin with small children waving palms and shouting, "Hosanna!" and end with a crucifixion.

If pastors aren't fixated on death when we arrive at the church on Palm Sunday, we are by the time we reach home. It's as though we think we have to get Jesus down off the cross single-handed, and every year it's a close call, and finally Easter Sunday dawns, with no help from us, and we get to stand in the pulpit and proclaim resurrection.

Adding to the stress is my own personal idiotic conviction that I have to preach the best sermon in the history of Christianity for the benefit of people whose annual visit to a church is on Easter. Some clergy mutter darkly about such visitors, but they make me happy. I like to think Easter draws them to a light whose glimmer once held meaning for them. I want to give them a sermon that will sustain them through whatever life throws at them in the coming year. Of course I can't, but each year I have to come to terms with my limitation.

▲   ▲   ▲

The spring of 1998, I didn't even try to write a perfect sermon. Instead, on Monday of Holy Week I reread the lectionary passages for Easter, did a bit of research in the commentaries, and went outside to dig three azalea bushes out of the front yard. As I worked, I mulled over my relationship with the church. I'd lived according to my notions of who I was, what I thought the congregation needed from a pastor, and what was appropriate and acceptable. I'd lived three years of chaos, trying to fulfill the congregation's expectations as well as my own. Church members are adamant about what a pastor should know; about what radio stations, television shows, and movies a pastor should enjoy; about how often he or she should laugh, how loudly, and at what. Often members' expectations conflict, even in matters as nonsensical as dress codes: one-third of the members expect serious professional clothing night or day; another third think jeans and sweaters are formality enough; and the final third don't care one way or the other. While digging, I concluded it was a good and proper thing for me to leave the chaos behind. I wanted a more orderly life, the kind in which crisis would be a foreign invader rather than a familiar companion.

How do you preach the resurrection when you're not sure it has any more significance than a hot-air balloon ascending? I did it by sitting with the text, John 20: 1–18. Mary Magdalene goes to the tomb while it's still dark and sees that the stone has been rolled away. She runs to get Peter and another disciple, who return to the tomb with her. Both of the disciples see the burial linens discarded inside the tomb. The two men leave. Mary remains, crying. She sees two angels who ask why she's weeping.

She says, "They have taken the Lord out of the tomb and we do not know where they have laid him." Then she turns around and sees a man, whom she assumes is the gardener, and asks where Jesus' body has been taken. The gardener, it turns out, is Jesus, but she doesn't recognize him until he speaks her name—"Mary!"—and then she knows it's him, and she answers, *"Rabbouni!"* which means "Teacher."

I was held by the image of Mary outside the tomb crying. *Could it be possible she had the same sort of questions that I had now? Could she, too, have wondered "Can there be anything here that matters?"*

▲   ▲   ▲

The piano got me through the week. I'd decided to play slowly and to concentrate on the shape and movement of my fingers. They resembled the water squirter my grandchildren ran through in the summer. The squirter had a dozen plastic tubes like long flexible straws attached to its base. Water pressure sent the tubes flopping this way and that as water spurted out. My fingers were equally floppy. When I played a key with my second finger, my thumb pointed toward my chin, my little finger pointed at the wall to the right, and my other fingers splayed upward. Forging new muscular and synaptical connections was grueling. When Brian arrived on Holy Thursday for my lesson, my hands were stiff from practicing, but my finger control had improved. Brian was impressed with my skill until late in the lesson when I was playing through an unfamiliar piece of music and Brian told me to back up and start from the G. I looked at the music, studied the keyboard, looked at the music again, thought hard.

"What are you doing?"

"I'm figuring out where the G is."

"What do you mean, figuring it out?"

I explained that to find a key on the piano I started at the C and recited the alphabet up the scale until I reached the note I was seeking.

"You mean you don't know where the notes are on the keyboard?"

"No. Am I supposed to?"

"Yes. I thought you already knew them." He drilled me for half an hour, plunking keys and insisting I call out their names. I was fretful and kept asking if we could stop (I believe I may even have whined).

Brian persisted. Finally he named the obvious: "You hate this part, don't you?"

"Yes. It feels like a test I haven't studied for that I'm failing. And I hate failing."

As a reward, Brian played the piano for me. I sat on the couch listening and watching, through the picture window, a squirrel jumping from one tree limb to another. Brian began a new piece with a series of runs. After the first dozen measures, I felt as though I'd have to get low to the ground to keep from levitating into the tops of the trees. I rolled off the couch and lay on my back on the living-room rug. Once in a while I lifted my right hand to smooth the tears off my face.

Brian's shirt and hair were wet with sweat when he finished.

"My God, what was that?"

" 'It Is Well with My Soul.' It's the music I played at the church the day Chris died. Don't you remember?"

Remember? No, not in intellectual terms, but my spirit or soul or whatever piece of me still clung to the holy clearly remembered. Fred joined us to say, "Why did you stop playing, Brian? Don't stop. That was wonderful," but Brian was spent. Listening to the music had taken a lot out of me, too, but it had given me as much as it took. I walked through the stripping of the altar at that night's Holy Thursday service with the same sad tranquillity I'd felt the day Chris died, and the music was still feeding me when the next night, Good Friday, I went to my friend Heidi's for the Passover seder. Heidi and I had met the week after Chris's death when I was seeking a therapist to lead a grief-support group at the church. She'd come highly recommended, and I was impressed when I phoned her to talk through the congregation's needs.

We'd nearly finalized our arrangements when she said, "I need to tell you I'm Jewish. I know some people have a problem with that, especially some church people."

Too focused for niceties, I blurted out, "I don't care if you're the devil himself if you can help these people."

She laughed, and from then on we were friends.

Fred was to go with me to Heidi's, but when the time came to get ready he begged off. After a day on the golf course, he was worn out. I'd read about seder meals as a teenager, probably in Leon Uris's books, and knew there was a point in the meal when the youngest child present opens a door to welcome in the prophet Elijah, but I was unprepared for the power of the moment when it came. I watched as Heidi's daughter left the dining room. I heard her party shoes click against the kitchen flooring, and then I heard the creak of the back door opening. A moment later a light breeze passed through the room. A chill ran down my back. Nobody else seemed to be expecting a miracle, and it seemed silly, really, to be having a spiritual experience while waiting for a child to return to the dining room. She came alone—Elijah didn't accompany her— but the chill persisted. It was, I realized on the drive home, the chill of hope.

Hope: a concept I hadn't thought much about, or felt, in a year.

What was I hoping for?

I don't know. Deliverance? Redemption? Freedom? Peace? The possibility that someday I would again feel safe in the Church? Any of the above?

All of the above.

▲   ▲   ▲

On Easter Sunday I began my sermon by naming the deep reason we were there, which is that the power of God, the power of the resurrection story, has a hold on us that never lets go, and on Easter we choose to let the story hold us one more time.

The story begins—well, where does it begin? Not with the resurrection. Not with the crucifixion. Not with the Last Supper, nor with Jesus entering Jerusalem while crowds cheer and wave palms. Not with Jesus' ministry, either, or even in Bethlehem at his birth. The story begins at the beginning, the beginning of creation, of time, of space, a beginning documented in the first chapter of John's gospel: *"In the beginning was the Word, and the Word was with God, and the Word was God. . . . The Word became flesh and lived among us."* Between the verses it says, *"He was in the world . . . yet the world did not know him. He came to what was his own, and his own people did not accept him."*

It's no wonder we didn't accept him. It's all so very unexpected. God in the flesh doesn't look like the God we carry around mentally. The Word—the Word who was with God and was God, God of God, Light of Light, very God of very God, being of one substance with the Father— became flesh . . . looking like a gardener.

The gardeners I know don't resemble the ordinary image of God. The ones I know are like my dad, who was foreman of a grape vineyard for a number of years. Gardeners are regular people with mud on their hands and under their fingernails and on the knees of their pants. If it's a warm day they have a line of sweat across their foreheads and sweat stains on their shirts and a slight mixed aroma of dirt and sweat.

That's what God looks like, or at least it's what God looked like to Mary Magdalene on Easter morning. She didn't even recognize the muddy, sweaty, smelly gardener God.

Now I ask you: What kind of God is this?

God was even harder to recognize a few days earlier when he was dying on the cross. He'd been flogged; a crown of thorns had been put on his head; he'd been dressed in a purple robe; and he'd carried his own cross to Golgotha. He was crucified with a sarcastic sign beneath his feet that said, in three languages, THE KING OF THE JEWS.

Now I ask you, What kind of king is this, hung out to die while soldiers divvied up his clothes and cast lots to see who'd get his robe? What kind of God gets thirsty and the only drink he receives is a sponge of sour wine; says, "It is finished," bows his head, and dies; and later a soldier comes by to break his legs but finding Jesus already dead shoves a spear into his side?

That's what God looks like: bruised from a flogging, wearing a crown of thorns, a sarcastic sign, sour wine, dying, dead.

The whole story is so very unexpected: God hanging out with sinners, God getting hung out on a cross, God reappearing looking like a gardener.

"So what?" is the question we usually don't get around to asking on Easter. So what that the resurrection took place? So what that we worship a God who does unexpected things?

The story of Mary not recognizing the gardener is the answer to our "So what?"; Mary's story is our story, because she asks the same questions we ask: Can there be anyone here? Is there meaning to our lives and our deaths, or is our search for meaning just a game we invent to ease our fear of the dark?

Mary reminds me of us, wandering in a garden at dawn, not knowing if the thing or person we're looking for is there, believing yet not knowing if the belief is real, showing up anyhow, looking, wanting, without even knowing for sure what we're looking for.

God the gardener is invisible, the way a clerk in the grocery store or a bank teller or someone in four layers of clothes pushing a shopping cart down the sidewalk in front of us is invisible. Those people don't look the way we expect God to look, any more than Jesus looked like God to Mary.

Only when Mary was desperate and Jesus spoke her name did she recognize God. And that's like most of us most of the time, able to recognize God's presence only when we're desperate. Every once in a while, though, we don't have to search. Once in a while we come across an Easter moment, a resurrection moment when we suddenly see God's grace right there in front of us. Sometimes it's a quiet thing; sometimes we knuckle away tears; sometimes the chill of hope runs down our spines. And that's why we're gathered here today: because the resurrection gave us a chill of hope that will live within us, world without end, amen.

᛫   ▲   ▲

On Easter Monday I planted more wildflower seeds, watered everything, and transplanted some of the hostas. The thought whisked through my mind a second time: *Brian and I should do the Pentecost sermon together. It would be my parting gift to the congregation.* I shook my head. No. No. No. It was too big a project. I wasn't going to do it; I was not.

The first Hanon exercise was beginning to take shape, as were "Drink to Me Only with Thine Eyes" and "Stars and Stripes Forever." Each song had a sticking point for me, though, one chord at which I came to a dead stop while I thought through the necessary position of my fingers and then, very deliberately, played the chord incorrectly.

Brian wondered why I expected complete command of my fingers. "You've been taking lessons a month, and you're playing 'Stars and Stripes Forever.' You're progressing faster than anybody else I've ever known."

"I'm only progressing this fast because I practice more than any other student you know of."

He shook his head. "No, it's more than that. You bring something unusual to the piano. Now play." After observing me, he said, "I know what the problem is. The two songs you're playing are in different keys, which means the chords are different. You're confusing the two sets of chords." I wasn't to worry. Determination and natural ability would make up for the difficulties I was causing myself.

At the end of the lesson, he had me stretch my fingers across the keys from middle C to the next higher C. "Can you press any keys?"

Why, yes, I could: both Cs, the F, and the A.

"Can your little finger reach the D to the right of the higher C?"

Lo and behold, it could. Already the nature of my hands was changing as my muscles and tendons stretched and strengthened. The proof was in front of me: I could reach an octave plus one key.

▲   ▲   ▲

Molly called to say, "We got through Easter. Now it's time to set the date for the party. I know it's still two months before you get out of there, but we need to get the party on the calendar."

I knew she meant the party to celebrate our mutual departures from our churches, but I felt weary at the thought. "I suppose you want us to invite people."

Molly was amused. "Yes. That's usually what happens before a party."

"I don't think I can stand to be around a crowd of people right now. The only person I think I can stand other than Fred and you is Mary Flowers. Is one guest enough?"

"Sure, if that's all we want. But you like Heidi. Wouldn't you like to invite her?"

Oh, that's right, I did like Heidi. Thinking about Heidi reminded me somehow of Nancy Hardesty, and Nancy's name somehow reminded Molly of Brian.

"Did you want to invite him?"

"Maybe. He told me he's an introvert, and he hates going to parties, but I'll see."

We scheduled the party for Friday, May 8, and then turned to the question of what the baker should write on top of the cake. Molly thought "Hot Damn!" ideal.

Scheduling the party meant it was time to start unplugging myself from the church's emotional circuit, time to begin the distancing required before the end arrived. With time running out, I discovered a thousand things I wanted to preach on. I'd never preached from the book of Job, or from Esther, or from Jonah. I wanted to return to some texts I'd preached on in my first year and think the ideas through again. I wanted to preach a lifetime's worth of sermons with them, which was impossible, even if I crammed each sermon so full it exploded from the inside out.

I practiced the piano whenever I could: an hour or two each night, four hours on Mondays when Fred played duplicate bridge, moments I could grab during the day, ten minutes, forty, seventeen, whatever I could spare.

Everything changed the day I took a lover, a brooding Russian named Pyotr. Brian introduced us. The fact that Pyotr died in 1893 did nothing to limit the passion invading me the first time I heard Brian play Tchaikovsky's *Pathétique.* The music is like a pot of water set on the stove to heat. Sometimes there's a stillness, and sometimes there's a mild simmer, and sometimes there's a full rolling boil with bubbles breaking on top of the water and the water level rising so rapidly that you rush to move the pot from the heat before everyone gets scalded.

Anthony Holden, in his biography, says that as a child Tchaikovsky drummed his fingers constantly on any hard surface. One day his sister Fanny found him sobbing in his room, and he said to her, " 'Oh, the music, the music! . . . It's here . . . in here!'—he struck his forehead— 'and it won't leave me in peace.' " Tchaikovsky has so much passion even the grave can't stifle him.

I had a lot still to learn before I could manage Tchaikovsky: more about shading, and about arpeggios (the first, third, and fifth notes of a chord), and I had to start using the pedal.

"I can't," I told Brian.

"Why not?"

"Because I read a book about teaching people to play the piano, and it says students shouldn't be allowed to use the pedal too soon; they won't live up to their potential if they're indulged too soon."

As though Brian didn't indulge me. As though he didn't let me skip songs I thought were boring. As though he restricted my playing to pieces he'd assigned. As though he didn't enjoy our arguments over the piano. One day at a lesson I was trying to figure out a note in "Drink to Me Only with Thine Eyes" when he said, "It's a C."

"Are you sure?" I asked him.

"Am I sure?" he answered. "Am I sure?"

He'd studied piano for eighteen years. I was in my third week of lessons. Yes, he was sure, the same way he was now certain I had to use the pedal to play *Pathétique.*

"Okay, fine. How do I work it?"

"Just put your foot down on the pedal and lift it off when the sound gets muddy."

After Brian left, I worked through the first six measures and then tried them again with the pedal, curious as to how I was supposed to know what muddy sounded like. Luckily, it was easy to recognize. The sounds tangled together as though they didn't belong in the same space.

▲   ▲   ▲

An iris bloomed in the side yard, my first one ever.

Several years earlier my mother had sent me a Ziploc bag filled with dirt and gnarly, evil-looking dead weeds. When it arrived, I vaguely recalled a conversation with her about plants. I couldn't remember what kind she'd promised to send, but I was afraid they were irises.

When I was in fifth or sixth grade, my teacher, Mrs. Kuemmel, had stuck several irises in a vase and told me to draw them. I was of the crayon-and-glue persuasion when it came to art, but I dutifully drew thick dark lines with my pencil and just as dutifully erased them because they didn't look right. When Mrs. Kuemmel checked back to see my progress, my paper was full of eraser detritus and holes. She decided I was finished drawing, and from then on irises had carried with them the faintest scent of failure.

I didn't plant Mother's dead weeds the day they arrived. I didn't plant them the next day, either, or the next. By the fourth day they were buried under papers on the kitchen desk. A few months later I stashed them in the cedar closet. They moved from there to the bookshelf in the living room sometime later and then disappeared. I rediscovered them in a drawer in the bathroom a year or more after their arrival.

Enough, I decided. *I'm not looking at these ugly things any longer.*

I was on my way to the trash can when I thought *Oh, don't be ridiculous. Go get the shovel and plant them.*

I stuffed them into the ground and forgot about them. Now, two years later, a tall green shoot was climbing into the air from a clump of fronds in the middle of a patch of daffodils.

"What kind of plant is that?" I asked Fred.

"Don't know," he said.

After a week I was curious enough to approach the thing and investigate. When I saw the tight bud of purple, I knew it was an iris. Ah. Just what I always wanted.

A week later my iris launched itself into bloom. It stood tall and purple, regal in the sunlight, proud of its lapping tongues and the three new buds below it on the stalk. It banished all thoughts of failure. Suddenly I was a kid once more, riding my bike home from the post office with the mail and glancing to my left to see, on the far side of Mrs. Fischer's house, a mass of what must have been two hundred irises, each as regal and joyful as the one in my yard. I'd raced home on my bike (blue, with chrome fenders, received on my seventh birthday) to tell Mom what I'd seen.

I went to find Fred.

"Oh, come look, you have to see what's up. It's gorgeous."

All of April was like that: patches of pure beauty mixed in with the sadness and excitement I was feeling.

▲   ▲   ▲

Some things—marriages and life come to mind—often end before any official expiration date. Pastoring is like that. The moment was coming, for me and for the congregation, when our relationship would change from "congregation and pastor" to "departing pastor and congregation preparing for a new pastor." The moment would not coincide with the calendar. Nobody could predict the time, but it would arrive, and the wind would shift, and we would all know that everything crucial about our life together had been said and done. I considered summarizing the current state of the church in a sermon, but what is the state of the church? I wondered.

Lurching on toward the kingdom, I decided. Staggering drunkenly toward the kingdom, the way every good church must because, while bringing in the kingdom of God is the business of the Church, we never get it right. We lurch, we stagger, we fall, we rise, we resist, we refuse, we fail, we fall, we rise, we fall, we rise. Bad planning on God's part, if you ask me, making human beings responsible, but there it is: the pattern abides.

One night that week, I saw clearly that patterns abide in music, too. I went to a concert, a medley of Broadway show tunes interspersed with poetry readings. As I listened to "Summertime," "When You're Smiling," "If Ever I Would Leave You," "I'll Be Seeing You," and other familiar songs, I watched the hands of the pianist. From my viewpoint high above the piano, things were revealed that weren't evident when I sat beside Brian on a level plane. The most important revelation was this one: the pianist was playing patterns. Her hands weren't all over the keyboard in every song. Instead, each song was built from repetitions of particular patterns of notes and chords, with a few variations thrown in.

At last I'd been invited into the mystery. The notes in a song don't exist independently. Each is connected to other notes. The key to piano playing, then, was the recognition of the patterns.

The next day I went to the library and looked at pictures of hands. One illustration showed the bones, muscles, and tendons. The fourth finger has a tendon that branches off both to the right and to the left. The tendon of the fourth finger is thus biologically conjoined to the tendons of the third and fifth. No wonder I had difficulties getting those three fingers to operate independently. They are a trinity, three discrete units and yet yoked.

▲   ▲   ▲

Brian and I sat outside before my next lesson so that I could tell him everything I'd learned about patterns and tendons. I fixed a pot of coffee, and we sat on the steps and drank cup after cup and smoked cigarette after cigarette, talking, interrupting each other, speaking at the same time, and laughing. When Fred joined us, he said, "I thought you were having a piano lesson."

"We are. We just haven't made it into the house yet." And then Brian and I, laughing, brought Fred up to speed on the stories we'd been swapping. Fred shot me a look that said, *Why is it that such a nice man as I has to be surrounded by idiots?*

Fred knew I was infatuated with Brian. Isn't that ridiculous? Middle-aged married minister infatuated with a twenty-year-old. Life doesn't get much sillier than that. It was the music, of course—why else would women have thrown themselves at Liszt, at Elvis Presley, at every band member who plays at a hotel barroom? Music stirs us, and the stirring isn't just emotional or spiritual; it's physical as well. And Brian was so bright, so funny, so conflicted. If I'd been twenty years younger and he'd been twenty years older and I hadn't been committed to Fred and Brian had been willing, I'd have screwed his eyeballs out.

Fred knew, and he wasn't perturbed. One of the advantages in him being fourteen years older than I and having endured a great grief is that he knows the difference between the trivial and the critical. Besides, Fred is incredibly attractive to women. All of my friends, even the lesbians, want to sleep with him.

I once asked him why that was, and he said, "It's because I like women. I think they're beautiful."

"All of them?"

"Yes. Pregnant women are the most beautiful, but they're all beautiful."

Women know this about Fred, that he finds them beautiful. It's a hell of an aphrodisiac. And the aphrodisiac has a special potency because it's safe. My friends are free to be enchanted because they recognize the first and greatest enchantment is Fred's with me and mine with Fred.

Are we foolish to live like this? Would we recommend it to other people? Probably not. There are risks, the greatest being that in a time of great distress, if, say, one of us is having a really bad day, or if the mood and the moon are in precisely the wrong position, one or the other of us could topple into infidelity. That thought is frightening, and yet neither of us is fearful. We are safe, because neither of us goes so close to the edge that we lose sight of the other, standing firm and tall, awaiting the other's return.

▲   ▲   ▲

Brian and I eventually moved to the piano. He was pleased with my tonal shadings and pedaling on "Drink to Me Only with Thine Eyes." He was less taken with my rendition of *Pathétique*. It was the first time I noticed Brian's pathological commitment to counting time.

"Those are dotted half notes. Why don't you play them that way?"

Oh, bloody hell. Playing had been straightforward as long as the music was divided, in an orderly fashion, into quarter notes, half notes, and whole notes. I didn't need to count to play correctly; I knew the proper timing at a glance. But then along came the dotted half note. Intellectually I understood the note is to be held for half again the time of the regular half note, but physically I couldn't stop playing in the simple time patterns I'd grown accustomed to.

▲   ▲   ▲

That night I went to visit Kathy Flynn. I hadn't seen her in several months, and I wanted the chance to say good-bye to her personally.

Kathy welcomed me and introduced me to the man she was dating. We spoke a little, the three of us, about Chris and mused a little about life and living and happiness, which somehow prompted me to tell Kathy I wanted to dye my hair purple.

Does the idea of my dyeing my hair purple seem out of character? It did to me. I don't know where the thought of it originated, but I do know it felt outrageous. I first noticed my desire during the written exercises I was doing for my class on creativity. The first night of class we had to complete the following sentence: "If I could do anything I wanted to do, I'd _____ (fill in the blank)."

The first thing I'd written was "Dye my hair purple."

Six weeks later we had to list ten things we weren't allowed to do. The first item on my list was "Dye my hair purple." Now the idea had popped up for the third time. Kathy was laughing at me.

"Do it! You need to do it!" she urged.

"I don't think I can."

"Of course you can. And I'll tell you what: If you dye your hair purple, I'll come to church to see it."

Ordained ministers in South Carolina don't go around dyeing their hair purple and, even if they did, I wouldn't. I may think outside the box, but day to day I try to live inside it. My hair is brown, a pretty brown, thank you very much. I put highlights in it once when I was in my twenties, but otherwise it's always been brown. Anything else is too extreme, which is the same reason the only jewelry I wear is my engagement ring, wedding ring, and the band Fred gave me on our fifteenth wedding anniversary. I've never received a speeding ticket, a traffic ticket, or a parking ticket.

None of which changed my wish for purple hair, so Friday afternoon I went to a beauty-supply store and wandered the aisles, mesmerized by the options. My sister, Amy, has colored her hair on and off since she was in high school, so I was aware of the available shades of blond, brown, and red colorings, but I didn't know about the blue, magenta, green, pink, and purple. I bought a can of purple hair spray and a box of purple hair coloring, took them home, and put them in the bathroom closet. I couldn't dye my hair purple; I had to conduct a wedding the next day.

Saturday afternoon I stood behind the altar in my black robe and white collar as bridesmaids gowned in jewel tones gathered to my right. Then the double doors at the back of the sanctuary opened, and the bride appeared, escorted by her father. A few months earlier, I'd sat with the bride, her sister, and her mother outside an intensive-care unit, waiting with them to learn whether the father of the bride was going to survive a major medical crisis. Seeing the father and daughter walk down the aisle together, both of them healthy and happy, made for an awfully nice wedding.

I got out the box of purple hair coloring when Fred and I returned home from the reception. He watched me pull the directions from the package.

"You're not really going to do that, are you?"

"Yes, I believe I am."

"What if somebody dies? You can't do a funeral with purple hair."

"I could dye it back to brown."

He shook his head in resignation. "If you're going to do it, you really ought to have some help."

I called an acquaintance who lived nearby. I meant to wait for her to arrive, but I was on a mission from God and didn't have time to waste. By the time she arrived my face, neck, and scalp were a vibrant purple, as were my hands up to my wrists.

She lifted a lock of my hair to examine it.

"It's purple," she pronounced.

"Are you sure?"

"Oh, yes, I'm very sure."

I felt like weeping from the great, reckless abandon of it all. A recording of an inquisition I'd never faced played in my head:

Why don't you want to be a pastor?

Because I can't dye my hair purple.

Why do you want to dye your hair purple?

I don't want to. I just want to have the option.

Claiming the option was, somehow, redemptive.

▲   ▲   ▲

When I showered the next morning, the water ran lavender. When I dried my hair, the towel turned lavender. When I blew my hair dry, my hands—scrubbed clean along with my face, neck, and head the night before—turned lavender.

I kept lifting pieces of my hair to study them in the mirror. Was it really purple? No, not strikingly so. In dim light, it appeared that I'd tried to dye my hair black using a really cheap dye. I took a hand mirror outside and looked at my hair in the sunlight. Ah, that was better. I saw purple.

At the worship service that morning, I told the congregation that God had been giving me pointers all week that it was time for us to talk about my leaving.

Last Sunday I counted the bookshelves in the church office that still have my books on them. If I empty one shelf a week between now and Moving Day, I'll run out of weeks before I run out of bookshelves. That tells me we're running out of time together.

I'm certain that noon on June 10 is not going to be the moment when we separate from each other. Our time together will end sooner than that. I'll still be your pastor, but the real leave-taking, the moment when we're no longer in relationship, will occur before Moving Day. The moment is different for each congregation, and different for each leave-taking, but the moment will come at a time when we're not even expecting it. Knowing this, I know that we're running out of time together.

I told them my spirituality group was studying John Wesley, and that one member of the group had asked me early in the week how the transition with the church was going.

"Really well. We're all in denial," I told him.

Oh, we're doing what needs to be done. We're making plans for the summer, and I'm deciding what to include in each worship service to honor our life together, hymns like "Lord of the Dance" last week and "Here I Am, Lord," this week, some words that I want to say one more time. I want us to share together one more time the things that have become flesh of our flesh, that have defined who we've been together. I want to honor our life together with a few precious, holy things I can give you one last time before you step into the future with your new pastor.

I don't have to do this preparation with you. In some ways I'd prefer not to. The trouble is that it isn't a faithful response. If we don't acknowledge the life we've shared, you won't be ready for your new pastor. You'll be refrigerators filled with emotional leftovers. At best, those leftovers will postpone your continued ministry, and mine. At worst they'll poison them.

I congratulated them on their commitment to diversity, accessibility, and inclusivity. I reminded them that to have a woman as pastor was an act of courage. For all of our commitment to inclusivity, many United Methodist churches refuse to allow women as pastors, and I knew my congregation had endured raised eyebrows from their neighbors and even from some church members who stopped attending in defiance of my gender. I reminded them that the district superintendent had said he was sending me there to find out if the church wanted to live or die.

We were all so innocent then. Nobody told us how difficult it would be to rise from the deathbed. It taxed us all. There must have been times when some of you wanted to slap me, and I know there were times when I wanted to slap one or two of you.

Whoa! Where did that statement come from? Startled, I paused and thought it through. Yes, there were times we had been exactly that angry with each other. Heck, there were times they'd have burned me at the stake if they could have agreed on where to build the pyre. But to have said so?

Blame it on the purple hair.

I turned to an enumeration of the emotions congregations experience when a pastor leaves: grief, anger, resentment, paranoia, and excitement. I said I knew it was a good list because I was experiencing all of those emotions, a different one for breakfast, for lunch, for supper, and for between-meal snacks.

Maybe you feel some of those same emotions. And maybe you feel a little fear, too, because a new pastor is coming, and it's a mystery what kind of church this will be under his leadership. My strengths, my gifts, matched the needs of the church when I arrived: administration, leading worship, involving more people in church leadership, preaching, visitation. The new pastor's strengths will complement mine and build on them. I know he will love you to the best of his abilities, just as I have loved you.

For the next few weeks, everything is likely to feel either really flat or really jangled. Anger may come spilling out. I try to imagine what shape the anger will take. The budget's always good for being mad about, and you haven't had a major fight yet over the rest-room renovations. It might be good for you to get that squabble out of the way before the new pastor gets here. That's my suggestion, but it probably won't be where the anger surfaces. It will probably surface over trivial things, like the color of my shoes or who forgot to turn off a light switch. That's what people do: fight over trivialities because we don't have access to the deep pain, the true source of our anger.

The final stage in parting is acceptance. That's the stage we're fumbling toward. The stumbling is okay, because the real mystery is how we formed our pattern of life together, and in only three years. I'm not sure you understood at the time what a risk you were taking in accepting a pastor in her first appointment. And there was the woman thing on top of that. And you were a congregation trying to understand if you were called to live or to die.

Nobody told us our time together was guaranteed to be painful. Whether I as your pastor led you through the burial of the hopes and dreams of the church or the unearthing of its hopes and dreams, it was going to hurt. Neither you nor I had the experience to know the pain wasn't about us but was about the hard, hard work we were doing.

Yet somehow in the midst of the difficulty we formed a pattern of life together. Or, to be more precise, God formed a pattern of life within us, a pattern in which holiness kept showing up, sometimes in spite of everything we did. Our life together, for all the pain, has been holy.

In the weeks to come we're going to walk together down a dark hallway fumbling on the wall for a light switch. We may not want to take that walk, but it's the faithful thing to do. It's what we disciples have done since the very beginning, walking and fumbling, patting the wall, looking for the light switch, trusting there is a light, hoping that our hands and bodies are in the right place and that we're fumbling on the right wall. That's what disciples do: they trust a light is there even when they can't quite find it.

The good thing, the holy thing is that together we know the name of the light, and together we fumble and follow, knowing the light is real and present and lighting our life together even while we grope in the darkness.

Amen.

I was fine until I got to the "amen." Looking out at their faces, it struck me how many of them I'd seen with oxygen tubes running up their noses or fear hiding behind their eyes, these people I'd baptized, served communion, laughed with, loathed, argued with, prayed with and for, celebrated with, mourned with, pushed to set goals, and cheered into mission work, and I unexpectedly heard myself say, "Oh, my God, who would not love you?"

I repeated the words I'd spoken at my first funeral: *And now we have to learn to live together differently.*

Our time together has been precious, I said. *Our time together has been holy.*

And then I said, *And now I'm going to cry.*

And then I did. I offered them the gift of my tears.

Tears for the love that would have to be lived differently.

Tears for the grief.

Tears for the frustration.

Tears for the grace.

While I cried, I babbled about the multiplicity of deaths we'd endured, of all we'd lost together and gained together, and how beautiful it had been.

When I finally stopped blubbering—when I and a number of other people finally stopped blubbering—I announced the closing hymn. It was "Here I Am, Lord," the hymn we'd sung together my first real Sunday at the church, and one last time we sang, "I will go, Lord, where you lead me/I will hold your people in my heart."

On the porch, only a few people mentioned my purple hair. One was a visitor who owned a beauty-supply store. She was trying to be helpful when she said, "I can sell you something to fix your hair."

I shook my head. "No, thanks. I did it this way on purpose. I wanted it to be purple."

"My goodness: you a preacher and telling a story like that." She never did believe I'd intentionally done such a disastrous thing to my hair.

That's okay: my hair was an outward and visible sign that I was making choices for myself, whether they made sense to anybody else or not. And I do know there was a direct connection between the permission I gave myself to dye my hair and the permission I gave myself to speak the vital words that honored our life together.

chapter nineteen

THAT SAME WEEK, FRED AND I CAME UP WITH A NEW
plan. We'd had sex, and afterward one or the other of us had remarked,
as we frequently did, "That was so good, I don't know why we don't do
it every night."

Our average was twice a week. We intended it to be higher, but life
too often interfered. We'd have a busy day and be worn out, physically or
emotionally; or we'd watch a West Coast basketball game that didn't
end until one in the morning; or I'd get a call from an emergency room
and Fred would fall asleep before I got home; or we'd go to bed at a rea-
sonable hour but just not be quite in the mood. It was as though our
default mechanism for sex was set on "Not tonight, honey." Very often it
took more effort than either of us was willing to expend to override the
default switch.

On that night in May, half asleep in the pastel lull between moans
and snores, I came up with a question: *Why did we not have sex every
night?*

I couldn't think of a good answer.

I studied on the idea a little longer, and then I nudged Fred.

"Are you awake?"

"No."

"I've got an idea."

"What is it?"

"I think we ought to have sex every night."

"Okay, now I am awake."

I told him about the default mechanism and that I thought it
needed to be reset. It took us twenty minutes to come up with the plan.
Instead of assuming that we would not have sex unless one of us took
overt action, we would instead assume from now on that we were going
to have sex every night.

251

You know how when you first start having sex with someone and all day long you know that the moment the two of you get alone together behind closed doors, you're going to take your clothes off? You know how the knowledge colors everything you do all day long? Everything you smell or touch or taste is different, tangier or richer or edgier? And you know how when the two of you finally meet in the same room, even when you have all your clothes on, your very pores are aware of the other person's presence, and your less-exposed body parts are busy humming a little song that goes something like "Soon, soon, gonna get me some of that soon"?

That's what happened to Fred and me when we changed our default mechanism: lots of high-frequency humming. All I really wanted was to receive all the joy my body and Fred's and the universe had to offer.

▲   ▲   ▲

Monday's piano lesson went smoothly: "Thoughts at Twilight," with accidental sharps and flats; "For He's a Jolly Good Fellow"; and the trickier "The Fairies' Harp." That one had a broken chord. With standard chords, you press the keys simultaneously. For a broken chord, you play the notes consecutively, very quickly. The resulting sound sparkles like Tinkerbell in the movie *Peter Pan.* By then I'd resolved my troubles with the pedal. When the notes got muddy I could not only hear them, but I could also feel the hair on the back of my neck rise.

Brian approved. "Good. Now I want you to start taking your foot off the pedal the instant before the notes get muddy."

What? I'd thought the goal was to identify muddiness, and now I was supposed to identify it before it occurred? "How will I know when that is?"

"You'll know. Just keep practicing."

My next assignments were "Greensleeves," "Go Down, Moses," and "Fascination." "Fascination" was my choice, not Brian's, and he was not especially enthusiastic.

"Why a waltz?"

"Do you remember at my first lesson when you asked what kind of music I want to play?"

"Yes."

"I finally know the answer: I want to play it all." I wasn't joking. I wanted to have under my command all the textures and rhythms of music, whether folk songs, classical, waltzes, marches, Motown, jazz, or music I hadn't yet heard. I wanted to experience the variety and the richness through my hands. I recognized the drive as identical to the one that had compelled me when I arrived at the church and wanted to employ every hymn in the hymnal and some outside it; perform every liturgy; and use every baptism and communion ritual. I wanted a totality of experience, wanted to investigate the nuances of tone and language until all the riches of worship—and now of the piano—became flesh and heartbeat and tendon of my flesh, because that's how I learn, how I understand, how I search for meaning. The difference now was that I was self-indulgent enough to say out loud, without apology, "I want it all."

▲   ▲   ▲

At the church, I was trying to invent ways to make life easier for the pastor who would follow me. Perhaps if the congregation more clearly understood the obligations of ordained ministers and, specifically, of pastors? I was to preach on the passage in the ninth chapter of Acts where Peter raises from the dead a woman named Tabitha. I decided to focus on Peter and the particular gifts he offered to the Church. And then I'd take a detour.

Christian theology holds that people offer their gifts to the Church in particular ways. Ministers, for instance. Most people don't know or especially care what ministers do, but I thought it might be helpful if, just once, a congregation was told the sacred obligations of ordination.

Instead of reading them all, I settled for the list of a pastor's duties in *The Book of Discipline:* preaching, overseeing the worship life, reading and teaching scripture; administering the sacraments; giving oversight to the educational programs; providing leadership in funding; leading in ministry with people with disabilities; leading evangelistic outreach; marrying, counseling, burying, and visiting; participating in community, denominational, ecumenical, and interreligious concerns; and ordering the life of the congregation for discipleship in the world.

When I concluded, I admitted simply reading the list made me tired, but before I went into the ministry I'd had an additional list of expectations.

I expected clergy to have toddlers who never had tantrums, teenagers who never got speeding tickets, and wives who never got runs in their hose. They were to have perfect relationships, be spiritually strong, and be able to spell, punctuate, and read my mind. I never realized ministers were human beings.

When I said that last sentence, the congregation stopped breathing. It was as though a giant had put his mouth over the building and sucked all the air out. No one coughed, no one twitched, no one moved.

I examined their faces. Nobody seemed annoyed, provoked, or resistant. I think they were in shock—not at my statement but at what the statement revealed to them about themselves.

I tried to talk them through their misery by setting the issue in a broader context, saying the coming of age of the baby boomers like me had irrevocably changed notions of ordained ministry; how we—they, I, the United Methodist Church, all the churches—are living in a time of great challenge; how difficult it is for everyone, on both sides of the pulpit. I talked about hope and the power of God. I introduced the closing hymn, and they all stood up to sing, but the air in the sanctuary still wasn't moving, so I signaled the pianist to stop. I said, "You are all so quiet. I worry about you when you get so quiet. I don't want you to be troubled." I told them a seminary professor had suggested that perhaps the reason pastors have an impossible list of duties, both written and unwritten, is to remind us we're dependent on God, and maybe their silence was because they, too, had realized how dependent on God we all are.

The congregation didn't buy it, any more than I had, so I stopped talking.

They were still subdued as they left. One man said, "I hadn't realized we'd stopped breathing until you said it, but you were right. I don't know what happened to us."

Nobody else spoke to me about the sermon, but what I believe happened is that for the first time they saw me clearly. Me. Not the comforting presence who prayed with them in times of crisis. Not the firm administrator who required fiscal responsibility. Not the stubborn preacher who held a hard line on which version of the Bible I'd use. Not the laughing pastor who celebrated the achievements of their children and teenagers. Not the powerful preacher. Me: a human being. A well-trained, capable, faithful human being.

The Lord's Prayer says, "Forgive us our trespasses as we forgive those who trespass against us." Before I was ordained, I trespassed against clergy by holding expectations of them both contradictory and impossible to uphold. As a clergyperson, I bore the same burden from others. The depth of silence of the congregation suggested that perhaps, in that moment, they understood. Perhaps in that moment I began to forgive all the trespasses of the last three years—not only theirs, but mine as well.

▲   ▲   ▲

"Stars and Stripes Forever" was too uplifting and "Drink to Me Only with Thine Eyes" too sweet, so I spent that afternoon with Tchaikovsky. *Pathétique* has, in its middle, seven measures filled with left-hand chords. None of the chords were familiar. I played the seven measures over and over with my left hand. A dozen repetitions, and I was no better than when I began.

I couldn't see the chords as a unit. It was like when I was learning to read and couldn't see words as a unit and had to sound them out one syllable at a time. Ba. Na. Na. Ba. Na. Na. Ba-na-na. Banana! I'd thought the same method would apply to chords, that repetition would promote recognition. It wasn't happening. Another hour on the seven measures, and I was still glancing from written music to keyboard, keyboard to written music. Perhaps if I were to memorize the chords and *think* the notes. But no: I was too inexperienced; the notes were too foreign, too complicated.

Thinking, trying, rejecting, thinking, trying, rejecting, trying— and then it happened, a moment when Brian's comments and the memory of seeing the pianist play in patterns at the concert coalesced, and not only did I know what I'd been doing wrong, but I also knew how to learn to play.

What I'd recognized, finally, at last, thank you Jesus, is that chords aren't isolated, independent entities. Until then, I'd approached each song as though the essential task were to play one chord, and then another, and then another, but that isn't how it works. Chords are connected to other chords, just as fingers are connected to other fingers and people are connected to other people. The most difficult part of *Pathétique* wasn't playing the chords. The difficult part was the transition from one chord to the next.

What I'd done until now was look at a chord and tell my fingers, *Play the E, the B flat, and the C sharp simultaneously.* I'd then look at the next chord and think, *Play the F, the A, and the D.* The breakdown happened as my fingers moved from one set of keys to the next.

The answer was to concentrate on the movement, not the destination. I broke the first transition into its elements—*Move the fifth finger from the E to the F. Move the second finger from the B flat to the A. Move the first finger from the C sharp to the D*—and I watched my fingers move.

I mastered that first intersection. It took me nearly an hour, but I did it. And when I did, I dragged Fred in to watch.

He'd have been interested even if we weren't having sex every night. "Tell me again exactly how you did it."

I demonstrated on the keyboard while I talked. "My brain can't do it alone. My hands and my brain have to learn at the same time."

"And they're learning."

"Yes!" We high-fived each other. "They're learning!"

To celebrate, we went to bed.

▴   ▴   ▴

Learning the transition between the second and third chords took half as long as learning the first transition. By the time I finished practicing the next day, I could play each of the transitions in *Pathétique,* which meant I had mastered the entire piece. I was satisfied. As I left the piano, a thought crossed my mind for the third time: *Brian and I should do the Pentecost sermon together.* My general rule says if a good idea occurs to you three times, chances are you should act on it, because it might be God. I called and left a message for Brian: "Pentecost is May 31, and I'd like you to do the sermon with me that day, with you on the piano and me preaching. Let me know if you're interested."

He called the next morning. Yes, he was available. Yes, he'd do the sermon with me.

▴   ▴   ▴

Given my achievement, you'd think my next piano lesson would have gone well. Instead, I played briskly through the Hanon exercises—I was now doing four of them a day—and then thrashed my way through the Tchaikovsky. When I finished, Brian's expression was guarded.

"That was pretty loud. Let me play it for you so you can hear the limits of loud."

I moved from the piano bench to a chair and watched him pedal as he played. When he finished he said, "Louder than that is blaring."

I responded, "I intended to blare."

"What's up with you today? Do you need to take a break?"

I didn't know what was wrong. I felt on edge, or was it melancholy? And why? I was handling things at the church smoothly, but something was not right. All I wanted to play were dirges.

We went outside for a cigarette and to talk about the Pentecost sermon.

"What exactly is it that you want me to do? And what exactly is Pentecost, anyhow?"

"Don't Southern Baptists talk about Pentecost?"

"I don't think so. If they do they call it by a different name."

"Pentecost is the day the Holy Spirit came to the Church. Wait a minute, and I'll get a Bible and read it to you."

When the day of Pentecost had come, I began, and then I moved through the rest of the first chapter of Acts, the words about wind and tongues of fire and people all together in one place. I got caught up in the rush of the wind, and speech became a music form with quarter notes, whole notes, eighth notes, dotted half notes; slurs, staccatos, and broken chords; piano, pianissimo, mezzo-forte, forte, slowly, faster, wildly, then slowly, gently, quietly.

When I finished, Brian's mouth was open. He blinked. Then he swallowed. "Is that really in the Bible?"

"Well, yeah. Haven't you heard this passage before?"

"Not read like that."

I closed the Bible and balanced it on the porch railing. "Neither have I. Now do you see why I want us to do this sermon together?"

"No. What do you need me for? Your voice is enough."

"But can't you imagine what it would be like for the congregation to hear both of us?"

I could see the glimmer in his eye that said he'd already begun to imagine.

"What would you want me to play?"

"I don't know. Music that goes with the words."

"Religious or classical?"

"Classical." I sighted a wisp of a frown on his face. "But you're the pianist. You get to choose."

"I can do that," he decided.

"I know you can."

"I'm going to be nervous."

"So am I. It's okay. In sermons like this one, it's as though you're dancing on the edge of a knife. If you fall, you know you're going to get slashed to pieces."

"Pentecost is like that?"

"Pentecost is always like that."

      ▲   ▲   ▲

I had a church member named Vicki whose sister-in-law had died. Visitation was that evening in a nearby small town. Driving there, I passed the cemetery where Chris and Beth were buried. To my surprise, when I got to the funeral home, it was deserted. Apparently the small town had more mortuaries than I was aware of. I was headed for a gas station to ask directions when I came up on the cemetery again. I thought, *I could go there now,* and at the same instant I turned through the gates. I'd been listening to Mozart while I drove, and I left the car running, the door open, the Mozart still playing when I approached the graves. Some flowers had blown out of the arrangements on Chris's and Beth's headstones. I gathered the azaleas to replace in Beth's arrangement and the magnolias to add to Chris's, and while I worked with the flowers I breathed and relaxed. It was a balmy evening, the slanted rays of the ebbing sun coloring everything in a tremulous light. There was no pain in the air.

What I'd responded to most deeply in Chris, and was responding to now in Brian, was the vitality. Both young men had the same rare, rangy, rascally power to set fire to the air around them; to captivate with a glance, a glare, or a snicker; to be captivated in turn. When Chris died, I regretted the loss of his fire. That evening I felt the radiance of its banked coals.

Late as I was getting to the funeral home, only a few people were still there to pay their respects. Vicki and I stepped aside to talk. She and I had met my first summer at the church when I performed her son's wedding. Later she started visiting the church, and, later still, I baptized her. When she was young, in her twenties, Vicki was in love with a man. One day he was diagnosed with leukemia. In less than two weeks he was dead. Her nascent grief reignited when Chris was diagnosed, and she'd followed his progress with prayer and then joy until once again her joy somersaulted into mourning.

I told Vicki about my mistake, how I'd gone to the wrong funeral home, and added, "Since I was right there anyhow, I stopped at the cemetery to see Chris."

Vicki is quick to catch the nuances of the spirit. Her eyes began to sparkle. "How's he doing?"

"He's doing very well." I sparkled back at her.

I'd come a far distance. I would never be reconciled to death, that pernicious destroyer of dreams, but if I carried with me no other good memories from the church, Chris was enough. I wouldn't have missed him for the world.

▲   ▲   ▲

Molly and I lost a final piece of innocence that spring when I read *Ordaining Women: Culture and Conflict in Religious Organizations* by Mark Chaves. For this sociological study on women and ordination, Chaves researched the one hundred largest denominations in America. His research revealed no significant difference between denominations that ordain women and those that don't. For example, although the United Methodist Church has been ordaining women since 1956, thousands of congregations refuse to accept the appointment of a woman. Conversely, although the Roman Catholic church continues to refuse ordination to women, women perform the functions of priests in three hundred or so congregations in America. Polity and practice don't coincide.

Most interesting to me was Chaves's conclusion that the disparity between faith and practice had more to do with public relations than with theology. In general, denominations that want to be perceived as liberal ordain women; the others don't. In other words, women are ordained so that denominations can feel good about themselves, not so they can have women serving as clergy. The Church is like an eighty-year-old man who marries a twenty-year-old woman, not in celebration of who she is and the life they can share together but because he wants to show her off in public. I called Molly to report on my reading.

"Molly, they didn't ordain us because they want real, live women to be clergy. They ordained us because they want to be known as denominations that ordain women."

"So the churches feel about you and me being in the ministry the same way I feel about homeless people," she responded.

"What do you mean?"

"I want homeless people to have homes, to have food, to be warm and safe and dry, but I don't want them sleeping in one of my bedrooms, using my bathroom, and being in my kitchen. I want them to have those things. I just don't want them living in my house."

I said, "You mean the Church doesn't want us."

"That's right. The Church doesn't want us."

I remembered a recent comment from another colleague. He and I were talking about Barbara Brown Taylor's preaching, and he said she wasn't isolated in being female and a great preacher, that women have a rare capacity, that they're willing to name realities and dimensions of experience within the biblical texts that male preachers never even notice. My friend was excited, bouncing a little on his toes, when he said, "The difference between men and women preaching—well, it's like me talking to my dog." I must have twitched, because he immediately added, "No disrespect intended." He went on to say that he meant women do preaching, and ministry as a whole, differently enough from men that it's as though we're two different species.

One of my friends questions whether ordination warrants the sacrifices it requires from women. "I see the energy my friends put into surviving within institutions that don't honor their contribution, and I think about what their energy could achieve elsewhere, and I just don't know if the Church is worth it."

Another friend told me most of the clergywomen she knows live in constant tension over whether or not to remain ordained. "We have a spiritual duty to question, often, whether or not to resign our ordinations—and then we need to stay, as long as we can."

It appears from Chaves's conclusions that denominations don't care much whether we stay or go. Perhaps that's why, according to *United Methodist Clergywomen Retention Study* published in 1997, women leave local church ministry at a 10 percent higher rate than male clergy, and nearly a third of the clergywomen aren't serving as pastors. There's a

limit to how long some people will stay in situations where they're neither wanted nor honored.

▲   ▲   ▲

Brian wasn't satisfied with my Tchaikovsky. "You're still not putting any
expression into it. And you still aren't using the pedal enough."

"Show me." As he played, I watched his hands, catching in my
peripheral vision the telltale movement of his knee as he pedaled. Then I
got distracted. It was raining. I could hear and see the raindrops splat-
tering the picture window. Brian finished, and I asked him to play the
song through again. He did.

While the last note lingered in the room, he said, "Now let's do
this. Let me sit in the rocking chair and look out the window and not
watch you. You play it as though nobody's in the room with you."

So we did. He sat and rocked and looked out the window. By now
it was storming, rivulets of rain streaming down the window. When I
finished, I turned to face him. He looked far away, as though while I
played he'd gone on a tour of the world and was staring at a sight he
didn't want to know existed.

"Yes," he said, after a pause. "That's how you play Tchaikovsky.
Your pedaling isn't quite there yet, but the rest of it—the tone and the
feeling—is all there."

We stayed together, held by the storm, talking softly about nothing
much. At times I confused Brian with my younger self. Other times I
just listened, fascinated by how life lived with an intellect and spirit
similar to mine sounded coming from someone who wasn't me. I felt
both ways that afternoon, as though I was seeing myself and myself-the-
stranger simultaneously.

Eventually Brian asked what I thought about heaven and hell.
Having been raised Baptist, he'd absorbed apocalyptic imagery, hellfire
and howling for the damned, streets of gold and pious gloating for the
righteous. It must have been my blue jeans, or maybe my language, possibly even the cigarettes that suggested to him I might have a different
understanding.

"I'm not interested in hell. Heaven? When somebody's dying or
when I'm doing a funeral, I believe it all: the resurrection, life everlasting, a place where people are connected in a whole different way than on

earth. The rest of the time I don't know. Except . . ." I told him about my British grandmother's death in December. "Whatever's true about heaven, the one thing I know absolutely is that my grandmother hasn't been extinguished. She's out there somewhere, twirling in the galaxies maybe, still radiating energy, and still loving me."

Brian was in a state of confusion, unsure whether I would go to hell for my beliefs, whether he would go to hell for listening to my beliefs, whether hell wasn't the product of mass psychosis. He changed the subject. "Tell me what you want on Pentecost."

I wanted to read the first chapter of Acts early in the service, with accompaniment, to familiarize the congregation with our methodology before they heard the sermon. In the first chapter, the disciples are gathered in Jerusalem after the resurrection, not knowing what's going to happen next, sticking around together because Jesus had told them to wait for the Holy Spirit.

"Can you play something that matches the unsettled feeling they must have had? Something a little mysterious, but hopeful."

"Sure. Mysterious but hopeful. Nothing to it." (Brian could be sarcastic when the spirit moved him.) Could I give him a week to work through possibilities?

"Sure. So are you coming to the party?"

"Probably not. I've told you I don't like crowds."

"It's not going to be a crowd, exactly. But I know how you feel. Come if you can."

The party was the next evening. The purple had washed out of my hair, so, still feeling the need for color, I'd bought two bottles of nail polish, one hot pink and the other schoolbus yellow, and painted my fingernails in alternating colors. The cake was in pink and yellow, too. After much thought, and knowing children would be at the party, I'd substituted "We did it!" for Molly's "Hot damn!"

⋆　　⋆　　⋆

Nancy Hardesty was the first arrival. Fred welcomed her with a hug and was still at the kitchen door when Heidi and her two children arrived. Mary Flowers and her daughter Jessica came next, and then Molly with her husband and children and a huge container of hot dogs and hamburgers already grilled.

I'd had two bites of my hot dog when I remembered the box of

New Year's Eve supplies I'd found on sale for a dollar in February. I located the box on the top shelf of the cedar closet and was ripping it open when Brian arrived. I did the introductions, sat him down with a plate and fork, and started handing out hats.

"Nancy, do you want a hat?"

"No, thank you."

"Melissa, would you rather have a tiara or a top hat?"

Nancy rose from her chair. "Tiaras? Do we have tiaras?"

"Of course we do. Would you like one?"

Of course she did. She chose purple. I picked out a green one. Melissa wanted a gold top hat. Fred, being Fred, didn't need a hat.

We'd reached the stage of blowing noisemakers when Heidi's husband, Bob, arrived from a late meeting at school. We fed him, and then everybody ate cake and ice cream, and then I dragged everybody into the living room to listen to me play.

I might have been nervous if I hadn't been so excited. I began *Pathétique*.

I played the song right every note, every chord, and every transition. I pedaled, and I took my foot off the pedal the instant before the sound got muddy. The music emerging underneath my fingertips sounded like ice, wind, great streaming globs of rain and, beneath it all, fire. I let the waves of the last notes linger until finally lifting my hands from the keys and turning toward my listeners. Mary Flowers was bawling.

"Mary, why are you crying?" I whispered.

"Because I remember when you couldn't do this, and it's like watching a miracle to hear you play."

Brian was staring at me, transfixed. "That was incredible. When I left here yesterday, your pedaling was still off. Tonight it was perfect. How did that happen in twenty-four hours?"

How? I don't know. How did my grandmother, staring into the coals in the fireplace the day the *Ark Royal* was sunk, see my father carrying his kit bag? How did I, standing in a parking lot at eight o'clock on a crisp Christmas night, know Terry's father had died? How do we reach beyond the capabilities of the physical? Mysteries can be miracles, and miracles can be mysteries. If I wanted to, I could speak of imagination, of delusion, of expected leaps attributed to extraordinary causes, but I don't need to do so.

Much later Nancy and Brian were the only remaining guests. Brian was at the piano. Fred was in the kitchen loading the dishwasher. Nancy and I were side by side on the couch, handing a copy of the Bible back and forth as we took turns reading the first two chapters of Acts out loud and discussing the tone, the tempo, and the tenor of the Pentecost story.

Brian began to play a piece I couldn't identify. At least, my head didn't recognize it. My soul did, though; my soul recognized the agony and the silence. And my bones—my bones recognized the intensity and the beauty. There wasn't enough air in the room, but I didn't want the music to stop one bit. I was in a lane of mystery, trees surrounding me, fairy lights in the distance, the woods waiting, the lane waiting, Tinkerbell and her kin waiting, and where I might step—toward the trees, up the lane, toward the fairy lights—didn't matter because in the moment all directions were possible, all were precious, all were holy, as the music surrounded, entered, bathed, embraced me, and promised it was okay, I was okay, whatever might come, the beauty, the miracles, the mysteries would sustain me, world without end, amen.

"What *was* that?" I asked Brian after the last notes had faded.

" 'My Tribute.' "

"Where have I heard it before?"

"I played it that Sunday with Chris."

"Oh. That's the one—" The one that touched me so deeply, the one that propelled me into my *yashab* sermon on the day Chris said, "I'm afraid," and we cried with him.

"That's the one."

"I want you to play it at the end of the Pentecost service."

Fred held up a cautionary hand. "I don't know if that's a good idea, Mary Jo. How are you going to preach? Listening to it takes too much out of you."

Brian said, "Fred's right. And not just you. The music is so powerful, people will need time to collect themselves."

I nearly agreed, but then I remembered who I am. "I've done funerals. I can do this. It'll be hard, but the congregation needs to hear this music one more time."

That's where we left it.

▲   ▲   ▲

Claiming the freedom to dye my hair purple let me claim other free-
doms. On Mother's Day I preached explicitly, for the first time, out of
my experience as a woman. Until then it had been too risky; even Molly
was accused of preaching a feminist diatribe the time she used mothers
in scripture as sermon illustrations. I made no bones about my inten-
tions, telling the men in the congregation,

You're welcome to sleep through this sermon if you want to, or you
can listen if you'd like and maybe know something about your wives, mothers, and daughters that none of them has ever told you.

In the biblical text, Jesus said the greatest commandment is to love
God with all your heart and soul and strength and to love your neighbor
as yourself. I said my family is as cantankerous as anybody else's, but I've
experienced a trove of love, and recently I'd been asking myself, *Oh, is
that what God's love for us is like?* I talked about corresponding with my
grandmother in England and how even from that distance her love was a
real force in my life. *And I wonder if God's love is like that. Does it ever seem
that way to you?*
Then I talked about my mom and the Betty Crocker spoons she
sent when I was in my teens and the Ziploc bag of dead weeds filled
with potential, and how first one big purple iris came into bloom, and
then another, and then another, and then another, and how Mother had
known all along what a wonderful gift she'd given me and how much I'd
enjoy it when it blossomed.

And I wonder if God's love is like that. Does it ever seem that way to
you?
I have one other example of family love to offer you this morning. I
don't know that I've heard anyone else name this feeling, but I'm going to
try. When my first daughter was born, I was nineteen. She was about ten
days old when I felt something deep and powerful that I'd never experienced before. It was the middle of the night, deep night, not long before
Halloween, and I was sitting in the dark in a wide-armed yellow upholstered chair. She'd finished eating and was drifting toward sleep, this tiny
girl with her little bald head and perfect ears.
From somewhere, from nowhere, arose in me the conviction that if

anyone or anything ever hurt her, I would destroy them. I would destroy them with my bare hands. *I paused. Waited. Let the words sit in the sanctuary, let them be fully heard and known.* The feeling was not civilized. It was animalistic, biology and emotion, survival of the species and love.

I've been thinking about that feeling this week, my fierce animal rage, and I came up with a question I've barely begun to ask, because it shakes me so. The question is, Is that what God's love is like? I don't mean the animalistic part, intent on destruction. I mean that fierce, protective, urgent, gorgeous, wild wave of love that penetrates every atom of your being. Could God's love be that strong?

And could God be like us watching our children and grandchildren? Does God watch us walking through life and want to protect us, to keep us from all harm, and is God helpless because to do so would mean imprisoning us, never letting us learn how to turn over, never giving us a chance to fall off a bed or to be comforted?

Jesus said we're to love the Lord our God with all our heart and soul and mind and strength and to love our neighbors as ourselves. If you're trying to figure out how to do that, maybe the best place to start is with this question: Is it possible God's love for each of us might be as strong as the love we experience?

Afterward, somebody said, "What is this? You say you're leaving, and then you give us the best of the best."

At first I was bemused by the statement, but later I was amused, announcing to Fred, "I've been giving the best of the best since I got here." Amused because it meant I'd finally made peace with my failures. I'd arrived at the job knowing that my inexperience was a detriment, knowing that however much faith and urgency I brought to tasks, it couldn't be enough. Often I was in water over my head, my legs cramping, flailing on through the pain. Always, always I left things undone. Sometimes I was weary, sometimes frightened, sometimes in despair. A congregation requires a pastor's life blood, and some weeks they didn't get it from me. Some weeks I hadn't loved them enough to give it; some weeks I'd needed every ounce to keep my own heart beating; some weeks I'd given so many pints the week before that to have given more would have been self-destructive.

At long last I'd acknowledged that failure was inevitable. Even Jesus couldn't heal every leper, any more than the Highway Patrol can ticket every speeding driver. Whatever my sins, whatever my mistakes, I'd done what I could do, done everything I saw to do or knew how to do or could figure out ways of doing. I'd given it my best. It was up to God to bless the work, and to bless the workers, and to bless the work to come, but I offered my own benediction when I said to Fred, "I gave it everything I had. Now I can relax."

▲   ▲   ▲

A few days later, on May 13, I got a phone call from Goucher College, the graduate program I'd most wanted to attend, announcing I'd been accepted into their master's degree program in writing creative non-fiction. A week earlier, word had come down that I'd received a summer fellowship to Columbia University. At last I had some answers, albeit incomplete, to the question of what was to come.

The day was sunny, full of hope and promise. To alter just a little a statement sixties poet Rod McKuen made in his poem "Listen to the Warm," for an hour I had everything.

chapter twenty

———

FRED AND I WERE BATTLING OBNOXIOUS ROBINS. TWO WEEKS earlier they'd claimed the narrow space on my car between the driver's window and the door panel as a rest stop. Three, four, five times a day, a bird would perch in that peculiar location and, on departure, leave the side of the car festooned with droppings.

Fred had been in and out all day, to the post office, to the country club for lunch, to the hospital to see a friend. Between trips he hosed down my car. He'd headed off for the grocery store when I got the phone call from Goucher College. I went outside to wait for Fred so that I could greet him with the good news. A robin was perched on a wooden post in the driveway. I watched him hop down to the ground and cock his head this way and that, inspecting me, inspecting the ground, inspecting my automobile. When he fluttered up to the door frame, I clomped down the stairs to scare him away. I was still waving my arms when Fred's car turned into the driveway.

My news got tangled up with the bird's antics; even as I was walking toward Fred, the robin was perching again on my car. "That bird's got an attitude," said Fred. "Get out of here!"

The bird hopped down from the car and across the driveway to the stone wall that edges our property. From there he fluttered up ten feet to the branch of a dogwood tree, then up and across another twenty feet to the high branches of a poplar.

"Maybe I can make him nervous." Fred picked up a pebble and tossed it into the tree's lowest hanging branches. The robin thumbed its nose at him. He tossed a second pebble. I'd grabbed several bags of groceries and was almost up the steps to the kitchen when I heard, "Stupid bird," and then nothing, and then my name.

I turned back.

Fred was bent double, clutching his right arm just above the elbow and staggering toward me.

"You have to take me to the emergency room. My arm's broken. I heard it snap."

I dropped the groceries on the kitchen floor, grabbed my purse, ran out and caught up with Fred just as he began to crumble. I tried to steady his descent, but his dead weight carried him past me, sideways onto the ground, his broken arm the point of impact. A quick howl, and he lashed onto his back, his breathing harsh and labored.

"Fred. Fred." No answer. I thought he was unconscious. "Fred, I'm going into the house to call 911. I'll be right back. Fred? I'll be right back."

How could his arm break? He wasn't throwing a boulder; it was a pebble, for Christ's sake. And what about his breathing? Is he having a heart attack on top of a broken arm? Oh, God, what's happening?

By the time I returned, his breathing was more nearly normal. I called his name, got a grunt in response. *Good. Grunting is good. He's alive.*

The rescue squad checked Fred's pulse, respiration, and blood pressure; put his arm in a sling; loaded him onto a stretcher; asked both me and him if they could give him oxygen and start an intravenous line. We both said yes. I went in the house and called a committee chair to excuse myself from the administrative board meeting that evening. Following the ambulance I thought, *A broken arm. And unconscious. A heart attack? Did he have a heart attack? That doesn't make any sense. Nothing makes any sense.* I skittered away from one recurring thought: *Bones don't break for no reason.*

Twenty minutes later Fred's oxygen mask and blood pressure cuff were gone, so I knew his heart wasn't the problem. Within forty-five minutes we were staring at an X-ray film the emergency room doctor had clipped to the light box. The bone in Fred's upper arm, the humerus, had broken in two at a sharp angle. Something more than the break was amiss, though. The bone didn't look like bone. It looked like tattered lace.

"Why does it look like that?" Fred asked.

"It appears to be a tumor," replied the doctor.

While the medical staff gave Fred painkillers and fitted his arm into a sling, I thought about the word "tumor." I went for a short walk, out to the rest rooms in the waiting room, and, by the time I returned, the orthopedic surgeon we'd requested was already talking to Fred. We both listened intently, but when the doctor turned to leave, I realized I'd been distracted again by the word "tumor." I followed him out of the curtained room.

"Tell me again what you think the tumor is."

"A plasmacytoma."

"And tell me again what it means."

"It means he might have multiple myeloma."

Plasmacytoma. Multiple myeloma. Rhyming words. So pretty together. So destructive.

"He'll need surgery on the arm. I don't know if I'll schedule it for Monday or Wednesday, but I'll let you know. Now don't get alarmed. It might not be multiple myeloma after all."

"What's multiple myeloma?"

"It's a cancer."

"A cancer of the bone?"

"No. A cancer of the blood."

"Like leukemia?"

"Something like that."

Fred might have cancer, a cancer of the blood, a cancer like Chris Flynn's.

Once home at nearly midnight he went straight to bed. I stayed up long enough to send an e-mail to my parents and to Amy in Arizona, and then I turned off all the lights and went to bed. Later I got up and turned them all on again. Morning broke. The phone rang at eight-thirty, the orthopedic surgeon with instructions on where to take Fred for oncological tests.

"When?"

"Now, if you can."

I'd never had to help Fred dress before, nor had I ever hovered, fearful that he would collapse. We waited for hours at the doctor's office. New at the game of illness, we didn't know to bring additional pain medication with us, and Fred's chin sank lower and lower on his chest as the pain increased. On the way home I ran into the orthopedist's office to sign the consent form for surgery—the receptionist thought Fred was a minor—and when we got to the house, Fred leaned most of his weight against me to climb the stairs. By the time he was seated in the kitchen, I was in the middle of a mental tornado from too much action, too much novelty, too much fear, too little control.

Information: I needed information, fast.

Fred shook his head. "Not me. I don't want any more information than I already have."

"Is it okay with you for me to get more?"

"Get all you want," he said.

He was drugged and again sleeping when the oncologist's office called.

"He didn't get a chest X ray this morning. He has to have one."

"When?"

"Now."

I balked. "No. He's sleeping. I'm not dragging him out again."

"But he has to have it before the surgery on Monday."

"Last night the doctor said the surgery could be either Monday or Wednesday."

"But in either case he's got to have a chest X ray before we can schedule the surgery."

"Why?"

"Because the oncologists think he has lung cancer."

Lung cancer? Oh bloody hell fuck me shit.

I dragged Fred from bed and to the hospital. When the radiologist, a family friend, came into the room with the X ray in his hand, his first words were, "I'm so sorry." His next statement was "We're certain it isn't a localized cancer. It traveled to the bone from somewhere."

Metastasized. Our nice friend said the word and then went on to say the cancer could be in Fred's bowels, or in his liver, or in his kidneys. It could be in all three, or in his colon or in his prostate, or in all of them and additional internal organs as well.

Bowels. Liver. Kidneys. Bowelsliverkidneys. Bowelsliverkidneys and more? Lungs? Was it in his lungs, too? I didn't remember the first part of the conversation, so I asked, "Is it in his lungs?"

"No. The chest X ray didn't show any cancer."

A flood of relief: the cancer might be anywhere, but at least it wasn't everywhere. Humans are like the grass that withers and fades, but we are also like well-cut diamonds, reflecting any glint of light, of hope, that comes our way.

That evening Fred and I sat at the kitchen table and talked. He thought I should preach on Sunday. ("Why wouldn't you?" he wondered.) I said we should call the children. He thought calling the children was foolish: we didn't know anything yet. I said, "You're having a rod installed in your arm because cancer has eaten away so much of the bone it can't heal. The children deserve to know."

I called the church to say I wouldn't be there on Sunday. I called my children. Fred called his.

Amy called the next morning from Arizona; she'd read my e-mail and was on her way to the airport. After that, I turned off the phone's ringer. I couldn't speak, because a nest of goblins had hatched in my brain, and I needed all my powers of concentration to keep their howls from coming out of my mouth. If the cancer were everywhere, how long might we have together? A month? Six weeks? Three months? Not enough time, not enough time, never enough time.

My worst fear was that the withdrawal both Fred and I were experiencing would remove us emotionally not only from the outer world but also from each other. Lying in bed that night, under the safety of the darkness, I said, "Fred, I can do anything as long as you don't go away from me. I won't be able to bear it if you lock yourself away and don't let me in."

He was quiet so long I thought he was pretending sleep to avoid me, but he must have been thinking things through, because at last he took a deep, deep breath and said, "Okay. If it's what you want, we'll do this together."

The weekend was filled with commotion: children and friends and food arriving. I had Fred-watch; Amy took over Mary Jo–watch; everyone else fended for themselves. Amy got me out of the house Sunday afternoon. Driving through town, we passed a plant shed.

"You need something bright and alive," she said, so we wrestled a flowering mimosa in a wide wooden tub into the trunk. We placed it in the yard where it was visible from the kitchen window, and late that afternoon I watched a hummingbird, the first I'd ever seen, zip up to a full-throated red flower and drink deep and long.

I spent all day Monday in the surgical waiting room. Tara was with me, and Amy, and Mary Flowers, and Terry's sister Maureen, and Molly. I almost cried when Kathy Flynn came in the door, knowing what it must have cost her to appear; I fought for control again later when Alva, his face grim with concern, arrived. The other visitors—Fred's relatives, our mutual friends—were a montage of movement in which I couldn't distinguish faces.

I'd kissed Fred good-bye on his operating-room gurney before nine, so when the orthopedic surgeon came into the room around noon, I thought the surgery was over. It hadn't begun. "We had to send out to Home Depot for another piece of equipment," he said, wanting me to laugh and relax. I obliged.

As the afternoon lengthened, the temperature in the room rose. I withdrew into myself, barely cognizant, except to hear somebody say that the way to get rid of obnoxious robins is to put paper bags over a car's side mirrors, that birds perch on cars in order to see themselves in the mirrors. In the second—or was it the third?—hour I concluded that the doctor had encountered unforeseen problems and was amputating Fred's arm. Nobody had mentioned amputation, not a single person, not a single time, but what other explanation could there be for the duration of the surgery? I pondered whether Fred would prefer to pin up the sleeves of long-sleeved shirts or wear short-sleeved shirts.

I gave up on the question, rested my head on the wall behind me, and retreated more deeply inward. Somebody sat down next to me and began talking, but I couldn't find my way up to respond. The room was stiflingly hot. I opened my eyes, and the first face I saw was that of Mary Flowers, directly across from me. I struggled to my feet and said, "You have to come with me."

"Where are we going?"

"I don't know."

I walked the length of the waiting room and around a corner where I found a small room with a couch, a table, and a telephone. The air was cool in there. I sat down on the couch and studied the gray carpet. It looked profoundly inviting.

I said, "I'm going to lie down on the floor." I could have explained my reasoning, that warm air rises and therefore I'd be cooler on the floor, but I didn't seem able to talk.

Just as I stretched out I heard someone say, in one breath, "The doctor's here—oh, my God, has she fainted? Why didn't you tell someone?" Mary Flowers was laughing (her standard response to great stress) and replied, "I just found it out myself."

I shook off the dizziness as I scrambled to my feet. "I'm all right." I brushed past the two women and walked straight to the surgeon. Friends and family—there must have been a dozen, maybe fifteen—encircled us with their bodies as though the night were bitter cold and we were their campfire.

The operation had gone well. The surgeon reported he'd gone through the shoulder to install a titanium rod in the humerus. He'd attempted to retrieve a sample of the tumor, or plasmacytoma, or whatever it was, to have it biopsied. Fred was in recovery. Then the surgeon said a lot of other words, about how he'd woken up at two in the morning thinking about the surgery and how, if there were a kidney problem, the adrenal gland could stimulate uncontrollable bleeding and he'd have to pack the arm with cement. Somebody laid a cold wet washcloth on the back of my neck, and the doctor kept talking, and I fought to follow his thoughts, but the words "uncontrollable bleeding" were circling in my head. I was puzzling over the question of whether Fred might yet bleed to death or whether the bleeding-to-death crisis was over, and the surgeon was still talking, and suddenly the effort to pay attention while "bleeding to death" was dive-bombing me was more than I could sustain, and I burst out with, "What in the *hell* are you talking about?"

The surgeon stopped talking.

I inhaled. "Is there still a chance Fred's going to bleed to death?" I asked quietly.

"No, no. That danger's over."

"Okay then. You can go on," and he did, saying I could take Fred home in an hour or so and telling me the schedule for radiation treatments.

Fred slept all afternoon, all night, and until noon the next day. After lunch, he went back to bed. I went with him and lay down, fully dressed, beside him under the freshly laundered yellow sheets. We were paddling in a rowboat down the river Styx, the two of us, and we both knew it. Death and destruction were to the right of us, death and pestilence to the left of us, death and despair straight ahead. Fred looked so hollow and frigid from pain that I was afraid to touch him. The air-conditioning was throbbing, the sheets felt cool and crisp. Resting there, I meditated on how quickly the seventeen years of our marriage had passed. Might this really be all we were going to have of life together? How was that possible?

Regrets poured over me, all of my failures of commission and omission. My abrupt temper. My distractibility. My stubbornness. Thoughts of all the things I might have done differently, of failures of attentiveness and open-heartedness, cascaded through my mind. Eventually they coalesced into a single regret, not terribly important in itself but a signifier of the largesse I would have shown if I'd known our life together might be this short.

I thought of a way to make amends, but before I could tell Fred I had to think through how to word the sentence, whether I should begin with the word "if" or with the word "when." Finally I spoke.

"When we get through this . . . " I began.

Fred jumped. "What? You startled me." He'd been half asleep.

"When we get through this," I said, "I'm going to give you a blow job every night for the rest of your life."

Fred was silent, and then he laughed, a weak, happy laugh. "Oh, good. I can't wait."

▲   ▲   ▲

That evening, in a fluke of timing that was either coincidence or God, Charlie, my younger brother, who flies for a commercial airline, had a layover in town. Amy picked him up at the airport.

"Is that the piano you're learning to play?" Charlie asked, gesturing to the Yamaha.

"Yes. Would you like to hear me?"

"Not especially, but go ahead," said Amy.

I played "Jingle Bells," missing not more than half the notes (my concentration was a little off).

"That was good," said Amy, "but here's the big question. Do you know where middle C is?"

"Why, yes, I do," I said. I pointed the key out to them, directly under the lettering of the name of the piano manufacturer, and then I presented a short lecture on how there were other Cs on the keyboard, all the way up and down.

"Wow, that's really something," Charlie said admiringly.

Clearly any fool could play "Jingle Bells," but only a real pianist knows where to find middle C.

"Jingle Bells"? Why "Jingle Bells"? Why not *Pathétique?* Because I was as precisely balanced as a piano that's holding between eighteen and thirty metric tons of tension within itself. In her book *The Highly Sensi-*

tive Person, Elaine N. Aron writes that music is always a stimulant. If I'd added Tchaikovsky's passion to my careful balance, I might well have exploded from the inside out.

▲   ▲   ▲

That first week, I never touched Fred at all. In bed, I avoided skin contact, not knowing if his other bones were fragile from cancer, not wanting to interrupt his concentration on pain control, afraid I'd bump, bruise, or break him. I didn't notice the absence of touch at first, and then I did, or, more precisely, my skin did. You know how you feel when you haven't eaten a green vegetable for a while, and one day you notice you'd kill for a serving of Brussels sprouts? That's how my skin felt.

▲   ▲   ▲

By the time we saw the oncologist, I had researched multiple myeloma. It's a relatively rare cancer, diagnosed in roughly 13,000 people in 1997. Most of them were male—more often African-American than European-American—and most over the age of sixty-five. Multiple myeloma can be defined from two directions: as a cancer of the plasma cells that weakens and destroys the immune system, or as a cancer of the immune system that causes uncontrolled reproduction of plasma cells. Plasmacytomas are tumors that develop because the cancerous plasma cells release a chemical that leaches calcium out of bones, most often the long bones of the spine, the ribs, and the pelvis. The calcium that's been leached travels to and blocks the kidneys, so kidney failure is an expected side effect. Patients are also prone to the same opportunistic diseases AIDS patients endure, such as Karposi's sarcoma, because, like AIDS, multiple myeloma impairs the immune system. The average life expectancy after diagnosis is twenty-eight months, with or without chemotherapy.

The oncologist began by assuring us Fred's heart was healthy, that the collapse in the driveway was due to the pain. There was no evidence of cancer in his lungs, kidneys, bowels, prostate, colon, or liver, or in any other organs. The cancer might be localized in the single identified plasmacytoma, or Fred might have multiple myeloma. Further diagnostic tests were necessary. Would Fred care to have a bone-marrow biopsy right now?

"Only if you've got good drugs." Fred, who entered the world in a home birth and had never been hospitalized or undergone a major medical procedure, knew from Chris Flynn's experience what the procedure entailed.

The doctor assured Fred they had good drugs. The nurse practitioner who was to perform the biopsy asked if I'd like to be in the room with Fred.

"Yes, I would."

"It's not an easy procedure to watch," she warned me.

"I'll be okay."

That's how I came to be standing on the right side of the gurney, watching marrow be extracted from the bone in Fred's right hip. He'd been given a dose of a sedative called Ativan, and then a second dose when the first one had no impact. I observed the moment the drug kicked in; Fred's facial muscles unclenched into the relaxed smile I was accustomed to seeing only after we'd had sex.

The nurse practitioner took up her instruments—what appeared to be a steak knife, a can opener, a melon baller, and a corkscrew—and extracted samples of bone marrow and of bone to send for blood and chromosome studies. Fred moaned only once, when she extracted the sliver of bone.

"I got it," she said.

"You and the fifteen burly truck drivers pushing against me," he responded.

▲   ▲   ▲

As Fred's spirits lifted, my fear of hurting him began to fade. Finally, one night I slowly, gingerly, moved my left leg up against his. Slowly, carefully, I lay my arm across his chest. Flesh against flesh: our first and last luxury. For the first time since his arm broke, I slept eight hours straight.

Within a week he was off all the painkillers, doing physical therapy twice a day with a wide red elastic band, and enduring the radiation with no side effects. I was doing less well. One day I leafed through a book Heidi had given me about living with cancer. The book suggested I pick a word or phrase on which to concentrate when I needed to calm myself. The first word I thought of was *life,* but every time I thought of the word, I sank into existential meditation: What is life, really? Why are we here? Does eternal life, as in dead and buried and gone to live with Jesus, count as life?

No. Forget eternal life. I wanted Fred alive in real life.

I settled instead on the word *breathe*. *Breathe* is a holy word. "Breathe on me, breath of God," we sing. "God breathed life into *adama*, the first human," we say. Breath, breathe, breathing, breath of air, breath of God, wind of the Holy Spirit, my lungs expanding and emptying with the rhythms of my own breath, calm and turbulent, breeze and gale.

Concentrating on *breathe* I could acknowledge that Fred and I were not in the middle of some weird, chaotic event. We were there because of the nature of things. We are human beings. We have bodies. Bodies break, the same way toys, mirrors, dishwashers, pianos, shoelaces, ice floes, coffee mugs, bicycles, and boughs break. It is the nature of physical entities. Some of the entities can be fixed. Some can't. It's how things are. This was happening to us because things happen to everybody. It's life. Things happen, some good, some not. There is nothing personal about it. Neither God nor the universe works that way.

When Fred's test results showed no evidence of multiple myeloma, he emerged from crisis mentality. He'd need a follow-up bone-marrow test at the end of August, and perhaps he might be back on the golf course by September, depending on whether there was enough new bone growth in his arm to stabilize it. Fred assured me the test results proved the power of prayer. I said if he believed his own words—if he honestly and truly believed prayer had the power to change the course of events— then he had a moral and spiritual obligation to pray every day that no child in the world would ever again die of starvation. He put his arms around me and held me close.

I didn't believe the test results. Why should I? Chris Flynn had a bone-marrow biopsy that showed no sign of leukemia, and two weeks later he was dead. I wanted, fiercely, to paint the walls of the house, recaulk the tile in the bathrooms, repair a crack in the ceiling, paint the exterior, destroy the kudzu in our woods, plant flowers in bloom around the perimeter of the yard. I also wanted to grow stronger, to build up my endurance for whatever lay ahead. The end was coming. I didn't expect it that week, or that summer, or that year, but the time was coming when Fred's death would be stone-cold reality. That's how life works, even when there's not a fourteen-year gap between your age and your husband's, and oh, what a nightmare and oh, what life.

It is a fucking nightmare. It is life. Maybe life is a fucking nightmare. Could that possibly be true? Of course it's true. Even God makes more sense from the premise that life is a nightmare. Who needs God when nothing bad can ever happen to you because you have a late-model car, health benefits, and a retirement account? In that circumstance, God's a sidekick, a buddy, a fuzzy blanket you sleep with at night because it's comfortable, and then when disaster comes you whine because God was supposed to be your personal defense system, keeping you safe. On the other hand, if you know life to be a nightmare, then the presence of God is a sanctuary, like the shell of a turtle, traveling with you wherever you go, rain or shine, in sickness or health, for better or worse.

▲   ▲   ▲

The second week of his radiation therapy, Fred and I had sex three times, because we wanted to and because we could. It wasn't desperation sex, sex as an antidote to death, but fun sex, good and careful and satiating sex.

Where do you go after the nightmare? Into each other.

▲   ▲   ▲

Fred's radiation ended, and he was ready to get back to living. "Pretty soon you'll be making good on your promise to give me a blow job every night for six months, whether I want one or not," he told me.

I grinned at him, not bothering to correct his time-frame error.

By then I'd decided my congregation was going to have to manage without me for the final two Sundays before Moving Day. I wasn't going to wrench my attention away from Fred to give it to the church. It was clear to me that the urgency I'd felt the year before (the urgency the executive committee of the Board of Ordained Ministry refuted when they suggested I postpone ordination) grew out of my knowledge, however subconscious, that Fred wasn't himself, that he wasn't well. I'd ignored my own urgency in order to satisfy the denomination's committees and boards, and I'd continued to work as though my job were my life, when in truth my real life was standing beside me all the time.

I was steadfast in my decision until Fred said, "I'm going to church on Sunday."

"You are?'

"Yes, I am."

"Who's going to be preaching?"

"You are."

"I am?"

"Please. I want to hear you and Brian do the Pentecost sermon."

I groaned. The idea of having to regroup, to rip my focus from my own hearth to the flames that danced on the heads of the disciples on the day of Pentecost, exhausted me. I studied his face in the sunlight pouring through the kitchen's plate-glass window. I noticed, for the first time, that his hair had turned white on the sides. It must have happened over time, the blond gradually fading away. His eyes were on me, watching me sort things through. Was he waiting to see if I could understand, without him having to articulate it, that he was choosing life and hope and wanted me to join him? More likely, he meant the statement at face value: he wanted to hear the sermon.

In either case, my answer was the same. I leaned toward him and pressed my cheek against his. "Whatever you want, Fred."

chapter twenty-one

"PENTECOST IS *THIS* SUNDAY? WE'RE GOING TO DO THE sermon together *this* Sunday? Are you sure that's a good idea?" Brian clearly did not think so.

"Fred thinks so. If you think we can pull it together."

"Of course we can pull it together. At least, I think we can. I have to go practice now."

The earliest we could get together was Thursday evening. In the meantime, Brian would choose and practice his selections, and I'd do my final exegesis, play with the text to find its natural divisions and its rhythms, and choose where the piano interludes would occur. I would also have to sit still long enough to *write* the sermon.

First I needed to choose the responsive reading. I ached to read Psalm 139, which reads, in the archaic King James language preserved in the 1964 hymnal, *Whither shall I go from thy Spirit?/Or whither shall I flee from thy presence?/If I ascend to heaven, thou art there!/If I make my bed in Sheol, thou art there!/If I take the wings of the morning/and dwell in the uttermost parts of the sea,/even there thy hand shall lead me.* I wanted us to attest together one more time that God is always, everywhere, with us, in the middle of life, in the middle of death, in heaven, in hell, everywhere; but in the end I couldn't because of a minor spiritual crisis: I couldn't remember why God's ubiquity mattered in light of the news that someday my husband would die. I settled finally on Isaiah 40, the verses Bishop Leontine Kelly had proclaimed at the ordination service where so much began in 1991, rearranging it a bit to read, *Have you not known? Have you not heard? The Lord our God is an everlasting God . . . God does not faint or grow weary. . . . Even youths shall faint and grow weary, and the young shall fall exhausted, but they who wait for the Lord shall renew their strength, they shall mount up with wings like eagles, they shall run and not be weary, they shall walk and not faint.*

281

Right now, my energy surpassed Bishop Kelly's. I could give the lines a power I'd only dreamed of before.

By the time Brian arrived on Thursday night with music in one hand and a bucket of fried chicken in the other, I'd roughed out the sermon. At the supper table Fred teased us about the coming service.

"So you think the two of you can do this without God striking you dead?"

I felt my eyes widen, and Brian laughed nervously. "Mary Jo says we can."

"We are professionals," I reminded them both. "Don't try this at home."

That night, with Fred's input, we reduced Brian's seven suggestions to five: excerpts from Beethoven's "Für Elise," Carl Koelling's "Hungary" and Beethoven's "Moonlight Sonata" at the beginning of the service, Schubert's Waltz in A Minor, No. 2 and Andrae Crouch's "My Tribute," as arranged by Dino Kartsonakis, during the sermon. We walked through the text, testing to see the most effective moments to bring in the music. Brian asked me to read a few lines at my top volume so that he'd know how loudly he could play before drowning me out.

Around nine o'clock Fred insisted we take a break. "Go get a cup of coffee or something."

"Are you coming with us?"

"No, I'm going to bed. But the two of you need to go." He pecked me on the lips and waved us off from the doorway.

We went to one of my favorite places, an all-night breakfast restaurant no cleaner than it should be. I ordered a trashcan omelet, Brian a sausage, mushroom, and cheese omelet, and we both talked with our mouths full. We spoke of cabbages and kings, of insolent older brothers and sisters, of what we might do with our lives when this segment of reality ended. We wondered if the congregation was going to know what hit them, and if we knew what was going to hit us. We confessed our mutual, moderate terror: allowing the power of God to take us over and spill out of us was one thing that Sunday with Chris. This was different. This event was premeditated, a deliberate choice to unleash the power of God on an unsuspecting congregation, not to mention ourselves.

"Somebody has to be in charge," said Brian. "It doesn't matter which one of us it is, but somebody has to be in charge."

"That would be me. I'm the preacher. I'm automatically in charge."

Our conversation had a subtext: we were evaluating each other's trustworthiness. If I couldn't trust Brian, I needed to back off, to tone down my presentation. He was less uncertain than I, but he needed to confirm that I wanted the pinnacle of what he had to offer. As our faith in each other grew, so did our courage. Around midnight, still at the restaurant and still ravenous, we cemented our friendship over a shared short stack of pancakes.

Saturday morning, we met in the sanctuary. The air-conditioning, shut off during the week to keep the power bill low, had been turned on earlier in the day. I could hear the equipment pumping and feel a touch of cool air moving in the sanctuary, but still it was at least ninety degrees. Brian was so tense, he was babbling. "Once in a while I have panic attacks," he said. No, he wouldn't have one Sunday. Yes, maybe he would. No, he wasn't okay. Yes, he was okay. It would help if we could walk through everything I was going to do the next day.

We walked through the first chapter of Acts, where Jesus tells the disciples to wait in Jerusalem for the Holy Spirit to come. I read the responsive reading, both my part and the congregation's. We reconsidered the sermon's construction, decided the first sound should be the piano rather than my voice, marked out where in "Hungary" I would begin to speak.

"How will I recognize it?" I asked, and Brian played it through half a dozen times.

"Got it?"

"I've got it."

We started over, and at the right moment I began reading the second chapter of Acts: *When the day of Pentecost had come, the disciples were all together in one place. And suddenly from heaven there came a sound like the rush of a violent wind.* I continued down to *All of them were filled with the Holy Spirit and began to speak in other languages, as the Spirit gave them ability.* I took a breath, and in the same instant Brian touched the opening chord of "Moonlight Sonata" and I said, *Now there were devout Jews from every nation under heaven living in Jerusalem,* and as I read the long list of foreigners gathered in the city, the Beethoven grew louder and stronger, and so did my voice as I searched for the spot where voice and music would collide and the resulting tension sear each syllable, each note, into the listeners' minds. Brian's hands were still when I read Peter's statement: "No, we're not drunk; it's only nine in the morning," but, as the passage moved into Peter's quotation of the prophet Joel, the Schubert waltz unfolded.

You can't really preach until you're preaching, but Brian insisted I give as much as I could. "If I don't hear the sermon until tomorrow, I might get caught up in your words. If I've heard some of it, even if it's not the whole thing, I'll at least know what to expect. It's the way you say those unexpected things when you preach that shakes me up."

I did the best I could. Then I stepped away from the pulpit while Brian moved steadily into "My Tribute." I couldn't stand still while I listened; I started walking, circling the outside perimeter of the pews to the rhythms of the music. At the rear of the sanctuary, I thought to rest for a moment. I lay down on a pew, closed my eyes, and let the music pulse in time with my heart. I felt Chris Flynn's presence, his vitality, his joy, his peace. By the time Brian touched the closing notes of "My Tribute," I was done crying.

                        ▲   ▲   ▲

On the morning of Pentecost, Fred woke up at six, in pain. If the pain continued, he wouldn't make it to church, but a pain pill would knock him off his feet.

"I'm going back to sleep. Maybe when I wake up again I'll feel better."

"I'll be back home before the service to check on you."

"Mary Jo, you don't need to do that. You have enough to do this morning." He looked like he had much more to say on the subject, so I patted the bald spot on the top of his head and said, "Okay, honey."

By seven-thirty I'd made some editorial changes to my sermon, scribbled some notes in the Bible I'd be preaching from, composed the pastoral prayer, printed out the final copy of the sermon, and was on my way to the church. Ten minutes after I arrived, Brian, wild-eyed and on the edge of a panic attack, burst into the office.

"Are you all right?"

"I don't know."

I wasn't too sure about myself, either. What was I thinking when I decided to do this? How dare I walk up to the eye of the storm, how dare I trust any of us would get out alive? I was as foolhardy as coastal dwellers who refuse to evacuate when a hurricane heads for shore.

There was nothing to do but continue. Brian and I rehearsed the service once, and again, and again, spending our greatest efforts on the transitions where I began speaking as he played or he began playing as I spoke. Our most worrisome spot was at the end of Peter's speech as he said, "Therefore let everyone know with certainty that God has made this Jesus both Lord and Messiah."

The clock on the back wall of the sanctuary showed 9:30. Rehearsal was over. We needed to leave before parishioners began to arrive, needed to preserve the isolation that would let us gather forces for the service. Life, real life, had become a distraction. The sermon was reality.

"Are you sure we can do this?" Brian asked.

"Yes. I'm sure." I'd compartmentalized Fred's illness, locked it away from the morning. I was focused and prepared to let God do whatever God wanted.

Back home I caught Fred drinking the milk left in his bowl of cereal. He'd eaten breakfast. As soon as he finished reading the newspaper, he was going to take a shower. He wouldn't ride to the church with me; he'd rather come a bit late and leave the service a bit early.

In the car again, I stopped fearing the power of the coming service. It wasn't going to be about me, or about Brian. It would be about God. I luxuriated, one more time, in the familiar happiness of preparation.

▲   ▲   ▲

I was draping the stole I'd received at ordination over my shoulders when Brian returned. Sweat stood on his forehead. His hands were trembling slightly. "I don't think we can do this," he said.

Was he out of his mind? We'd come too far to stop now. There was going to be a sanctuary full of people, and there was no way I could do this service alone. I stepped directly in front of Brian and clamped my hands on his shoulders. Speaking quietly but deliberately I said, "Brian. Stop it. This isn't about us. It's about God."

I could see shock in his eyes and then a transition from wildness to concentration. "What did you say?"

"This service isn't about you, or me. It's about God."

"God?"

"Yes. It isn't about our power or what we do out there. It's about God's power and what God does out there."

"Can I write that down?"

"Of course you can." I released his shoulders to hand him a piece of paper and a pen. Then he placed the scribbled paper into the notebook that held his music.

"I'm ready," he said.

"So am I."

Just before we entered the sanctuary, Brian said to me, "And we're not going to hold anything back in this service? Is that right?"

"That's right. We're not going to hold anything back."

▲   ▲   ▲

Pierre Teilhard de Chardin once wrote, "The day will come when, after harnessing the ether, the wind, the tides, gravitation, we shall harness for God the energies of love. And on that day, for the second time, [we] will have discovered fire." On Pentecost, Brian and I discovered fire.

The faces in front of me that morning were so filled with love that I had to fight for composure. I said, my voice shaking hardly at all, "Fred and I haven't been to hell since we saw you last, but we could see it from where we were standing. We're okay, and we thank you for the prayers, the calls, the food, and the support you gave us."

Sermons are sea foam cresting over the bow of a boat, gone in the same moment they exist. The first chapter of Acts is lost to me now. Before the start of the second chapter, the choir sang the sweetly invocative "Spirit Song." I sat with my head in my hands and allowed their voices to touch, and soothe, and hold me. Then I took the pulpit, and Brian the piano bench. We gathered ourselves before exchanging a glance. He began playing "Hungary," and I felt the flames pulsing from the keyboard toward me while I waited for the first run, and when it came I proclaimed, *When the day of Pentecost had come, they were all together in one place . . . Divided tongues, as of fire, appeared among them, and a tongue rested on each of them."* I pictured tongues of fire as "Moonlight Sonata" drifted through the sanctuary and I read aloud about the devout Jews gathered in Jerusalem, the Parthians, Medes, Elamites, the residents of Mesopotamia, Judea and Cappadocia, Pontus, Asia, and elsewhere.

Schubert was in the sanctuary as I crooned a variation on Joel's words: *In the last days it will be, God declares, that I will pour out my Spirit upon all flesh, and your sons and your daughters shall prophesy, and the young people shall see visions, and the old people shall dream dreams.* The passage, so often presented somberly, became a lithe and dancing promise, a song of love and hope as Brian's passion and mine melded into the wind and fire and flames, with power and beauty swirling through the sanctuary, the sun pouring in through the colored-glass windows, the sheen of concentration on Brian's face, the look of joy on Fred's, the tears coursing down Mary Flowers's cheeks, Alva's face stern as he held on to control. The piano faded, leaving nothing but my voice, and I gave the reading everything I had, left nothing standing between me and chaos, or perhaps I mean nothing standing between me and glory, but the thin veil of mortality. I danced on the edge of the knife, dipped and swayed, totally in control, absolutely out of control, and a voice came out of my mouth, a voice that should have emanated from someone nineteen feet tall, and I thundered,

Jesus has poured out this power that you both see and hear. Therefore let the entire house of Israel know with certainty that God has made this Jesus both Lord and Messiah.

I took a two-whole-note rest and said,

Have you not *known*? Have you not *heard*? The Lord our God is an *everlasting* God. Our God does not faint or grow weary, and our God shares God's power with us.

I switched tones, marking the boundary between words from scripture and my own words.

Pentecost is the day we celebrate God's gift of power. It is not a gift bestowed in antiquity that has nothing to do with us. It is God's everlasting gift, God's gift to the Church and to the people, the gift of a power that never ends. It is that gift, that holy, powerful, terrifying, life-giving gift, that we celebrate on Pentecost, the same gift from the same awesome, life-giving God that caused Annie Dillard to ask, in words you've heard from me so often:

"Does anyone have the foggiest idea what sort of power we so blithely invoke? Or, as I suspect, does no one believe a word of it? We as the church are children playing on the floor with chemistry sets, mixing up a batch of TNT to kill a Sunday morning. . . . We should all be wearing crash helmets. The ushers should issue life preservers to us; they should issue signal flares; they should lash us to our pews." *My voice had been gaining in strength, in authority, and I upped it another notch as I said,* For the waking God may draw us out to where we can never return, *and then I opened my arms wide and opened all the vocal stops and announced, in a voice ringing with majesty,* This is the power of God.

Utter silence. I held firm eye contact with the congregation, kept them at the same outer level of connection, peripherally conscious of Brian mentally collecting himself, holding the congregation taut until his hands touched the keys and the first demanding run from "My Tribute" pulled their eyes from me to him. I waited yet a moment longer before I took my one step backward from the pulpit, the step that would allow the piano's vibrations to slam against my body, to invigorate and revive me. I blanked my mind and let the music hold me up, and Brian played as though God's ear was longing for the music; as though the curtain between heaven and earth were gauze; as though we'd all woken up together on the last morning of the world and were celebrating the glory of the breaking day. He played as though the piano were his breath, his laughter, his soul, as though there was nothing we could ever want or need in our lives except to be here, here, in this sacred place with the sacred tones, and he skimmed the notes into our blood, into our lives, into our futures, daring us into the power of love. I tensed for the final, stirring chords, and, as his hands dropped from the keys, I stepped forward again, and when I looked at the faces in front of me, I knew how precious each one was, and how beautiful, and I asked again, this time, I'm told, as tenderly as I might say good night to my grandchildren,

Have you not known? Have you not heard? The Lord our God is an everlasting God. Our God does not faint or grow weary. And our God does not keep God's power from us.

When the day of Pentecost had come, the glory of the Lord shone upon the disciples. The glory of the Lord shone around them and within them and beyond them and out from them, out and out and out, the glory of the Lord of the violent wind, of the pulsing flames, the glory of the Lord in the power of the Spirit, upon them, beyond them, the power of the Lord in them, in us, from that day forward, to this day today, and forevermore. Amen.

I bowed my head and waited for the echoes of my words to fade. I asked then for them to bow in silent prayer, and Brian and I walked down the sanctuary aisle, protected on each side by rows of bowed heads. I leaned against the back wall of the sanctuary for support, noticed Fred standing at the end of his pew waiting to join us. I glanced at Brian's flushed, worn face and linked my arm through his, and then I pronounced the benediction:

May the Lord bless you and keep you. May the Lord's face shine upon you and be gracious unto you. May the Lord lift his countenance upon you, and give you peace.

And then we were in the sunshine of the sparkling day, and we sank down together onto the top porch step, half-laughing, half-crying, and I dragged my hair away from my face, hoping to catch a touch of cooling breeze, and there was no breeze, but there was Fred beside me, laughing— and, laughing, I rose into his arms.

"You did it," he said, his eyes glistening.

"We did it," I said, and by then Mary Flowers had her hands on our shoulders, Fred's and mine, and to Fred she said, "Did you see them? Did you see *her*?" and to Brian she said, "I've never heard anything so beautiful," and to me she said, "Until now I never knew what the word 'power' meant. Mary Jo, you were radiating light."

That light, the light: sometimes it amazes, even me.

▴   ▴   ▴

For the next week I lay low. I dug holes and planted vinca, a butterfly bush, evergreen grasses, and hosta. I hadn't touched the keys of the piano since playing "Jingle Bells" for Amy and Charlie after Fred's arm broke, but on Tuesday I made myself sit down long enough to play Hanon. I had four of his finger exercises in my repertoire now, and I didn't want to lose the facility of movement I'd achieved. Later in the week, I picked up *Pathétique,* but I had to put it down: Tchaikovsky's intensity was more than I could bear. Instead, I turned to more recent, and much perkier, assignments: "Greensleeves," "Fascination," and "Scarborough Fair."

In his classic book *Human Values in Music Education,* James L. Mursell wrote, in 1934, "Music is a refuge for the spirit, a wellspring of water in a thirsty land." I was too parched for the music to fill me that day—all I could do was sip a bit—but I knew the time would come when once again it would satiate me.

I spoke with the Flynns and told them, stammering in my uncertainty, that I wanted, if it was all right with them, maybe, I didn't mean to intrude, I didn't know if I ever would but I wanted to, to write something, I didn't know what, about Beth and about Chris, about all of it, and they said yes, anything, everything. Throughout the week, I prepared for Sunday, my final Sunday. I thought to do a collage of the scripture readings I most treasured, so for two days I skimmed the Bible. When I finished, I had a list of forty-three passages I wanted to read. On Friday I trimmed it down to fifteen; the next day I reduced it to nine.

Church liturgy tells us that in the very midst of life we are in the midst of death. The reverse is also true: in the very midst of death we are in the midst of life. Reading the verses we knew and loved together, I knew that whether in life or death, this congregation and I had made music together. Not the kind I expected, but a different music, the music of eternity, the music of redemption, the music of life. And the music we invented, hummed, and sang to each other had made us taller, stronger, braver, bolder, and more gorgeous than I could ever have dreamed.

▴　　▴　　▴

Early Sunday morning I entered the office that was no longer mine. My books, my wall hangings, the turquoise valences were gone. In the center of the room were stacks of shipping boxes: the new pastor's books and documents, ready to be unpacked and set into place.

I sat in the swivel office chair and gently rocked, breathing slowly and deeply, letting the memories hold me. Memories of the faces I'd seen in caskets, behind wedding veils, at youth groups and Easter egg hunts, at the altar and at softball games. Memories of my hands shaking when I baptized Bradley and Devin, of Vicki's happiness when I baptized her, of performing the marriage ceremony for a couple the week after I arrived at the church and, eighteen months later, baptizing their new baby. Memories of church lunches, all those Sundays when I preached into the smell of baking ham or roast beef, over the sound of my own growling stomach. Memories of sermons, the one with the bread machine under the altar; the one with the flying chickens; the one about groping down a dark hallway, knowing there was a light switch, trusting there was a light switch. Memories rained over me like baptismal droplets, cooling, refreshing, making me whole.

I knew the truth of what Molly had told me long before: that when I walked out the door, my life with the congregation would be as fully ended as if I'd never met them. But I also knew that I'd achieved what I'd been sent there to do. I'd spoken the truth as I saw it, preached the gospel, and tried to stay far enough out of God's way to let the Holy Spirit soar. I'd helped them replace the sewer lines, establish a coherent budget, start a men's group, and embark on mission projects. And I had loved them. Oh, yes, I had loved them.

▲　　▲　　▲

I started the children's sermon by showing them the clock from the sanctuary wall. I'd had it installed my first year at the church to make it easier for me to keep track of the time. I asked the children to guess why the clock was no longer on the wall. Nobody had a guess.

I said, "It's because a new preacher is coming. He's going to be different from me, and he may not want a clock, so I'm going to put it on his desk in the church office and let him decide whether or not to put it back up."

I told about my friend Julie who, in teaching a first-grade Sunday-school class in a church in North Carolina, was continually amazed at the children's vision of God. Julie had told me, "Sometimes the pastor drops by to visit the classroom. When he leaves, I always have to tell the children, 'Now, that wasn't God. That was only the pastor.' The children are always surprised. They think the pastor is God."

I said I'd thought about relaying the information to the first-grade Sunday-school teacher when Julie first told me. After all, I didn't want our first-graders confusing me with God. On second thought, though, I'd let the matter rest. Perhaps it wouldn't be so bad if, for a few years, they believed that God has naturally curly hair, notices when you lose your front teeth, and is not male. I said it might take a little time to get used to the new pastor. I reported my exchanges with the rising first-grader (now a rising fourth-grader smiling shyly as she listened) who for two years had informed me, "Our last preacher was a man." I said it would take time to get used to seeing the new preacher, but God would love them through it, and so would I.

After I sent the children back to their mothers, fathers, grandmothers, and grandfathers, I read scripture, and I lullabied the congregation one last time with "Surely the Presence of the Lord Is in This Place." I got a wild hair and walked up and down the center aisle singing the refrain from "Victory in Jesus," waving everyone out of the pews to sing it with me. I retreated to the pulpit, and as their voices faded into silence, I sang softly to them, one last time, "He loved me e'er I knew him and all my love is due him."

That's all I've tried to say to you for the last three years, *I said*. It's what every pastor you've ever had and every pastor you ever will have has tried to say about God. God loved us before we knew God, and we get to love God back.

I don't know if it was spite or delight that made me schedule "The Battle Hymn of the Republic," but I laughed, as always, when I sang, "Oh, be swift my soul to answer him, be jubilant my feet," and when we sang the phrase "song of my Spirit, rejoicing and free" from "True-hearted, Wholehearted," I thought of feet dancing free, jubilantly. In and amongst the scripture readings, I told them a few last things I wanted them to know.

We have been in this place on days when you were so hungry for God that you weren't sure you could put one foot in front of the other unless you got a glimpse, a hint, a whisper that God was real and present.

Our time together has been short and intense and passionate. I thank you for all that you've given Fred and me.

I mean no disrespect to the hard work you do when I say it's the grace of God and the power of the Holy Spirit that have brought you this far, and that will lead you home.

You are feisty and gorgeous and passionate, and you are faithful.

▲   ▲   ▲

After the last benediction, the last handshake, I walked through the sanctuary unsnapping my robe. I draped it over my arm and piled my sermon notes and Bible on top of it. In the office I laid in the center of the desk the keys that were no longer mine. It was finished.

To be an ordained minister is to be asked to share the nature of God. I had much still to learn about that nature, much to explore no